Stephanie Hemelryk Donald is Professor of Film at Monash University Malaysia and Head of the School of Arts and Social Sciences. Since 2018 she has worked in the Justice, Arts and Migration Network (Lincoln-Sydney-Hong Kong) on artivist interventions that highlight state injustices against people, including children, on migrant journeys. This work was made possible by Natasha Davis (The Big Walk: It Takes a Decade, 2020), Hoda Afshar (Remain/There's No Place Like Home, 2019), the SYMAAG, Maison de Femmes, and Right to Remain organisers in Dunquerque, Manchester, and Sheffield, and the curators at Mansions of the Future (Lincoln 2018-2020).

'*There's No Place Like Home* stands out for its immediacy, poignancy, and elegance. By capturing the fragility and elasticity of childhoods, this book makes a compelling addition to world cinema, and the real world of precarious migration.'
— Ying Zhu, City University of New York; author of *Two-Billion Eyes: The Story of China Central Television*

'*There's No Place Like Home* is a brilliant and timely meditation on migration and visual culture. Donald's rich readings on the powerful concept of "child life" – transient, formative, elusive – shows cinema's attempts to close the gap between the world we live in and the world we want.'
— Vicky Lebeau, University of Sussex

'Drawn from years of research, this book is an extraordinarily wide-ranging volume, mixing film analysis with forms of auto-ethnography. Donald highlights how the image of the migrant child in film provides a power commentary on the material and psychological consequences of social upheavals.'
— Paul Cooke, University of Leeds

Migrant Han girl, Xinjiang, © Tom Cliff.

WORLD CINEMA SERIES

Series Editors:
Lúcia Nagib, Professor of Film at the University of Reading
Julian Ross, Research Fellow at Leiden University

Advisory Board: Laura Mulvey (UK), Robert Stam (USA), Ismail Xavier (Brazil), Dudley Andrew (USA)

The World Cinema Series aims to reveal and celebrate the richness and complexity of film art across the globe, exploring a wide variety of cinemas set within their own cultures and a they interconnect in a global context. The books in the series will represent innovative scholarship, in tune with the multicultural character of contemporary audiences. Drawing upon an international authorship, they will challenge outdated conceptions of world cinema, and provide new ways of understanding a field at the centre of film studies in an era of transnational networks.

Published and forthcoming works in the World Cinema Series:

Allegory in Iranian Cinema: The Aesthetics of Poetry and Resistance
Michelle Langford

Amharic Film Genres and Ethiopian Cinema
Michael W. Thomas

Animation in the Middle East: Practice and Aesthetics from Baghdad to Casablanca
Edited by Stefanie Van de Peer

Basque Cinema: A Cultural and Political History
Rob Stone and María Pilar Rodriguez

Brazil on Screen: Cinema Novo, New Cinema, Utopia
Lúcia Nagib

Brazilian Cinema and the Aesthetics of Ruins
Guilherme Carréra

Cinema in the Arab World: New Histories, New Approaches
Edited by Philippe Meers, Daniel Biltereyst and Ifdal Elsaket

Contemporary New Zealand Cinema
Edited by Ian Conrich and Stuart Murray

Cosmopolitan Cinema: Cross-cultural encounters in East Asian Film
Felicia Chan

Documentary Cinema of Chile: Confronting History, Memory, Trauma
Antonio Traverso

East Asian Cinemas: Exploring Transnational Connections on Film
Edited by Leon Hunt and Leung Wing-Fai

East Asian Film Noir: Transnational Encounters and Intercultural Dialogue
Edited by Chi-Yun Shin and Mark Gallagher

Eastern Approaches to Western Film: Asian Reception and Aesthetics in Cinema
Stephen Teo

Impure Cinema: Intermedial and Intercultural Approaches to Film
Edited by Lúcia Nagib and Ann Jerslev

Latin American Women Filmmakers: Production, Politics, Poetics
Edited by Deborah Martin and Deborah Shaw

Lebanese Cinema: Imagining the Civil War and Beyond
Lina Khatib

New Argentine Cinema
Jens Andermann

New Directions in German Cinema
Edited by Paul Cooke and Chris Homewood

New Turkish Cinema: Belonging, Identity and Memory
Asuman Suner

On Cinema
Glauber Rocha, Edited by Ismail Xavier

Pablo Trapero and the Politics of Violence
Douglas Mulliken

Palestinian Filmmaking in Israel: Narratives of Place and Identity
Yael Freidman

Performing Authorship: Self-inscription and Corporeality in the Cinema
Cecilia Sayad

Portugal's Global Cinema: Industry, History and Culture
Edited by Mariana Liz

Queer Masculinities in Latin American Cinema: Male Bodies and Narrative Representations
Gustavo Subero

Realism in Greek Cinema: From the Post-war Period to the Present
Vrasidas Karalis

Realism of the Senses in World Cinema: The Experience of Physical Reality
Tiago de Luca

Stars in World Cinema: Screen Icons and Star Systems Across Cultures
Edited by Andrea Bandhauer and Michelle Royer

The Cinema of Jia Zhangke: Realism and Memory in Chinese Film By Cecília Mello

The Cinema of Sri Lanka: South Asian Film in Texts and Contexts
Ian Conrich

The New Generation in Chinese Animation
Shaopeng Chen

The Spanish Fantastic: Contemporary Filmmaking in Horror, Fantasy and Sci-fi
Shelagh-Rowan Legg

Theorizing World Cinema
Edited by Lúcia Nagib, Chris Perriam and Rajinder Dudrah

Queries, ideas and submissions to :

Series Editor: Professor Lúcia Nagib - l.nagib@reading.ac.uk

Series Editor: Dr. Julian Ross - j.a.ross@hum.leidenuniv.nl

Publisher at Bloomsbury, Rebecca Barden – Rebecca.Barden@bloomsbury.com

THERE'S NO PLACE LIKE HOME

THE MIGRANT CHILD IN WORLD CINEMA

STEPHANIE HEMELRYK DONALD

BLOOMSBURY ACADEMIC
LONDON • NEW YORK • OXFORD • NEW DELHI • SYDNEY

BLOOMSBURY ACADEMIC
Bloomsbury Publishing Plc
50 Bedford Square, London, WC1B 3DP, UK
1385 Broadway, New York, NY 10018, USA
29 Earlsfort Terrace, Dublin 2, Ireland

BLOOMSBURY, BLOOMSBURY ACADEMIC and the Diana logo
are trademarks of Bloomsbury Publishing Plc

First published by I.B Tauris in 2018
Paperback edition published by Bloomsbury Academic in 2022

Copyright © Stephanie Hemelryk Donald, 2018

Stephanie Hemelryk Donald has asserted their right under the Copyright,
Designs and Patents Act, 1988, to be identified as Author of this work.

For legal purposes the Acknowledgements on pp. xi-xii constitute
an extension of this copyright page.

All rights reserved. No part of this publication may be reproduced or
transmitted in any form or by any means, electronic or mechanical,
including photocopying, recording, or any information storage or retrieval
system, without prior permission in writing from the publishers.

Bloomsbury Publishing Plc does not have any control over, or responsibility for,
any third-party websites referred to or in this book. All internet addresses given
in this book were correct at the time of going to press. The author and publisher
regret any inconvenience caused if addresses have changed or sites have
ceased to exist, but can accept no responsibility for any such changes.

A catalogue record for this book is available from the British Library.

A catalog record for this book is available from the Library of Congress.

ISBN: HB: 978-1-7845-3423-3
PB: 978-1-3502-5238-7

Series: World Cinema

To find out more about our authors and books visit
www.bloomsbury.com and sign up for our newsletters.

Contents

List of Figures		ix
Acknowledgements		xi
	Introduction	1
1	The Dorothy Complex	17
2	*The Red Balloon* and *Squirt's Journey*: story-telling with child migrants	43
3	*Once My Mother*, *Welcome* and *Le Havre*: breath and the child cosmopolitan	71
4	*Little Moth* and *The Road*: precarity, immobility and inertia	95
5	*Landscape in the Mist*	121
6	*The Leaving of Liverpool*: Empire and religion, poetry and the archive	141
7	*Diamonds of the Night*	173
	Afterword: where have all the children gone?	195
Notes		203
Bibliography		243
Filmography		261
Index		263

Figures

Frontispiece: Migrant Han girl, Xinjiang, © Tom Cliff.

1.1	'Girl waiting for train to Xinjiang', *Railroad of Hope*, screen shot.	32
1.2	'Kylie's heelies in close-up', *Kisses*, screen shot.	37
1.3	'Dorothy in the tornado', *The Wizard of Oz*, screen shot.	41
1.4	'Maria Running', *White Material*, screen shot.	42
2.1	'Molly and her cousins on the whitening plains, early example of digital colour manipulation', *Rabbit-Proof Fence*, image courtesy Australian Film Archive, RMIT Melbourne, permission courtesy Christine Olsen.	49
2.2	'Molly and her cousins at the fence', *Rabbit-Proof Fence*, courtesy RMIT University Melbourne, Australian Film Archive, and Christine Olsen.	50
2.3	'Filling in reference grids, Guangzhou 2014', image courtesy of the author, the children and Ming Liang.	65
2.4	'Storyboarding, Guangzhou, 2014', image courtesy of the author, the children and Ming Liang.	66
2.5	'Storyboard for an animation, Guangzhou 2014', image courtesy of the author, the children and Ming Liang.	67
3.1	'Helen, the film-maker's mother', *Once My Mother*, source image, courtesy Sophia Turkiewicz.	82
3.2	'Refugee camp in southern Africa', *Once My Mother*, source image, courtesy Sophia Turkiewicz.	83
3.3	'Sophia, arms crossed, very upset', *Once My Mother*, source image, courtesy Sophia Turkiewicz.	84

Figures

3.4	Detail from 'Idrissa in the water', *Le Havre*, screen shot.	93
4.1	'Little Moth and Guihua begging, with narrative on ground', *Little Moth*, screen shot.	118
4.2	'Little Moth alone on the bridge, final scene', *Little Moth*, screen shot.	118
5.1	'Voula at the back of the truck after the rape', *Landscape in the Mist*, screen shot.	125
6.1	Illustration from the Father Berry Homes annual report, 1895, courtesy Nugent Archive, Liverpool Hope University.	154
6.2	Illustration from the Father Berry Homes annual report, 1895, courtesy Nugent Archive, Liverpool Hope University.	155
6.3	'Lily and Bert in Sydney', *The Leaving of Liverpool*, cast shot, image courtesy Australian Film Archive, RMIT Melbourne, permission courtesy ABC Archive.	163
7.1	'Ants on the boy's hand', *Diamonds of the Night*, image courtesy of TIFF Archive and Czech Republic Film Archive.	175
7.2	'The boys murdered by the old men, their boots and feet wrappings evident', *Diamonds of the Night*, image courtesy TIFF Archive and Czech Republic Film Archive.	181
8.1	Detail, 'Exuviate II: Where have all the children gone?', artist, Jin Nü. Courtesy White Rabbit Gallery, Sydney.	196
8.2	Detail, 'Exuviate II: Where have all the children gone?', artist, Jin Nü, image and permission courtesy White Rabbit Gallery, Sydney.	197
8.3	'Child adventurer facing the seas before the war, UK, 1939', permission courtesy the author, photographer presumed Fintan Kehoe.	202

Full film production details can be found in the Filmography on page 261.

Acknowledgements

This book has been a long time in the making. As ever, there are many people to thank. For funding and material support I thank The Leverhulme Trust for an International Visiting Professorship at the University of Leeds, the Worldwide Universities Network at the University of Sydney, the Australian Research Council for a Future Fellowship at the University of New South Wales (UNSW) and, of course, Madeleine and Philippa at I.B.Tauris. At (or through) UNSW I especially thank Vanessa Lemm, Dennis Del Favero, Yi Zheng, Anne Engel, Kath Albury, Kelly Royds, Lina Tao, Sarah Yan, Linda Bartolomei and Jodi Brooks. At RMIT I thank Jo Tacchi (then in Melbourne and Barcelona, now in London), Larissa Hjorth and Lisa French. For help with the Dorothy Project film-making workshops in London, Sydney and Guangzhou I thank Enda Murray, Inara Walden, Ming Liang, Tracy Mullan and Sebastian Liu. I am indebted to practical and creative assistance from Stefan Solomon, Zitong Qiu, Emily Baker, Claudia Stocker, Olivia Stocker, Sebastian Secker Walker and Jordana Bjelmar. A very big thank you to Jo Chipperfield for her interlocutory editing help. International collaborators and hosts for talks and seminars have included Bill Marshall (Stirling, SCMS, and IAS Senate House), Lúcia Nagib (Centre for World Cinemas, University of Leeds and Centre for Film Aesthetics and Cultures, Reading), Ying Zhu (City University of New York), David Goodman (Xi'an Jiaotong Liverpool University), Michael Lambert (Liverpool Hope University), Daniela Berghahn (RHUL), who gave me the opportunity to present at her symposium on diaspora and film, Christoph Lindner (Amsterdam KNAW Fellowship), The Finnish Youth Network, Tim Bergfelder and Erica Carter (panel colleagues at Society for Cinema and Media Studies, 2010), the Planning Institute of Australia, which provided a chance to address them on 'Boys running' and city environments, Tani Barlow at Rice and Cara Wallis at A&M, who gave me an opportunity to try out ideas in Texas

Acknowledgements

(where I breakfasted in a café decorated with Dorothy images, and visited the superb war photography exhibition at the Houston Museum of Modern Art), Karen Lury and her colleagues in Glasgow and at *Screen*, Elke Grenzer and Alan Blum, who invited me to discuss *Little Moth* in Toronto and Roger McKinley at FACT Liverpool, who hosted and co-curated *Libidinal Circuits*. Enormous thanks to my UK colleagues on our Leverhulme Network on *Childhood and Nation in World Cinema*, Sarah Wright and Emma Wilson, and to Eleonore Kofman at Middlesex for her continuing help, company and advice. Thanks to Angelos Koutsakaris and Mark Steven for their original invitation to think about Theo Angelopoulos's work. Archives consulted have included the Maritime Museum Archive at Liverpool, the Nugent Archives at Liverpool Hope (thanks due to Karen Backhouse), the AFI Archives at RMIT Melbourne (especial thanks due to Alex), TIFF in Toronto, the State Libraries in Sydney, Melbourne and Perth, ACMI (Melbourne), the White Rabbit Gallery, the National Screen Archives in Canberra, the British Library, the BFI and the Cinémathèque Française in Paris. I also applaud the Merseyside Refugee Welcome group for their moral example, the Refugee Council of Australia and GetUp Australia for their action and focus, and all the children who worked with me on watching films, making films and telling me to pluck up my courage and see more zombie movies, for their creativity, resolve and wit. Finally, I thank my UK friends who have offered support when it was needed: intellectual, demanding, generous and kind, especially Catherine Roe, Nadine Gurr and the health bosses at Primal. Also, to those in Sydney who welcomed me home, Ilaria Vanni, Karen Reid, Ming Liang, Paul Allatson, Greg Dolgopolov, Nina Danko, Maha Abdo, Genan Dadoun, Tracey Crawcour and Kirsten Seale. Thank you all very much.

    I dedicate this book to my darling migratory family – James, Morag and Ellen, and the cats.

Introduction

> Emotions, then, are bound up with how we inhabit the world 'with' others. Since emotions are in the phenomenological sense always intentional, and are "directed" towards an object or other (however imaginary), then emotions are precisely about the intimacy of the "with"; they are about the intimate relationship between selves, objects and others.[1]

One

I think I became so fascinated with child migration and its cinematic formulations when I moved to Australia as an adult. Almost immediately I was involved in the politics of child care for young people of Indigenous and non-Indigenous backgrounds, in educating international students and researching media and film projects with younger children and teenagers – who had themselves moved from China at the end of the 1980s, or had been born to first-generation migrants. These children were so busy. In addition to managing their own lives they were also teaching their parents the Australian customs and competencies needed to survive as political and social subjects.[2] I saw for myself what Daniela Berghahn has described in her work on diasporic families in film, that the role of the child in negotiating family belonging is emotional, exhausting and essential.[3] Or, perhaps I noticed this because I myself moved as a child from Malta to the UK to Singapore to Hong Kong to Malaysia and back to the UK as a 'navy brat,' as we were called. Once repatriated to the UK, the images I carried in my head were of places beyond the quiet drizzle of a southern British moorland. They were of darker green foliage than that in our grassy garden, of wetter seasons, and of friends who spoke Hindi and Bahasa Malay, and who could not attend my birthday parties because my Mum served pork chipolata sausages on sticks. They were my friends nonetheless but now they lived elsewhere, inexplicably lost along with our games in longer grass and our secret codes. Those passages of childhood provided a good education in mobility and adaptability – and an understanding of mobility-as-homelessness. Then again, perhaps the fascination became pressing when my eldest daughter, aged nearly four, told me after less than eighteen months in Australia that she was 'Australian'. And yet, looking at the world we live in today and knowing more about the world we lived in before, my memories seem to present peculiarly benign pictures of happiness forestalled. Indeed, the context of my own travels as a child – the disestablishment of the British Empire – marks my childhood out as code in global post-colonial ciphers left by a dead Empire tidying up, barely, after its own mess. Mine was a family chasing down a dissolving Empire. My father was a lieutenant in a colonial navy, and we spent most of the early 1960s traipsing round to places that 'we' – my erstwhile nation at least – were 'leaving' or about to 'leave': – Malta, Singapore and Malaysia (and Hong Kong, although in the 1960s it was still a geographically convenient watering hole for colonial servicemen, business people, bankers and civil servants).[4] Moving around as a small child teaches you some important things about mobility. One, you only belong for as long as you're there, and even then you only belong to your group of fellow transients. Other children will be your friends but you won't understand the true conditions of their lives very well and vice versa. Two, the people who believe that home and location are one and the same thing seem stronger and more authentically in place than you ever will, and sometimes they use that as a proof of superiority. Three, no-one tells you what is really going on. Four, your

Introduction

world is always mobile, period. There is nothing outside that persuades you inside that everything won't change again.

But while experience gives you insights, the profound difference between safe and dangerous uncertainty is more illuminating. I think I really woke up when I encountered the harsh resonances, discordances and equivalences between the Stolen Generations of twentieth century Australian Indigenous peoples, and the painful work of the Child Migrants Trust in the UK, which became better known in the late 1990s,[5] and then the failure of the Australian Government to care for the Tampa refugees in 2001.[6] In all these stories, distributed visual access to child refugees' faces was crucial to the creation of empathy and the delivery of justice, and it was denied. Comparing these instances of horrific displacement and endemic cruelty to the images captured in *Children of Europe* (1949), a book of photographs that did collect the faces and terrors of displaced children at the end of the World War II, I finally confronted the blindingly obvious: that what we do to fellow adults we do to children, and what has been perpetrated in history continues in other forms, or through other perpetrators, now.

What I did not realise even in the 1990s was the degree to which the devastating fact of global forced child migration would push itself so brutally into our collective consciousness in the years between first proposing a project on 'child migrants in world cinema' in 2010 and finishing this book in 2017. Images of child migration in cinema and the visual arts have proliferated in these years, whether through documentary footage of actual tragedies shared on social media, or staged re-tellings of current journeys, or fictional narratives based on encounters between the child migrant and an adult world, or activist works determined to bring these children to the attention of populations and governments who might be able to help them.

This book does not attempt to provide a comprehensive account of all films about all child migrants, nor does it confine discussion to recent films and immediate twenty-first-century causes and conditions of flight. In the following chapters I introduce certain films that have seemed to me as empathic, as peculiarly illuminating, or simply as representative of a zeitgeist. Some are familiar to film scholars and students, and as such are frequently referenced in the literature; others may be less so. I do not pursue a chronological trajectory but rather present a trans-historical circulation of images, tropes and themes that move between and across the disaster of the mid-twentieth century European war and its far-reaching impacts, the cruel pragmatism of late colonial England and that of erstwhile colonies themselves, the aggressive accelerated modernisation of China PRC since 1980, and – in front of our eyes and behind it all – the utter devastation facing many millions of children today due to the twenty-first-century Afghan, Yemeni and Syrian conflicts and ongoing dispossessions in East and Central Africa. Thus, when I discuss the television treatment of child migration to Australia in the 1950s later in this book, I find it essential to also look back at the nineteenth-century origins of that phenomenon, and to search out other children whose faces were not seen, and whose voices were not listened to. These stories serve to remind us that every crisis has its prequels in history, and that, while the cinematic-literary and archival relationships that I share with the reader are derived from my own journey through images, films and the archives, and thus contestable, they do nonetheless offer a method of connectivity and visual thinking that acknowledges complicity as well as shock. Like others before me, I am drawn to the philosopher Giorgio Agamben, and his writings on bare life (of which more below), but, although I am equally depressed and fascinated by the child in war, it is more precisely the child *after* war, or at least on the journeys that war makes necessary, that are most central to my discussion. Indeed, one can identify a panoply of heroic and tragic tropes in the cinema that reflects on the dark fairytale of a journeying child migrant. The children journey on a quest for home and family reunion, for liberty and safety, or simply for a space to breathe and grow up unharmed. They are frequently alone or in small groups of vulnerable young people, making strange and transient friendships to assist survival, overcoming obstacles (read 'national borders'), encountering monsters (usually in the shape of predatory adults) and sometimes sacrificed for a mythical greater good.

My project begins with the onset of the World War II in Europe in 1939. I use an *Ur*-text, *The Wizard of Oz* (1939), a film that both defines that pre-War moment and predicts the global turn to savagery. Specifically, the central protagonist Dorothy Gale is my lodestone and I continue through a suite of films that reveal aspects of how children migrate and explore how film-makers engage with that phenomenon. Every child in this book is Dorothy by this conceit but every Dorothy is different and not all are innocent – Dorothy Gale was a witch as well as a queen in Oz. One specific text that I have chosen to illustrate this point, Claire Denis' *White Material*, centres on Maria, a character who may be understood as an inverted 'Dorothy' figure. Maria is an adult protagonist who will not shift her thinking from a pre-colonial to a post-colonial frame, from a fantasy of long-gone innocence to a reality of immediate and extreme danger. She embodies *within the film* what other theorists of the child in film correctly identify as the 'over-determination' of the child in films about children made by adults. Over-determination, as pointed out by Karen Lury, refers to the role of children not just in film, but more broadly, as cultural metonyms for adult self-obsession and denial.[7] Claire Denis takes this to its logical conclusion, where the adult protagonist, dressed in a girlish frock, is embedded in the narrative and her refusal to give up her disingenuous relationship to her innocence as a coloniser comes at the expense of real children (in this case child soldiers in Cameroon and her own teenage son). I will also introduce other Dorothy figures in every chapter of the book, most of them more attractive personality types than Maria, but none are fortunate. They include males and females, internally and transnationally displaced children and youths in China and Europe (Chapters 3 and 4), forcibly migrated boys and girls in Australia (Chapter 6), wartime teenage escapees from genocide (Chapter 7), and siblings whose journey is 'over-determined' by prolonged national grief after a vicious civil war (Chapter 5).

Books are written as part of a conversation with colleagues, with the social world one inhabits, and ideally with those people whose circumstances demand an explanation or at least an acknowledgment. This book is my contribution to challenges posed by colleagues, by film-makers and by the world at large on the multifaceted question of child migration, child mobility and child homelessness, and it seeks to engage with the capacity of film-makers, artists and writers to visualise the courage, loneliness, trauma and fear that accompanies much of the work that children do in seeking out a place called home.

The films I discuss collectively capture shared features of the experience and impact of migration and mobility for children and open up enquiries into the past and the present. In some instances, the films have an openly activist, or consciousness-raising, intention. In others there is an implicit critique of the failure of hospitality in nations that are *not* suffering war, famine or environmental wreckage. There are films that celebrate child resilience and imagination. Others mourn the loss of children and young people whose lives are wasted by adult negligence. For every film I discuss, the reader will think of others. This is neither a manifesto nor a list, but a conversation.

The Dorothy Complex *operates as a signature* that frames an approach to child migration on screen. The grouping of films in this book is thereby conceived as a cinematic body that acknowledges socially and culturally discrete phenomena, demographics and populations, portrayed across 80 years of film-making. Dorothy evokes ideas of travel, of accelerated maturation, of dreams taking the place of real life, and of adults who exploit and lie to children in order to ignore the actual conditions of childhood. When Dorothy wakes up back in Kansas, she recognises where she is and where she is not: There's no place like home, she says. That is what migration teaches us, there is no place like home, except what you make of what you have, of the affordances of the place of arrival. In all the films explored in this book, this signature has suggested to me that the figure of the child has been crucial, not just as a protagonist and actually not always overdetermined, as a lightning rod to elicit a heightened ethical sensibility for what we do as adults to children travelling alone, for children travelling with imperfect adult companions and children for whom many adults represent immediate danger.

The methodology of the project underpinning this book included the usual work that scholars undertake in film collections, libraries and archives; looting, collecting and storing films, images and histories for our part in an inter-textual creation of knowledge. But that is not quite enough in this instance. I am adult, and, as I indicated in my opening paragraphs, I have my own memories which both inform me and leave me vulnerable to nostalgia. I will draw on them unapologetically in my writing but I will also depend on others to help me see things I miss. So, crucially, this book also relied on field-work in China, the UK and Australia, where I facilitated film-watching and film-making workshops with young people who have much more recent and much more traumatic experiences of migration than I do. The practice of working with child respondents in this way developed from my pre-academic life in children's theatre where participation is revelatory, and became a methodology in Western Australia where I worked with children of Chinese background to make stories and television shows that described their sense of connection with their parents' place of origin,[8] and again in Beijing and Shandong for a later book on children's film and media use.[9] It is essential that anyone who would like to read this current book allows that I offer a shared narrative influenced by all the children and young people that have helped me think about film. These contributory thinkers and film-makers have been displaced internally and across borders for social and economic reasons, or have been re-settled through refugee programmes, or have sought asylum with their families by other means and for a multitude of reasons. They also include young people who are systemically required to move regularly from a home environment to an institutional one for education. Their contributions are discussed in Chapter 2 both in terms of how they use film to reveal the complexity of lived experience and also in relation to how their work informed my own.

Two

Central to this opening discussion is what I call 'child life', and its visual representation through ephemerality as a form of image collection. Child life is a term coined in association with Agamben's ideas on 'bare life'.[10] However, while bare life indicates the least of living, the reduction of the human spirit and the destruction of sociality and hope, child life refers to the transient and crucial being-in-the-world that is childhood, an ontology that grounds us all. It is the quality to which the Dorothy Complex gestures and which films try to engender through the narration of childhood and the presentation of the child on screen. Child life is embodied in every child, and mourned by every adult. In bad times it is uprooted, trampled and forgotten, and society is disfigured. In the circumstances of child migration, child life becomes both more poignant and more vulnerable. In Chapter 3, I include a discussion of *Once My Mother* (2013), a film built on the scraps of memory shared between mother and daughter, and documented by rare and tiny photographs of the mother's migrations. In Chapter 4 I introduce a fictional little girl, Little Moth or Xiao E'zi, who presents impenetrable quietude in the face of a sustained attack from untreated disease and systemic criminality. Whether it is apathy or atrophy that we see in her face, the understanding between spectator and film-maker is that we are watching the slow and deliberate destruction of a child's life and of *child life* in the world of accelerated modernisation and forced mobility that China currently represents. That which is already ephemeral is damaged, truncated and lost in the rush for the transient goods of urban wealth.

In Chapter 5 I discuss *Landscape in the Mist* (1988) by the Greek director Theo Angelopoulos. This film has particularly powerful central performances by a young girl and an even younger boy. Indeed, Angelopoulos' entire oeuvre addresses childhood in tandem with his fascination with the problematic of history and the present which he describes through the repetitions and absences of political discourse across generations. In much of his work, Angelopoulos links the ageing male memory to fragmenting national discourses of the Greek Civil War (1946–9) and to images of childhood, often counterposed to the soft borders of the Mediterranean Sea. Angelopoulos presents the retrieval of childhood's fragility as the beginning of mature recollection and thus as the fitting end to a single life. His work is essential to a discussion of child migration and world cinema in so far as he is a film-maker who constantly investigates border crossings, border shifts, betrayals and national grief, and does so through a non-linear and collective approach to history and its affects. His protagonists embody child life with a luminosity that is rarely matched in cinema.

Child life indicates that the condition of childhood is a status of being alive that has absolute quality. My talk of 'fragility' does not suggest that a child has less or more resilience than another being, but it does insist that child life is not something we can replicate, and it is not something that humanity can lay aside. It is fundamental to our growth and to living and dying well. Generally however, adult nostalgia reaches into the treasure box of childhood for its substance and emotional pique, but fails to re-invent child life beyond the enigma of such material traces. Extreme old age that may mimic and obscure childhood is a different kind of wandering, a psychical double but not the thing in itself. Nostalgia belongs, as the Chinese *Book of Rites* reminds us, to only a 'very old' person, like a seven-year-old, that cannot be held accountable for his actions, a centenarian – like an infant – that 'must be fed'. While childhood is deeply integrated into adult personality and behaviours, it is emotionally distant, factually indistinct, irreplaceable. The space between us and children, including the children we once were, is immeasurable.

This seemingly inevitable disappearance of childhood entails, in the philosopher Paul Ricoeur's term, a 'profound forgetting' that hinges on the articulation of two traces: 'psychical trace, cortical trace'.[11] What is forgotten nonetheless grounds the present. What may be remembered emerges from what has been lost. The relationship between the adult and the child is then a series of mnemonic starts and recognitions, none of which make childhood truly available, but any of which can prompt partial access to the feelings and power of its affections, terrors and adventures. Meanwhile, still using Ricoeur's schema, 'documentary' or 'cortical' traces are the ephemeral remains of childhood that we have stored in our personal or occasional archives – photographs, books, film clips and the occasional object – a dress, a spoon, a favourite toy. The ephemeral is an utterance that makes sense only through its relationship to some other contingency. Charles Foster Kane's dying word in *Citizen Kane* (1941), 'Rosebud', the meaning of which is the central pursuit of the film, is simply the name of his little childhood sled, the one he was playing with on the last day he saw his mother. The disclosure is made only to the audience, just as this piece of ephemera is cast into the fire, dead wood to everyone but the now-deceased Kane. Thus, objects may structure and determine the memories that adults hold dear, because they open up deeper recall of who we have been and what we might be next, but only in so far as that 'might-have-been' is the work of adult memory and wishful thinking. Childhood is thus the ephemeral and transient epitome of life itself. Without its disappearance and continued possibility, the living of life has no centre, no beginnings and no good way to end.

Whether documentary or fiction, films are collections of ideas and emotions. They are part of 'how we inhabit the world "with" others' as Sara

Ahmed tells us.¹² In a certain way, this book is my collection, a reflection of how I inhabit the adult world and the world of my childhood. I pick things up and turn them upside down, wondering what they mean, and why they are here, why these. In Walter Benjamin's reading of childhood he claims that children are forging change through these randomly loved transitional objects from an adult world that has failed to change itself. In Chapter 8, I discuss two Chinese artworks that mourn the passing of childhood through immersing the spectator in its ephemeral traces. These works bring my book to a close as meditations on objects that can retain the freshness of childish hope, and the 'overdetermined' hope of adults that children will, after all the tribulations that we throw at them, regain hope for the world at large. The childish toy, or dress, or colouring book is less culpable than the fripperies of adult consumption, and more poignant of the child herself. In Andrei Makine's novel of a Russian childhood, *Le Testament Français*, his refugee grandmother, fleeing the onset of the World War II in Russia with her own children, recalls the strewn debris of a bombed train ahead of her own transport… so many of the objects are dolls, which tells her that so many of the dead are children.¹³ So when Susan Buck-Morss notates Benjamin's essay on childhood as an essay on enchantment and a quest for a better world, she rescues the object from a history of politically impoverished consumption. Benjamin, she avers, creates:

> A materialist history that disenchants the new nature in order to free it from the spell of capitalism, and yet rescues all the power of enchantment for the purpose of social transformation: this was to be the goal of Benjamin's fairy tale.¹⁴

So, adults and children approximate each other's world through a shared poetics of pastness on the one hand, and a promise of the future present on the other. Benjamin echoes the *Book of Rites* when he links the very old and the very young without claiming an exact equivalence: 'Animals (birds, ants), children, and old men [are] collectors'.¹⁵ The ephemeral object is both found and forgotten, it is both trivial and replete with meaning.

Ephemerality is a trace in time at the junction of remembering and forgetting, each of which has value and disadvantages, and neither of which exists without the other. In Chapters 6 and 7 I have drawn on innovations in memory scholarship – theories of prosthetic, multidirectional, post- and palimpsestic memory – in order to get under the skin of films that have present child life as cinematic, fragile and precious. Memory work and trauma discourse are socio-political innovations of the twentieth century, designed both to find and record the nuances of pain. Memory work is very much like the habitual scavenging of a collector. These theories of memory understand that forgetting is constitutive of the human condition, without the relief of which madness or sadness – or both – rage. The Man in Cormac McCarthy's book *The Road* (2006; see Chapter 4 for a discussion of the screen adaptation) dies of too much memory. The psychoanalyst Adam Phillips argues that memory sometimes needs to be rebooted after trauma, so that a human life can start again and see the world afresh, like a child. 'Forgetting has to be allowed for if memory – non-compliant, unmanufactured memory – is to have a chance'.[16] For the Man this is not conceivable, he is overgrown with memory, but for the Boy in the same book, there is a chance that objects can and will allow his memory to make sense of his future – and save his life.

Transience and ephemerality are, however, not of the same order. Transience indicates that which passes, but it may not be something that will be missed, or be the subject of nostalgia. By contrast, I use a definition of ephemerality lodged between *memory* – how we ground our future in the past – and *forgetting* – the pathway to the future after memory has been dissolved or absolved. The ephemeral is never entirely forgotten, but it is always fragile. Certain passages of life are ephemeral in that they are both exquisitely precious and fascinating, yet their material meaning, their ontological sensations, are not persistently available however much we wish or need to access them. Indeed, it is because the ephemeral is as it is that we invent nostalgia to cope with the inevitable loss of profound memory and with the excruciating ache for that perfect condition of no memory at all. We cling on to objects that may convince us that what we are missing was not in fact ever with us. Clearly then, the ephemeral is epitomised in childhood, a condition that every living adult has experienced but that remains opaque and intangible – except to children.

Ephemerality does not offer transparent revelation. It both remembers and forgets, but it does grant a kind of temporal simultaneity. Film delivers this triumph of ephemeral knowing. The camera (both that of the protagonist and that of the film-maker) is the apparatus that tricks and trumps the human eye. The 'chiasmus between ... clarity and indistinctness', is exemplified by the visual, literary and cultural critic Anne Friedberg's observation on 'seeing' the hyper-modern city of Los Angeles, namely that one encounters the city most authentically as a bright blur through the back window of a speeding car.[17] Likewise, the prosthesis of the camera provokes a memory of child life, but not as a speeding blur. Rather, it is a slowing image of the child disappearing as in a retreating telescopic lens, beyond our grasp, and we say, that cannot happen, we must be able to say no to this, and this.[18] The refugee shanty towns on the edges of Europe, far-flung detention camps in Papua New Guinea, the massive camps in Jordan, the great refugee cities of Africa where globally most refugees reside – are such blurs on the edge of our speeding consciousness. Children stand briefly in the sightlines of an NGO fund-raising campaign, or an activist video. They pop up on Facebook. Do we retain a retinal image of these children? Can we see street children in China, the inheritors of modernity, or have they also slipped into the passageways of non-place, tidied away like the invented stories of sadness lain out on the street after a day's work begging? Glossing Freud, Ricoeur talks of blocked memory as 'forgetful memory', 'the patient repeats instead of remembering.'[19] Film-makers who seek to create ephemerality, displacement and forgetfulness are in effect requiring that the spectator, the looker-on, truly considers the memories that must be hidden from the protagonist and the location. *At Home in the World* (2015) is a documentary about a Red Cross school that educates newly arrived refugees and asylum seekers in Denmark. It teaches them Danish and, as the teacher explains, 'skills that they can use in Denmark, if they're granted residency. Or anywhere else in the world.' The children in the film are all dealing with separation anxieties, memories of multiple migrations and multiple arrivals, and the acute uncertainty of their residency status. The documentary records the rigid facial muscles of children who daren't show emotion until they know it's safe to do so – we witness the small tremors of a child's face as his father tells him he'd rather be shot than endure 15 years in a Russian prison – and the sudden smiles when safety is secured, for now, by a temporary residency visa. The children apparently live in the present in their optimism, in their football games, their language learning, their cake-eating and their relationship with the trusted teacher. But the film-maker presents the subscript through prosthetic touches of childhood as it is always used, to get us closer to what this impossibly lonely life of arrival, residency, deportation and arrival might or could feel like… rain on the window, snow fights shot at a lonely distance, football games which end and people drift away, friends suddenly leaving school to be deported back East, lying awake while parents worry aloud in the next room…[20] So, then, one may argue that ephemerality is a state of complexity revealed on film through apparent incompleteness, trivia or forgetfulness. This definition coincides with its role in the traumatic reworking and collection of the ends of childhood and the beginning of old age. 'Children thus produce their own small world of things within the greater one.'[21] This quotation refers us to our ongoing status as the children of our parents, through Walter Benjamin's musings on fatherhood and children's literature (*Passagen-Werk*, 1927–40). Translated as the *Arcades Project*, Benjamin's voluminous notations on European nineteenth century life and thought, positioned within the architectural logic of mass consumption, create a huge prosthetic imaginary. Every section or 'convolute' requires the interpretative input of the finder, and indeed its hope resides in the 'politically explosive potential' of the 'child's fantasy'.[22] Benjamin makes a utopian trick out of the double consciousness of adult innovation and wish-work, and the child's capacity to dream with the leftovers of the past generation. The inventions and the fripperies of mass culture in one generation become historical consciousness in the next, with the added benefit (for humanity, for society) of finding newness in the past and present, and delivering change.

Why do I think all this is important in approaching the cinema of child migration? Well, I want to explain that writing on cinema and the image may be as simple as a kind of collecting, a way of placing transitional objects between the world that has failed to change itself and the world we want. Benjamin wanted childhood to stand up for the possibility of change, he believed in child life. The idealised future of Benjamin's Arcadian project was not wholly commensurate with the realities and capacities of the everyday child in an actual present.[23] But, as the cultural historian of childhood Maeve Pearson tells us in an essay on the modern child's burden of redemption: 'Walter Benjamin argued that when the dream of an ideal child coincided with the utopian projects of the early nineteenth century it represented the desire to redeem the past and to bring this dream into reality within the next generation.'[24] The theme of the child as a collector in Benjamin's work prefigures the modern subject as a reader of philosophy, a viewer of cinema, a consumer in a world of advertising, luxury and ephemera, a creature of random enthusiasms and cruelty, of animal instincts and obsessive memory. Nevertheless, the memory of childhood itself – retrieved through ephemeral material objects and images – allows the human society to become much more, and much greater. 'Collecting is a form of practical memory, and of all the profane manifestations of "nearness" it is the most binding.'[25] This optimism refers to a profound dreaming of the self as a pre-social inventor (though not to daydreaming – it is worth noting in this regard Freud's dismissal of daydreaming as 'two-dimensional', and the child psychologist D.W. Winnicott's delineation of 'playing, dreaming and living' on the one hand and 'daydreaming' on the other[26]).

The child's role is to collect the dreams of the past and re-imagine them, realise them, and thus enable actual revolution. Benjamin's insistence on this responsibility does not absolve any generation even after they have left childhood. The work of politics is immediate, history is unpredictable, and action cannot settle into a comfortable 'ism' but must always take place in 'a time as actual as now'.[27]

Three

In his account of his late childhood during the 1940s the author Italo Calvino tells of an incident where young Fascists, or rather boys recruited to be Fascists in Italy, travel over the border and loot an abandoned French town. Their expedition is a mixture of childish adventure and teenage hooliganism, encouraged by adult criminality. The protagonist (Italo) has been enchanted by fallen love letters in an empty house, while his friend has pilfered objects, some for profit and 'face' but some as secret treasures, chosen in a last gasp of childish fascination. Calvino muses,

Introduction

> Basically, I had been a fool not to take anything; they were not anyone else's possessions anymore. He winked at me and showed me his real finds, the ones he cared about and would not show the others: a pendant with a picture of Danielle Darrieux, a book by Léon Blum, and also a moustache curler.[28]

The childish instinct to collect random, beautiful, strange and discarded things is here perverted by war – and adolescence – into looting 'you could still find objects that were worth something'.[29] Even worse, the direct involvement of violent adults makes the targeting of the discarded objects a form of adult hate work: the commander of the boys shouts out 'any young man who is here today and does not take something away is a fool! Yes sir, a fool and I would be ashamed to shake his hand!'[30] His bullying prompts the young Calvino to find a dangerous and transgressive piece of loot – a key to a Fascist clubhouse. In stealing as his keepsake the very thing which must not be seen as ephemeral, he accounts himself braver and happier than the looters. But, in so doing he also admits that the town's transient status as an emporium of free items for thieves, and ephemeral fascination for teenage fantasy, is based on the violent disappearance of the previous occupants. His immediate nostalgia on finding the love letters is almost immediately revealed as misplaced and inappropriate. Again, there is Dorothy in Calvino's prose, a teenage child in a place full of stolen magic, slipping a key into a pocket/slipping into the shoes of a dead witch imparts magical powers. The signature of Dorothy is here in its many incarnations.

In the port city of Liverpool in late 2016 I heard the British singer Eliza Carthy give a concert where, in this time of the largest human displacement since World War II, she challenged her audience to think more positively about hospitality and migration. She noted that she was the daughter of a family of Irish Travellers on her mother's side, and that she had always been taught to lay an extra setting at the table, just in case 'they were visited by an angel unawares'.[31] Then she sang a song about the goodness of the fruits her country had to offer the visiting stranger (as a Traveller her country is the whole of the north of England). Her comments and her song serve to remind me that several of the films I discuss in the following chapters concern child migrants, but they also all reference the successes and the failures of adult hospitality to the travelling child, of lost and substitute families, and the theme of mobility-as-homelessness. Sara Ahmed, quoted at the top of this chapter, argues that emotions are created by recognition of the distinction between self and other, between one group's passionate identifications with itself, and – therefore – equally passionate rejection of another social entity. Yet, the boundaries between our body and the object, between one group and another must also serve to connect us, as Ahmed puts it 'the impressions of others'[32] are how we belong to the world, and to each other. Dorothy arrives in Oz as the saviour of the Munchkins. It's a good start. Most child migrants just turn up, with no fanfare, no marching Munchkins, and not much help along the road. This is a book about film, but I hope it also reminds us that new arrivals in our places of safety right here, right now, need guidance, love and 'skills that they can use' – and above all a recognition that our connections are somatic, historical and ethical.

The sudden shock of feeling a different being in the room might bring momentary fear, but – if we are growing rather than shrinking as our emotional selves and societies progress – we will recognise that there may be an angel at our table, a new child in our midst.

Notes on 2022 edition

Since this book was first published, the world has experienced a pandemic that has emphasised global inequality, the United States of America have experienced Trump's presidency and his campaign against children crossing the southern border, and the Chinese Communist Party has increased its re-education violence against Uighurs in Xinjiang, condemning parents to strategies of cultural and religious elimination and their children to forced assimilation. The films that will engage with these horrors are still in the making, but I would like to acknowledge the many art-ivists that I have encountered in the past four years, and their commitment to the lives and dignity of migrant children and adults.

1

The Dorothy Complex

One

Emma Wilson has referred to the 'missing child' in cinema, and called for a 'new [cinematic] politics of childhood'.[1] The starting premise for my response to this is that Dorothy from *The Wizard of Oz* (1939) is an exemplary actor in the cinematic politics of childhood. Her role in a fantasy film, based on a fantasy book for children,[2] acts out a version of mobility and homelessness that allows a certain kind of hope whilst revealing other, less positive feelings in the film's text. 'Dorothy' is an agent more than a character. Her story is not one of character progression and individual fulfilment. Rather, she broaches different scales and types of childhood and child mobility: forced migration, fantasies of escape, quests and, simply, running away from home. Dorothy offers a rhetorical principle or framework of resonance; a structure of attention for seeing the cinematic child through one particular but recurrent, symptomatic trope – the intrepid, intrusive 'orphan' girl on the yellow brick road dancing and darting between home, arrival and return, girlhood and maturation – what I am calling the Dorothy Complex. Dorothy is a starting point for a discussion of child migration and cinema since 1939, drawing both on films that cite

The Wizard of Oz directly and others that I have found easier to understand with the *Ur*-text in mind.

Dorothy Gale, from (Lynan) Frank Baum's *The Wonderful Wizard of Oz*, first published in 1900, is a country girl, an orphan living with her uncle and aunt in impoverished Kansas. She is swept up in a tornado and deposited (with her farmhouse) in a fantastical land, which she shortly comes to discover is named Oz. On arrival she is immediately hailed a heroine as her house has landed, fatally, on the Witch of the East who was, as she is informed joyfully by the newly liberated Munchkins, a tyrant. Oz itself comprises many smaller lands, or regions, including Munchkinland and the Emerald City. Dorothy travels down the yellow brick road through these lands in order to achieve her immediate goal, namely to find her way back to Kansas. She achieves this goal, and lands back in the dingy sepia-toned Kansas muttering 'There's no place like home'. On her whirlwind visit to the Land of Oz Dorothy copes magnificently with the challenges of the foreign, the strange and the downright dangerous. Yet, despite her triumphs, she chooses to go home, and indeed everything she does in Oz she does in order to go home because Oz is, as Salman Rushdie has commented, 'anywhere and everywhere' but not 'the place where we began'.[3] Dorothy's return to Kansas is a return migration to a place that will now be always disappointing but always formative to her being-in-the-world. It is not that she has really left home, but that home has been clarified, through the fantasy of travel, as both necessary and impossible.

The genesis of Baum's original story was the Great Depression or 'Panic' of 1893 and pro-worker progressive politics of the late nineteenth century.[4] Dorothy's Kansas was a wasteland of poverty and low opportunity, but also a land ready for changes to working-class culture as the pre-1924 wave of new immigrants negotiated ways of being American and avoiding starvation. A magical escape to Oz would seem just the thing for a fairytale for American children of the era, while the political allegories embedded in the structure of the work would not go amiss for adult readers. In 1961 Henry Littlefield, in an article that has informed many subsequent analyses, noted that 'Baum's immortal American fantasy encompasses more than heretofore believed'.[5] Littlefield pointed out that the plight of the Tin Woodman – to work harder and harder but without benefit to himself, and (when the rain sets in) to be rusted as though stilled by a localised great depression – is the plight of the working man in Baum's America, while Dorothy is an exponent of mid-Western optimism – a remnant of the romance of happier economic prospects.[6] Littlefield's perceptions are important on two counts. First, his allegorical reading reminds us that the original book was a fairytale of its time and, second, he notes that Oz is not the panacea of the woes of Kansas, it is just a more sharply delineated version of its tragedy. The fairytale is in essence a fantasy of the real, through which direct political allegories but also indirect fantasies of the human condition can be communicated between generations. Perhaps not coincidentally, the 1939 film adaptation coincides with tail end of the deeper and longer Great Depression (1929–39) experienced by the next generation of Americans, with its great tornados of grit swirling out of the dust bowls that Kansas and other central and south-western states became. Millions left their barren farms, blown out by dust storms; 'Toto,' Dorothy says after the tornado sets her down 'someplace where there isn't any trouble', 'I've a feeling we're not in Kansas anymore'. Littlefield's allegorical interpretation does not argue against the queering of the 1939 film in the work of Alexander Doty and others; indeed the queering of the text is precisely what allows cinema to open up the wide terrain on which both Baum's and Judy Garland's Dorothy make their multiple claims on the cinematic imagination and the social imaginary.[7]

Oz may be claimed as pure fantasy or it may be termed a fantastic representation of Kansas, of America and of the possibility of the Other in Technicolor, but with the same cast of principal characters – just more dangerous, more exotic and yet, oddly, more manageable. Dorothy and the tempest from Kansas have more power than the wickedest witches in Oz. The Wicked Witch of the East is flattened by Dorothy's falling house; the Wicked Witch of the West can be melted with a handy bucket of water. And, of course, this is Dorothy as portrayed by a 17-year-old Judy Garland – an actress already deemed by MGM as too womanly to be sufficiently childlike, too dangerously sexual for a family film. Garland's breasts were therefore bound flat and her hair braided so that the filmic Dorothy offers the *sign* of girlhood, but also the barely disguised *promise* of the woman. This Dorothy is more delightful than Baum's for the viewing adult, as the power of the child is excused in a barely disguised woman's body, which is in turn reduced by the gaze of those who might see her as an available child. In a similar folded paradox, Oz is more excellent than Kansas, for Oz is a place where Dorothy, teenager/child/migrant, can take control, solve her problems and those of others, and leave with a click of her heels.

The present argument is not so much concerned with how we can understand the various manifest or latent intentions of the book or film however, but rather to question what they have wrought collectively and what they make possible in subsequent cinematic work on migration. In particular, I hope to explain in this opening chapter how Dorothy can be interpreted as an archetypal cinematic touchstone for the migrant child and how her presence registers as a *signature* in many films dealing with the reorientations (or queering) of global history since the end of the Word War II. Taking my cue from Salman Rushdie's comments on Dorothy's mantra, to whit: 'There's no place like home … except of course for the homes we make, or the homes that are made for us, in Oz; which is anywhere and everywhere, except the place where we began',[8] I argue that Dorothy's pre-war hopefulness returns within the traumatic narratives of postwar childhoods in Europe, China and Australia, specifically as such childhoods have included periods of forced migration, de-colonisation and re-colonisation. Dorothy's signature, traced in the closing stages of pre-war Hollywood dreaming, loses its American specificity as it reappears across world cinema but gains a sense of the child at large in a brave new world. The idea of 'signature' I have borrowed from Giorgio Agamben's work on method in the humanities. It is the performative movement in his methodological triplet: paradigm, signature and the archaeology of method itself.[9] I use it here to indicate a lighter touch and a softer set of transcultural expectations than might be attached to the archetype alone, 'the sign signifies because it carries a signature that necessarily predetermines its interpretation and distributes its use and efficacy according to rules, practices and precepts that it is our task to recognize.'[10]

An archetype generally assumes a pre-formed narrative trajectory pursued by a protagonist in a formal relationship with the verbal and written traditions of the culture in question. The resulting story has thus a synchronic coherence and depth of reference for readers or audience, while retaining a diachronic freshness to the specific tale or plotline. The archetype may also – and this has been argued to be the case in Chinese literature, an argument I borrow in the first instance for Chinese film – refer not so much to the forward motion and cyclical nature of pre-loved narratives as to a shared understanding of relationships, abstractions and non-narrative qualities of person or place, 'movement and stillness, elegance and baseness, joy and sorrow, union and separation, harmony and conflict, … prosperity and decline'.[11] Such relational archetypes may be described in film through quite simple narrational techniques, as I suggest below in regards to Ning Ying's *Railroad of Hope* (2002), while the classic archetypal protagonist might be conveyed through character traits, plot choices, events and forms of closure.

A key archetype and one which has provided the most well-known 'complex' of European literary thought, and that touches both definitions, is the Oedipus myth. The Oedipus complex resonates with the Confucian horror of inappropriate relationships (its psychopathology forms the basis of the child's murderous attacks on his mother in Zhang Yimou's 1988 *Ju Dou*),[12] as well as defining a European sense of impossible desire that simultaneously repels and attracts. The notion of a queered archetype manifesting the *ur*-form for the expression of childhood transitions is somewhat counterintuitive but, combined with the idea of signature, it begins to account for Dorothy's returns in world cinema. Thus, I call the transnational reiteration of this signature the 'Dorothy Complex', by which I mean the various configurations of the character, relationships and narrative that make up the structure of fantasy that is 'Dorothy' in and beyond *The Wizard of Oz*. It is a structure of fantasy that we are tasked to 'recognise', however it is distributed across our cultural fields of identification. I further suggest that while the signature of Dorothy inscribes many films that attempt the scripting of maturation (the journey from child to adult), it is at its most intense when mapped onto narratives of migration. The recurrence of narrative patterns is then grounded in new specificities of space, time and movement, articulating the chronotopes of nationality and belonging, to account for both arrival and return and for multiple encounters along the way. As such, the Dorothy Complex provides a framework of resonance for cinematic fantasies of transition, migration and growing up across a complex world that is differentiated and yet intimately connected by the logic of movement. Dorothy, created in 1900 and filmed in 1910, 1912 and 1939, prefigures and valorises the child migrants of the post-World War II period.[13] Her adventures and her persona are at the heart of a fantasy structure in cinema, reiterating both the impermanence and multiplicity of home.

To ground my claim for the Dorothy Complex as a facilitating signature-archetype for childhood transition, I simultaneously suggest that the migrant child is a major trope in world cinema. Reflecting my interest in the intense politicisation of both the category of childhood and of the child migrant, this move draws on the work of Chen Kuan-hsing, who has suggested 'Asia' as method – for him a geopolitical approach to re-framing perspectives and analyses of global change.[14] Chen's Asia-as-method (*fangfa*) is a key stage of the post-colonial project, whereby the global system of referential value re-positions Asia as central to its own narrative, and removes the West to the margins. I proffer childhood 'as method'; however one does not want to make of this too perfect an analogy. *Asia* is not a child to the so-called *West*'s adult (although infantilisation – which is a different phenomenon – is a stratagem of racism and colonial management), but it is useful to understand Chen's concept as a springboard from which to consider childhood as another valid, internally referential cultural and social system, one that is central to its own narrative and that removes adulthood to the margins; or one could term this a *flattened ontology*, as does cultural geographer Nicola Ansell in a powerful analysis of the macro and micro scales of global experience.[15] The flattened ontology of childhood is a spatial-temporal construct, specific to the enunciation of childhood in academia, policy and in wider discourses of cultural value. It entails a horizontal re-scaling of experience for which the key points of reference are drawn from children's lives and ontological capacities and affordances. The global, national, regional, local and familial are not excluded but they do not necessarily assume the same dimensions that they might in adult visions of pertinence and meaning. Fellow geographers Tisdall and Punch have expanded on Ansell's intervention, nominating 'becoming' and 'being' as equivalent human conditions, and quoting director Ang Lee's simple but socially radical perspective: 'Lee (2001) …

takes a predominantly historical approach … to argue that adults lack finished stability in terms of their working lives and intimate relationships. With adults in a perpetual search as human becomings, then children and young people are equally in this "age of uncertainty".[16] This comment is a sociological plea to eschew the false dichotomy between childish being and adult being, and to refute the idea that children are 'becoming' while adults have 'become'. The space of being where adult and child are most difficult to discern as useful, discrete or combined categories are the teenage years, when bodily development, social expectations and responsibilities and hormonal stresses are intense, creating an alternating state of being that is neither child nor adult.

In the cinematic realm the slippage between adult, teenager and child is performative and spectatorial, produced by both the sexual maturity implied in the actor's (I use this as a gender neutral term) performance and through the ways in which the actor is perceived within the script. This perception is dominated by spectators who wish to read her (him) as sexually available without releasing the imagined power of adult over child. Such ambiguity is not necessarily unknowing or uncritical. It is central to films such as Ang Lee's *The Ice Storm* (1997); and Lance Daly's *Kisses* (2008), both featuring girls who are pre-pubescent but who reveal (in very different ways) close familiarity with sexual behaviours and dangers. In *The Ice Storm*, Wendy is a predator on a younger boy, while in, *Kisses*, Kylie is herself preyed on by older men, including close family members. The dilemma is in such scenarios of youthful desire on the one hand and implied carnal knowledge on the other.[17] How are we to look at these girls and how do we see them both as sexually knowing and as children? The two films offer answers to the second question in a voice aligned to childhood-as-method. We see the protagonists as children who are sexually active in certain registers, we make judgements about their knowledge and desires from their perspective (and both films make that possible), but we also retain the relational reciprocity of adult power, and thus a responsibility for guiding them, where a child is in danger of self-destruction or threatened by the violence or heedlessness of other parties. That responsibility is not applicable to film spectatorship as such, but it does pertain to the way in which adult spectators would need to watch the film and acknowledge the child's agency, retaining responsibility and reciprocity without assuming moral superiority or a saviour role, or indeed a predatory one. Crucially in both films, adult protagonists do not produce safety for the children without the intervention of children themselves. Kylie and her friend Dylan determine their own return to their homes (although this is facilitated by a policeman whom they approach for help), and in *The Ice Storm* it is a collective refiguring of family responsibility in the wake of the tragedy of a boy's death that allows Wendy's nuclear family to work together to achieve reciprocity and moral survival.

Garland's Dorothy undertakes her travels under the sign of girlhood (a child's dress, white socks and plaited hair) but with the shadow of adult trauma and change in play. Wendy and Kylie are, if you like, cinematic returns of this bifurcation of being and not-being, misformulated on-screen as child and adult but referring to a deeper, more enduring lost-ness in the human condition. That the producers found Garland 'too adult' is background knowledge that haunts the film itself and subsequent incarnations, and makes her Dorothy an even more multi-faceted signature, announcing the ambivalence of childhood on screen. Garland's voice as well as her suppressed curvy body belies her supposed youthful 'becoming'. She is somewhere between child and woman. She might be playing 11, 13 or 17, but she does so in the body of a 17-year-old, full-throated chanteuse, and so she errs towards the latter. Garland's teenaged Dorothy is very different from the much younger Dorothy of L. Frank Baum's own screen adaptation *The Wonderful Wizard of Oz* (1910). There, Dorothy is played by an actor who seems between 9 and 12 years old. Garland's age provoked Salman Rushdie to aver that this was not just a film about migration but also a film about growing up. The fact that Shirley Temple (then 11 years old) was also considered for the role is also notable, given all the ambiguities of pre-pubescent sexuality that go along with her cinematic persona. There is one moment of confusion at the end of the film, in the departure from Oz, when Dorothy's exchange of kisses and sorrow at parting with the Scarecrow is of a definitely more romantic tenor than her leave-taking from the Lion and Tin Man. And, crucially, queer theorists plot her relationship to her own female body as inherently sexual and rebellious. Dorothy's archetypal contribution is then, on one level, her capacity as a cinematic figure to pass as both adult and child within the same frame and between frames. As we will see later, one of the threats to actual child migrants is that they are judged against criteria of 'childishness' and 'adulthood' that are not appropriate to their situations and experience.

Dorothy's intersectional position is bizarrely prescient. The conditions of the signature (and the necessary recognition of the child on screen) could perhaps also be understood through what Laura Marks calls the juncture of 'intercultural cinema', operating at the 'intersections of two or more cultural regimes of knowledge'.[18] Marks is interested in hegemonies of geo-political entities and concepts, and what happens to 'Other knowledges' that 'may evade expression because of censorship, because memory is inaccessible, or because to give expression to those memories is to invite madness'.[19] If for an adult to think and know like a child is a form of madness, can cinema provide a fourth space in which children's thinking and knowing is scaled as appropriate, imaginative, sane and visible?[20]

Two

Postwar and post-imperial migrations have been fundamental to the changing demographics of European nations over six decades, with related impacts in postwar receiving countries such as Canada, Australia and the United States. Trans-continental migrations, often within the same geo-political entity (as is true in China, South America and Australia) have marked profound disturbances for populations and peoples over decades and indeed centuries. People have moved – and are still moving – driven by need, opportunity, crisis, foreign occupation and fear. The modern world is in constant motion, with populations configured and re-configured by arrival and departure, by fragmentation and re-constitution, by the dynamism and morbidity shaping individual and collective futures. The experience of migrant children, whose lives are determined by the requirements and challenges of forced relocation, re-settlement and displacement, have always been present in these waves and currents of human mobility. The rendition of such childhoods in social discourse and law is often highly problematic. Children are children, playing, living, working and growing up however they can and with what support is available, but *childhood* is a contested and emotive category of cultural identity, a measure of national morality, and a retreat for political uncertainty.[21] The expectation placed on migrant children to be both endlessly resilient and utterly flexible whilst retaining an aura of innocence and dependence, as well as finding the imaginative wherewithal to conform to the expectations of the places of arrival, is extreme.[22] The radical disjuncture between adult expectations and children's experience, and their impacts on public opinion and policy,[23] has been traced in the context of child detention and forced return by activists and scholars defending young migrants.[24]

Like everyone (arguably) child migrants are complicated people, but made more so because migration is a multi-directional, multi-scalar and multi-temporal project. All migration stories entail an origin, a journey and an arrival, or indeed multiple arrivals along the way, 'the way' being itself an unstable category. The Munchkins' chirpy directive to 'follow the yellow brick road' is an illusion of simple wayfaring. Dorothy is often forced off the road to discover friends and destroy enemies, and to get lost. Neither the road itself nor the countryside beside it is really secure. It takes a massive quotient of courage and imagination to leave, to travel, to settle and to survive. For most migrants there is no single grand plan and, if there is, it is very likely to be misinformed, misguided or impossible to achieve for external reasons. In the case of children, plans are usually made by others, but even where they do forge their own paths they must work around the many levels of exclusions foisted upon children in cities and across borders. One constant feature of the films I discuss in this chapter and in this book is the extent to which children are routinely excluded from everyday rights and options that are afforded to adults.

The Dorothy Complex indicates a response to adults' anxieties by reiteration of a queered and flattened presentation of childhood, requiring a child's-eye view, while maturation is signalled by endless returns to the recognition that there is 'no place like home'. Dorothy in 1939 represents a certain version of mid-twentieth-century America: youth, movement, opportunity and self-made heroism. She also echoes the poverty of the nineteenth and twentieth centuries' east-west migrations and prefigures the hopelessness of America's lost soul in the twenty-first century – no place like home anymore. The release of the film in 1939 appeared as if the angel of history was rushing forward and glancing back – it emerged at the tail end of the golden era of Hollywood escapism, not only at the conclusion of the Great Depression but also coincidentally providing anthems of optimism and irony to Allied soldiers in the 1940s and later to LGBT identity politics. The Dorothy Complex is not however restricted to the American context, and may be understood both as a signature in films that essay the darker passages of postwar transitions, including those we witness in twenty-first-century Syria, and a transcultural archetype in the creation of queered protagonists who refuse to remain locked in normative boundaries of behaviour and desire. My next case study is therefore, and I suggest necessarily, perverse; the Dorothy Complex presented through an adult clinging to an infantile politics of colonial privilege and belonging, falsely secure in her own indestructibility, and that of France in Africa.

We should recall that *The (Wonderful) Wizard of Oz* is itself not free of colonial inference. Debates about the book's politics and the film's assumption of the story include charges that Dorothy is a colonial adventurer, recalibrating time and space to fit the requirements of her quest. John Funchion positions Dorothy as an American abroad at the vanguard of twentieth-century imperialism, whereby the rest of the world serves only as a playground of high-cosmopolitan policy, a fantasy world order that claims and reinforces the centrality of the United States.[25] Funchion is austere and exact in his judgement on why the American child is allowed to wander on the yellow brick road: 'Baum does not so much reconcile nostalgia with cosmopolitanism as depict Dorothy's nostalgia for Kansas as the desire that compels her to develop a cosmopolitan ethos only as a means to return home'.[26] Funchion's point is one of analogy with the United States' hawkish foreign policy and domestic conservatism. Dorothy, he contends, is not an innocent abroad escaping Midwest Depression, but an American abroad in a period of growing US confidence. Funchion is not clear whether he refers both to Baum's Dorothy of the 1900s and the more famous Dorothy of 1939, but his reference to Baum suggests that he at least includes the former.[27] In both, Dorothy is both a child in the presence of American adults and a powerful witch in the face of child-sized adults, adult substitutes and talking animals. While this is the dreamwork of adolescence, it is also an articulation of postcolonial white identity. An associated pathology to Funchion's critique is that if a colonial adult retains and inhabits a fantasy of post-colonial belonging, this may become inextricably confused with the flattened ontology of childhood, creating adult myths of childish invulnerability. In other words, just as childish innocence can be invented and appropriated by adults so can the apparent innocence of the post-colonial other. This refers us to the problem of innocence and 'the infantilisation of adulthood', to whit; 'a mythical outside … the imaginary repository for all that is excluded from political life: sensual pleasure, emotional nourishment, as well as pleasure'.[28] So, perversely, in the following example of Dorothy in world cinema – Claire Denis' *White Material* (2009), Dorothy is a deluded adult. Her victims are the actual post-colonial children in the film – the main protagonist's white son and the local African children conscripted into soldiery by rebels and subsequently murdered in their sleep.

In *White Material*, Isabelle Huppert plays Maria, a French coffee farmer in a post-colonial African state. She is a lonely figure, living in a household with her ex-husband, his child with a local woman and her own teenage son. The political status quo is disintegrating and rebels are recruiting child soldiers to fight the incumbent government, which in turn sends out hunting parties to kill such children.[29] Maria refuses to leave the farm, despite the urging of French soldiers who fly overhead in a helicopter imploring her to leave. Rather, she convinces herself that she is in control of herself and her situation, right up until the destruction of her family, the death of her son, and the full flowering of her madness. Maria will not accept that she is at the wrong end of colonial history, 'white material', a human rag worth less than nothing in the current state of affairs. The flimsiness of white material, a metaphor both of the colonisers' non-human status in the eyes of both rebels and independent government and of Maria's thin grasp on the reality of her situation, is emphasised by her choice of girl-like cotton dresses. One dress is indeed stolen and worn by a teenage girl soldier. If nothing else would convince us that this Dorothy misunderstands her age, her ethnicity and the danger in which she places herself and others, the dress-as-transitional-object literally brings fantasy and materiality too close for comfort.

The film's chronology is organised through extended flashbacks while immediate events develop the unfolding crisis. Maria is frequently on a yellow dust road leading between the town and the property and some of her key discoveries – particularly of an injured rebel fighter whom she harbours and whose presence brings down the fury of government forces on her family and the workers – take place in the adjoining scrub. This place between places is Maria's way home, but is much more accurately referred to by locals as dangerous no-go zone. In the sequence that confirms her misrecognition of where she is and who she isn't, she stands alone on the road, shouting and flailing her arms at the French helicopter above her, refusing their offer to get her and her family away. Seeing these helicopters as the enemy, she misreads the sources of danger even as she retains a childish sense of inviolability in her particular Oz. But as we see in other flashbacks/flash forwards, to which she is not privy, this Oz endorses an intensified tragedy, not an escape. Her teenage son, François, joins up with the child soldiers on the road and they share medicinal drugs looted from the village pharmacy. Francois then takes them home, and that night the children are knifed in their poppy-induced sleep and everyone, François included, is burned to death (it is not entirely clear whether François himself takes part in the murders or at best directs the government troops in the child soldiers' direction, again recalling the trope of the collaborator in a colonial context). The slaughter drives Maria into madness and the co-location of the colonial property with the murder site emphasises the degree to which childhood is made grotesque both by the cruelties of war and the dangerous idiocy of personal delusions.

Many other sequences in *White Material* have visual echoes in Dorothy's trials on the way to the Emerald City and in her battles with the Wicked Witch of the West. These are not slavish analogies but signatures of cinematic license. Dorothy and her friends are sent to sleep by the Witch in a field of poppies; the child soldiers unwittingly prepare themselves for their murderers by ingesting pills as they sit in a deceptively quiet field. The French helicopter reminds one of the Witch's enchanted flying monkeys sent to attack Dorothy in the forest. The key difference is that Dorothy in Oz takes part in a fantasy of recognition of her power and release from Oz, but Maria's fantasies are premised on denial and as such are lethal. Rather than heroically finding her way home and saving her farm and her workers, she walks down a path – a yellow dust, rather than a yellow brick, road – to utter loss and abandonment. We remember that on arrival in Munchkinland Dorothy inadvertently kills the Witch (of the East). This feat renders her a (good) witch in turn, and endows a little girl with the responsibility of freeing the locals from the oppression of the wicked witch's attacks. As Maria travels up and down the dust road on more and more fruitless and foolish forays, all of which end in the death of others, her masquerade as a good witch crumbles and she is revealed in the final frames of the film as mad, bad and corrupted by her own colonial hubris.

In *White Material* Maria is a highly suggestive perversion of the frame of reference offered by the Dorothy Complex. The film is quite explicit that this protagonist will not be recuperated and will not go home. Indeed, as a long-term migrant, Maria has no home to return to in France. Maria's transformation from Dorothy, the girl-woman who could click her heels to return to 'no place like home', to a murderous witch in the ashes of the place called home, exemplifies the dynamics and fluidity of the representations of the child and the outsider, the colonist and the post-colonial child, the innocent who is always already guilty. This post-colonial guilt is darker than the 1939 colonial optimism of *The Wizard of Oz*. Funchion's American Dorothy gains prestige and power the further she is from Kansas, and deploys cosmopolitanism as a mode of parochial authority with strangers. As Glinda, the good Witch of the North, tells Dorothy before she goes home, she had a return ticket as soon as she became a witch and put on the silver shoes (ruby slippers in the film) – 'you always had the power to return'.

This is of course not true of most migrants for whom return migration is not always an available or desired option – even if enforced by inhospitable receiving countries or internal regions. In 2002, the Chinese director Ning Ying portrayed migration and re-migration between internal Chinese regions, Sichuan and Xinjiang. Made in collaboration with UNICEF, Ning shot *Railroad of Hope* (literally *Journey of Hope, Xiwang zhi you* 希望之旅) as a documentary vox-pop treatment of internal migration at the end of a decade of accelerated Han population expansion. Sichuan is China's major and richest western province. Xinjiang is further west but is a special autonomous zone, incorporated into the People's Republic of China after Liberation in 1949 but for many centuries operating within a larger geopolitics of the Silk Road Central Asian region.[30] Han is the dominant ethnicity in the People's Republic of China, while Xinjiang is a predominantly minority region, with Muslim Uighurs the largest ethnic grouping with a long history of resistance to Chinese occupation. The staged internal migration was part of a larger expansionist policy, 'Open up the West' (*Dakai xifang* 打開西方). In the 1990s, the policy prompted subventions for the cotton industry, which in turn fuelled a need for outside labour and population in-flow. The population ratio in Xinjiang in the year 2000 had jumped from under 10 per cent Han ethnicity to nearly 50 per cent.[31] Most migrants on the route from China proper to China's limits in the 1990s and early twenty-first century were therefore peasant farmers. Many of those included in Ning Ying's film are first-time economic migrants, for whom this three-day journey across western China is also their first time on a train. They expect to spend a short time cotton picking in Xinjiang and return home with enough extra cash to pay for their children's school fees, lay something aside for their old age, or just have a little fun.

The film is made up of short interviews conducted in the queue at the rail station and on the train itself. The film-makers sought prior approval from the Chinese Railway Authority and there are signs of this approach: pre-approved interview questions, a benign view of harried police and railway workers, and a film which ends as the train crosses the Gobi desert into Xinjiang proper, right on the brink of a contested terrain where cameras are not encouraged. There is certainly no overt discussion of the relationships between Xinjiang locals and incoming migrant workers, nor any comment on the political tensions between the two groups. This is to a large degree because the travellers are mostly people who have never been out of their home villages and counties before and who would be most unlikely to have any patience for, or understanding of, anti-Han feeling (also, not all of the migrants would necessarily be Han as Sichuan has long been the crossing point of cosmopolitan exchange and diversion in the various territories subsumed into the Peoples' Republic of China, and for centuries beforehand). Moreover, the film was made before the tensions between locals and incomers erupted into violence in 2000 and 2009, after which Han incomers could not fail to recognise that Uighurs were unhappy with their growing presence.[32]

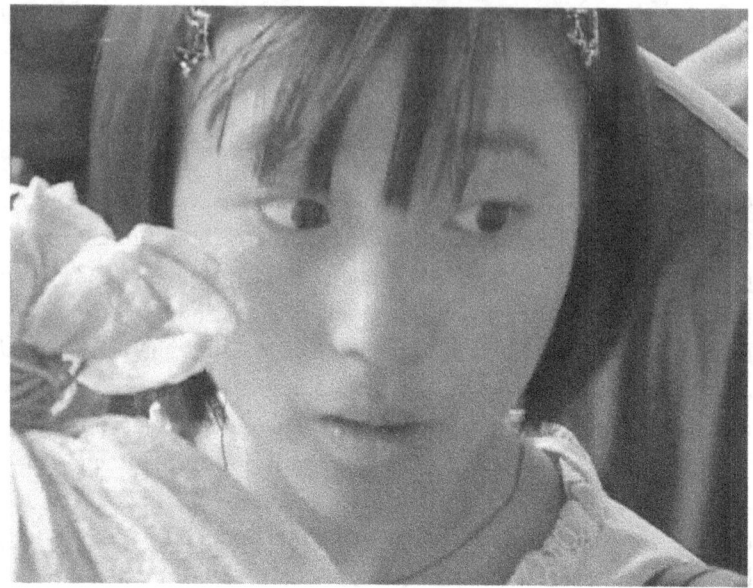

Figure 1.1 'Girl waiting for train to Xinjiang', *Railroad of Hope*.

The interviews are very short and offer only tantalising glimpses into the motivations and expectations of the travellers. However, while the structure of the film is episodic, there is a relational sensitivity that supports a notion of collective experience and the group. Despite the long wait in line and the uncertainty around boarding trains (whether or not one has a ticket in hand), the crowds, the police and railway staff charged with managing the migrants are not portrayed as if in conflict but as parts of a chaotic but nonetheless functioning systemic whole. This is the order in chaos, harmonious dysfunction and fearful certainty that Plaks' theory of Chinese relational archetypes (described above), might deploy.[33] Watching the film, my interest is piqued by an unnamed girl standing in the queue (Figure 1.1). She appears to be travelling alone, whereas others are in larger groups from various villages. The interview reveals that she is 14 years old and is not making the journey to pick cotton, but to attend school. Her near family – mother, father and brother – are all in Xinjiang already and she hasn't seen them for four years. She has to be there by the 28 January.

The Dorothy Complex

She comes from the county of Pingchang. As she imparts these staccato slips of information she begins to cry as though the expression of her duty, her loneliness, and the stress of transition has suddenly become overwhelming. The emotional pressure on the girl is caused and emphasised by an unrelenting extreme close-up, such that the intensity of the camera's focus on her own image is surely complicit in reducing her to tears. For several moments screen space is reduced to the bewildered face of a single child, and in those moments on screen, the uncertainties of migration, settlement and occupation are rhetorically assumed through a singular, unnetworked persona. She is just a child travelling alone in search of family, but she embodies multi-occupancy of space in recent history of contested Chinese expansionist politics. She is the Han invader, the victim of history, and the child migrant.

One may not easily contradict the Confucian expectation of family centeredness and group endeavour. Chinese children are 'born into a web of human relatedness; [s/he is] a link in the human nexus'.[34] Nevertheless, I suggest that the child in *Railroad of Hope* is accorded a different quality of close attention than any other interviewee or protagonist on the train, and analysis of her situation benefits from a deterritorialised cinematic analysis, based on the Dorothy Complex and the flattened ontology of childhood. Admittedly (and unsurprisingly) Ning Ying does not explicitly recall Dorothy in her film, but she introduces an abstracted and relational version of the child migrant that carries the signature of the Dorothy Complex: a child migrant who is an outsider, who has no control over the decision to move between home and family, who queers the script of Confucian belonging to a secure family network and 'relatedness' apparent in the bustling village groups elsewhere on the platform and in the entire network of human action at the railway station, and that manifest the workings of a colonial enterprise. If we recall Wilson's idea of the missing child, we might ask what if the body is both visible and missing, or seen only as a crowd or as a thing to be controlled or saved – the rampaging child, the vulnerable child, and the already-dead child? The cinematic child is then riveted to its own non-being, its own always-becoming. The child in Ning Ying's film is visible in close-up for a few moments of extraordinarily close questioning, but then she disappears. Her narrative is both rhetorically framed as special, and deliberately truncated as transitional, but she is not at any point collective. In a Chinese term that has become more widely used since 2002, she is a 'left-behind child' (*liushou ertong*, 留守兒童). Her family have undergone the process of migration without her and now she is trying to catch up. Her situation reminds me of a singular interview I held with a professional woman in the UK in 2014. She was Korean and working for an Australian educational company. On discovering that I was an Australian too she talked freely to me about her childhood in Australia, and mentioned that her parents lived in Sydney. On further discussion, it transpired that she had in fact lived in Sydney from the age of 11 to 18 with informal foster parents, as her parents had sent her away for schooling in Australia. She did not see her birth parents during her entire adolescence. She offered that she could not be away from her birth parents easily now as it had taken a long time to repair the relationship. Yet I wondered at this, as her particular job involved massive travel and long periods of absence. She had been sent away but had a very strong sense of having been left behind. Her constant travelling to use her education and fluency in English seemed hardwired rather than what she thought were choices about what she was doing and why she was doing it. There is another interview in *Railroad of Hope* with a 16-year-old boy, also travelling alone, on the Sichuan-Xinjiang train. After a few moments and a few partial answers he turns his face to the window. This may be symptomatic of overly probing, even unethical, questioning, or it could be understood as a knowing demonstration of the vulnerable subjectivity of child migrants, who go missing even in the grip of their own stories. Ning Ying perhaps does not want to fool us into thinking that these are tales that can be resolved through narrative closure and the clicking of red heels.

Domestic migration in China is massive, and child migrants there are accordingly numerous. In addition to children who travel with their parents it was estimated in 2015 that there are 20 million left-behind-children, many of whom will themselves migrate to join parents or seek out their own opportunities. Caught between family, livelihood and place of origin, the homelessness of these children is profound.[35] There is no easy solution either to their drive to migrate and catch up with parents, or their desire to be parented, or to the emotional deprivation of being left behind. Most of these children's parents are travelling eastwards to larger metropolitan centres rather than westwards to the ethnically diverse hinterland of Xinjiang. And surely – as the riots of 2009–11 confirmed – this anonymous Dorothy's presence in Xinjiang will be experienced by young Uighurs as an imperialist incursion and a threat to the remnants of their cultural autonomy. John Funchion's stern appraisal of the American abroad, poor or otherwise, rebounds both on Maria, the French colonial farmer, who misleads herself, and the Han Chinese girl in *Railroad of Hope*, who is simply following her family into an internal exile.

Referring to another anonymous girl, photographed *in* Xinjiang and pictured on the frontispiece of this book, Tom Cliff says:

> She is of course a migrant, at that time and no doubt now living a very precarious life; the building, and indeed the whole area of the city, behind her was due for demolition when I took the photograph around or about May 2008. ... we are intrigued to see her again, but would we be disappointed? She would be an adolescent, weighed down with the burden of study in the Chinese school system. She would be gawky and tired. With the photograph, we have the luxury of extending momentary voyeurism forever.[36]

Three

In *Kisses* (2008) Lance Daly pays direct homage to *The Wizard of Oz*, quoting it explicitly. The film splits the adventuring protagonist into two children, Dylan and Kylie, and introduces as companions on the metaphorical yellow brick road actual migrants within the context of Ireland following the expansion of the European Union in 2003–04.[37] The narration shifts between fantasy and realism, a strategy that marks the film's metaphorical intent as well as its interest in taking the plight of ordinary children into the world of high cinema and taking cinema into the ontological sphere of the child. As with *The Wizard of Oz*, *Kisses* is structured as an escape from an untenable situation (Dorothy is trying to save her dog Toto; Kylie and Dylan are saving themselves) and after that it operates as a road movie and a city film. Dylan and Kylie run from violent family situations in the suburbs of Dublin and set off to the city to look for Dylan's older brother. The film relates different scales of access to the city, double occupancy and a flattened ontology from which to enter a developing European city. The theory of double occupancy is Thomas Elsaesser's and realises a Europe that has spatial dissonance between populations, but produces conflictual as well as productive, hyphenated identities.[38] Daly's strategy of quotation and re-use allows the film much greater scope than would a social realist drama of abuse and danger confined to a poor suburb of Ireland. Rather, characters and protagonists are imbued with an archetypal quality that is drawn from cinema. For instance, the sequence in which Dylan escapes from a violent father quotes Stanley Kubrick's *The Shining* (1980), a film that describes an adult's misrecognition of himself (Jack, played by Jack Nicholson) through his displacement of his own violent tendencies onto ghosts. In *The Shining*, mother and child escape from a bathroom window as the father lashes at the door with an axe. Nicholson's face leering through the gashed wood is the iconic motif placed on posters and VHS covers. In *Kisses*, Dylan scrambles out of a high window as his father breaks down the door to continue his attack, his face distorted with fury. *The Shining* requires our active collaboration as spectators to buy into the ghost story so that the tension and denouement of the film can build to its climax. Jack's decline into madness materialises as a murderous assault on his family. In *Kisses*, the borrowed attack sequence squarely insists that the 'ordinary' domestic violence of modern Ireland is as horrific as its manifestation in Kubrick's most frightening film. The structure of *The Shining* also bears similarities to the structure of *White Material*, where Maria's sense of herself is delusional, yet the narrative tension requires a level of collusion from the spectator to maintain disbelief until the final slaughter is revealed. Maria and Jack are both adults who retreat into madness to avoid the responsibilities of adulthood. As children, Dylan and Kylie are allowed a journey that returns to a more positive and playful approach to the Dorothy signature. Daly uses monochrome in the opening sequences at the children's homes, moving into colour as they travel to Dublin. Oz is revealed just at the point that they jump a barge and start their journey. A

The Dorothy Complex

brightly lit shopping centre, where the children spend drug money stolen from Kylie's brother, is a microcosm of the Emerald City (on the Emerald Isle). The dark streets of the city at night are much more dangerous – a forest ('lions and tigers and bears – oh my!'), or perhaps a witch's castle.

The children's companions are all migrants or street workers. The first is an east European bargeman who breaks into song (Bob Dylan) when he hears Dylan's name, the second is a local street entertainer who impersonates Bob Dylan for a living, and the third is a sex-worker who offers magic kisses in the dark. The children use the drug money stolen from Kylie's brother to buy new clothes, sweets and flashing 'heelie' trainers with inbuilt skeeler wheels (Figure 1.2). These are their ruby slippers, and Dylan later rescues Kylie from abductors by clinging to their car and skating along on his heelies. This dramatic allusion to Oz is a fantastic plot device that both represents the heroism of the children and is proof of the magical world that they bring with them to the city. And the film is indeed full of glimpses of magic, making us privy to the experience of the city as it unfolds from the perspective of these two children. When Dylan meets the sex-worker, she recognises his maturing masculinity and proffers a magic kiss. These are the friends of Dorothy, outsiders who help the children and welcome them into the parallel world of outsiders and strangers. Across the passage of the night, the children's quest fails in so far as they do not find Dylan's brother. But, like Dorothy, they do discover an internal, mutual self-recognition through acts of courage that are real

Figure 1.2 'Kylie's heelies in close-up', *Kisses*.

enough but which lie outside the real world of their homes, the places they have escaped but to where they must return. When Dylan saves Kylie from sexual predators of Dublin at night, he demonstrates the possibility of being saved from the predations she suffers from men at home and proves to himself the chance of re-framing a life in the future that is loving rather than violent. The quest is for a life that can be lived, whether in a miserable residential suburb or in the city itself. Home is where we are, the film tells us, and the travelling self is our vehicle to get there. As Dylan and Kylie return to their dystopian family lives, they are cognisant of their intrinsic worth as children and as people who will mature into adults with their hearts intact. This temporary migration from monochrome to Technicolor does not release these child migrants from the bonds of family. Rather it accentuates the relationship through distance and regret and manifests in homecomings that must be managed and recuperated as a place called home – for now.

Four

The twister carries Dorothy from Kansas to Oz and she (with her ruby slippers) takes herself back again. Oz and 'Oz' are not the same place, but the place of Australia in the global imagination (and its own) as a lucky country of sun and sumptuous flora and fauna is not entirely divorced from the idea of Dorothy's Oz, with its lush forests, sunlit fields and gleaming cities. It is also a country whose soul is beset with the crimes of Empire, the murderous destruction of Indigenous culture, society and kinship, and the institutionalisation of child removal and child slavery.[39] Baz Luhrmann's high-camp, textually promiscuous epic *Australia* (2008), teases at this worldly Oz as a place of transition, a regional war-zone and a cultural metaphor for the ongoing appropriation of Indigenous land and livelihood. Luhrmann's white adults are as wild and wicked as the Wicked Witches of the East and West, or as inadequate as the Wizard. The Indigenous child at the centre of the film, Nullah (Brandon Walters), is the focus of their fantasies of control and emotional connection to each other and to the land itself, a land which has made them extremely rich. As a fair-skinned son of an Indigenous woman and white man, Nullah is threatened with a

The Dorothy Complex

forced migration from his ancestral lands and into white man's 'protective' custody.[40] The practice of removal from Indigenous mothers was part of systemic dispossession of children.[41] Nullah's mother drowns in a water tank where she hides with her son during in a raid by men sent to abduct him on behalf of the State. Nullah escapes but is nonetheless appropriated by an English woman played by Nicole Kidman (and the intertextual reference to Kidman's early role in a film about Sydney – *Emerald City* – is not irrelevant here) who informally adopts him.[42] Luhrmann's point in an entirely parodic epic (which didn't communicate to UK audiences perhaps because they do not recognise their ongoing complicity in post-colonial violence) was that Kidman's comedic performance as Lady Sarah Ashley in the opening sequence 'off the boat' and 'into the bush' presented her character as an archetype from *The Wizard of Oz* – she is a coloniser and a witch, not an entirely bad one, but a witch nonetheless. Nullah and Lady Sarah Ashley in Luhrmann's Oz present a composite Dorothy, a signatory flourish by Luhrmann that makes an acute comment on colonial appropriations of Indigenous values and spirit albeit sodden in Australian sentimentality. The Englishwoman Lady Ashley is in colonial exile, whereas Nullah is always close to home and will describe it physically step-by-step on walkabout. In Luhrmann's retelling, the pair becomes a combined characterisation of Baum's characters. When Nullah does finally take his walkabout with his grandfather King George (David Gulpilil), there is a sense that he is also teaching the colonial Dorothy/Lady Ashley the magical skill of travelling a long way across land whilst carrying the principles of home. The act of walkabout is after all a coming of age ritual which creates a physical description of home by walking the place into a spiritual existence for a newly mature member of the group. Walkabout is a ritualised, heroic journey of maturation, binding the young to their ancestral lands and testing their practice of survival and self-management. The casting of actor David Gulpilil as King George is ambivalent. Gulpilil played the young Aboriginal man in *Walkabout* (1971), a film about Anglo discovery and Indigenous dispossession made by a British film-maker (Nic Roeg). In *Walkabout* Gulpilil plays a young man on his walkabout who suicides at the end of that film. Is this casting anything more (or less) than cinematic nostalgia, giving not just *Australia* but also *Walkabout* a retrospective happy ending, returning Oz to itself through the walkabout of the otherwise dispossessed Aboriginal child? It's a matter of judgement. Nullah/Walters embarks on his walkabout with a better protector (George/ Gulpilil) to support his survival, a pair whose journeys to adulthood are captured in films made by whitefellas (Roeg/Luhrmann). Would that survival not only include survival as a character but also as an actor in a whitefella business? As the man and boy leave the property, King George offers a hand of peace to Lady Ashley, welcoming her to 'our' country. The nostalgic affect is comparable to that in (*White Material* director) Claire Denis' *Chocolat* (1988), whereby the children engender a 'might-have-been' cosmopolitanism through a nostalgic 'encounter between children and adults resulting in more understanding, more kindness ... an increase in moral goodness'[43] that can surely only be ironic in the contemporary Australian context.

Just as Dorothy's dream helps her escape from sepia to Technicolor and enter a place that helps her make sense of herself, Nullah leaves the pale-skinned, needy Lady Ashley for King George, a man who makes sense of the country and who protects Nullah from the white (but let's call them sepia for now) evil men who have taken it over. By reducing sepia to a place from which she can bounce into a cinematic dreamscape, Dorothy encounters her more powerful witch-self in another world without ever leaving Kansas or the farmstead. Likewise, Nullah encounters his more powerful, culturally grounded adult self on walkabout, without leaving Country. Dorothy makes sense of herself in her dream; Nullah in his Dreaming. So, looking at film, might we also look past the difference between fantasy and actual experience, and recognise children dealing with change on many levels simultaneously? With this multi-scalar and palimpsestic experience in mind,[44] 'Oz' becomes an elaborate metonym for cinema and its capacity for such revelation. Dorothy is a migrant on the right side of 18, a child becoming something other, not an adult after all, but a child who assumes sudden, extreme and occasionally violent responsibility. Whereas in Kansas she could not save her dog from a nasty lady on a bicycle, here she must save herself and others from their own demons and really bad magic. In a 1925 film version of *The Wizard of Oz*, Dorothy stays in Oz and becomes a queen. Dorothy the child-woman adventurer becomes a

The Dorothy Complex

Figure 1.3 'Dorothy in the tornado', *The Wizard of Oz*.

cinematic figure who becomes more truly cosmopolitan the more she is repeated and remade.

The Wizard of Oz works as an organising text for thinking about migration and what parts of the process a film might represent: it shows us the components and stages of a journey: the place of origin and the problems that beset it, the decision (or imperative) to leave (Dorothy sets off down a road with Toto, then the tornado takes over), departure, journey, arrival and the long process of settling, and/or re-migration. In the 1939 film Dorothy's departure from Kansas is forced, sudden, terrifying (Figure 1.3 and parallel *White Material* image, Figure 1.4). The place called home is rendered totally unsafe by an external incident (for tornado read climate disaster, war, famine, family breakdown). Adults disappear into a hole and shut the door against her, whilst the wind tears apart the material fabric of her world. Her journey is haphazard, a whirling house with just two dear possessions – a dog and a basket. The journey is a continuation of the confusion of her departure

There's No Place Like Home

Figure 1.4 'Maria Running', *White Material*.

and it goes on after arrival – one of the aspects of experiencing migration first-hand is that it is a process, not a defined action. There is much more one can say about Dorothy; her temerity in forming relationships with the three strangers on the road, the first opaque encounter with the city and the unimaginable tasks she is set by the Wizard in order to regain her right to go home. We know that similar tasks are set for the right to stay put:

> The right to the city manifests itself as a superior form of rights: right to freedom, to individualization in socialization, to habit and to inhabit. The right to the oeuvre, to participation and appropriation (clearly distinct from the right to property), are implied in the right to the city.[45]

2

The Red Balloon and *Squirt's Journey*: story-telling with child migrants

– if you were going to make a film about your home – what would be the soundtrack?

Maybe *Travelin' Soldier* by Dixie Chicks because I've always sung it with my mum, or in the car or something, so it's like heading back home, that feeling of going home, so yeah. Probably country, or just like songs on the radio, pop songs or old songs. Stuff like that …

… It's a sad song, but it's about – she meets this guy at a café, she's the waitress and he's going off to war and he wants someone to write to, and he's only just met her and he says 'can I write to you?' and so they kind of fell in love because of that. But then he doesn't come back home, the letters just stop. But it's just a song that even though it's sad it just reminds me of home. Home's not sad but the song just reminds me of home.[1]

One

The films I have discussed in the previous chapter offer various configurations of the migration story, drawing down the cinematic sign of Dorothy.

The fantasy structure that seems so deceptively simple, a mere dream, turns out to be a complex of encounters in which the child criss-crosses between monster and liberator, colonised and coloniser, migrant and settler. I presented films that subtly or overtly show an affinity with the character of Dorothy and to the 1939 film *The Wizard of Oz*. This has entailed excursions into a post-colonial setting, in-country resettlement and also internal movement. Katherine Slater has suggested, in her fine thesis on twentieth century regionalism in children's literature in America, that Baum's 1900 bestseller represented, amongst other achievements, an exercise in cosmopolitan regionalism.[2] As such, she argues, it built on both the social-populism and the local realism of the mid-West which flourished in tandem with the postbellum rise of Chicago as a modern metropolis to challenge New York and Boston. Baum's young Dorothy Gale embodies the unselfconscious cosmopolitanism inherent in a settler region, where many people have migrated from other American states or further afield and where, despite a sometimes conservatively expressed desire for security, their everyday lives are impacted by population shifts, wildly uncertain weather and an unspecified distance from a dimly remembered place called home. Dorothy is white, female and American, albeit an American in a period of great poverty for settlers and a time of challenge for new migrants to the wide open plains of the states of Kansas, Dakota and the rest of the mighty agricultural heartlands. As a fictional heroine, and subsequently a cinematic one, Dorothy's *whiteness* compensates for her low social status and her regional location. As a *female* she is a safe image, in the safe mid-West, of an adventurous spirit. She occupies and extends domestic space, from which she pivots into the fantasy of Oz, a country both within her imagination and within the psycho-geography of a farmstead. A white girl could not easily – whether in fiction and in the social myth of peculiar White vulnerability – walk down a yellow brick road across the diverse and sometimes dangerous landscape of America. In reality, thousands of girls were doing just that in the context of domestic migration. As an *American*, she embodies a country that lauds a settled tradition and belonging, but that is built on colonial conquest, the displacement of native peoples, and constant movement to and from other sites of conquest or influence. Beyond America, *The Wizard of Oz* provokes us to imagine still wider regional configurations, but ones which also draw us into considering the ongoing displacement of nations and peoples, evidenced in the historical and continuing movement of children.

Two

In her famous intervention on the subject of children's literature, Jacqueline Rose declared that it was an impossible construct.[3] How could an adult produce a child's voice? In similar vein the film director Tian Zhuangzhuang has argued that children's film cannot exist.[4] Their claims are logical but also idealistic and open to dispute. Certainly some adults do retain a capacity to talk, write and visualise in ways that communicate effectively to a child and for children in ways that the intended spectators and readers enjoy and accept. In making his documentary *In This World* (2002) Michael Winterbottom collaborated with a child who had travelled and survived a difficult migration process, and in that measure the film has an aspect of authenticated, ontological, child life presence. In thinking about the child migrant through compiling a canon of films that approach their multifaceted lives and histories, it seemed important in my own work to involve co-researchers with immediate experience and a more recent, indeed current, embodiment of a child's-eye view. The preparation for this book has therefore involved interviews and film workshops with first-generation migrant children (transnational and domestic) in Australia, China and the UK. One major point of this hands-on fieldwork was to develop the emotional insights necessary for an informed engagement with contemporary migrant and refugee children – ordinary cosmopolitans, if you like. I wanted to discover how they might pursue their own film-making and introduce their own sense of scale and ontological film thinking into questions of travel, space and the stages of mobility. The process was designed within a framework of collective film spectatorship and discussion, structured approaches to colour and space in life and on film, freeform personal or group discussion and film-making.

I worked with children of refugee background in Sydney and in London, migrant workers' children in southern China and Indigenous high school students in New South Wales, Australia. Thinking around questions of home, journeys and transformations wrought by mobility, my co-locutors crafted their own films – about friendship, transition, zombies, ghosts, starting school, bullying, religious ceremonies, early death and treasure hunts. The project design[5] responded to current debates and practices in childhood studies, where theoretical discussions on children's subjectivity are increasingly nuanced away from the notion of children as perpetually innocent or passive and towards an acknowledgment of complex and layered subjective states.[6] Children's studies address class, ethnicity, identity and citizenship in the frame of competing intercultural expectations and in respect to cross-cultural linguistic and political competencies. These insights derive from post-colonial inflected political critique[7] and from a global (albeit Eurocentric) understanding of mutuality and risk.[8] However, despite the fact that child refugees and child migration have become ever more prominent features of global, and especially urban, life since the end of World War II in Europe and Asia in 1944 and 1945, the topic has not been prominent in considerations of social inclusion and exclusion, cosmopolitanism and 'human flourishing'.[9] Jens Qvortrup has pointed to the continuing 'conceptual homelessness of childhood', and noted that the 'structural analysis' (class, race, caste, ethnicity, gender and so on) were all 'reserved for adults'.[10] Furthermore, where children's subjectivity has been discussed, it is often from the perspective of the needs and fantasies of the adult subject. Child subjectivity is invoked to explain, prefigure and reform the philosopher-adult. Castañeda observes that 'working from one's own adult subjectivity to make claims about the child is fundamentally compromised by the fact that the child has been so consistently constituted as the adult's pre-subjective other'.[11] This observation is pertinent in that the use of participatory methods in revealing child perspectives on cultural objects and social practices is both a counterweight to the primacy of the adult subject and a valuable tool for developing a shared critical consciousness between adults and younger people.[12] Sara Ahmed's cultural analysis of emotion as the 'impressions left by others' also evokes the sense that the child migrant on screen will provoke cosmopolitan engagements of some intricacy.[13]

The first workshops were with a group of young people in London of Afghani heritage, run by myself and a research associate, Tracey Mullan, whose own work focussed on Traveller children's experience in Britain.[14] When working with young people (8–16 years of age), the terminology simplified from 'migration and mobility' to 'journeys'. This allowed those who had experienced a variety of more or less turbulent, disruptive or extended journeys to share a language with their peers without having to divulge personal differences and experiences by dint of insensitive or voyeuristic categorisation. When participants wanted to share personal stories they had the opportunity to do so either to the group or in one-on-one debriefs with a researcher.[15] It was also not appropriate to suggest that children who are now ordinarily resident in the UK or Australia are refugees or migrants first and foremost, as that might serve to re-establish feelings of deracination or uncertainty in their new home. An insistence on reifying 'migration' also forecloses on subsequent experience.[16] What we did seek to do was to valorise *journeys* as subjects of narration in film, and to indicate that films with children or young people as key protagonists were as important and as complicated as any other kind of cinematic storytelling. The underlying premise in conducting the workshops was, then, not that all participants were simply 'migrants' and therefore interesting, but that – due to their exposure to migrancy and relocation – all participants could lay claim to a status of grounded, active and visceral cosmopolitanism that could afford insights and deepen everyone's thought.[17]

In the first week we worked on building a shared vocabulary and visual database of film segments. We discussed space, colour, emotions and journeys, using screenings, reference grids and camera exercises. The discussions were both conceptual and pragmatic. What colours evoke or indicate what emotions? How long is a journey? Are all journeys physical transitions from one place to another, or are there journeys that are more about the self, growing up, changing direction? How does space work on screen, and how can one work with small spaces to show greater truths about feelings and events? In week one we watched the Australian film about the Stolen Generations, *Rabbit-Proof Fence* (2002).[18] The film is based on the story of three girls who, in 1932, escaped the Moore River Children's camp in Western Australia (a detention settlement for children taken from their Aboriginal mothers to be raised as domestic and agricultural labourers in semi-slavery).[19] The girls evaded their captors for several weeks to reach their home in the far north of the State. The sequence that we watched first concerned the decision to escape and the girls' first successes in avoiding capture. The film's tones are blue and brown in these scenes, portraying a landscape that is beautiful but also a demandingly tough space that the girls need to make their friend if they are to survive and move safely across it. The tracker, an Aboriginal man (another uncompromising performance from David Gulpilil), uses his understanding of the country to follow their tracks. They in turn use their intuition and their own in-country intelligence to outwit him. The workshop participants picked up on the drama of the escape but also on the betrayal evidenced by the tracker. One boy commented that the tracker reminded him of spies in his home town. Participants also noted the unreliability of 'law' that did not protect children, but rather pursued them. In this regard one might see that the child philosopher sees the child subject of the law as integral and complete, not the 'pre-subjective other' of assumed adult identities in the making (in that case young Aboriginal people being prepared for manual labour), but young people deserving of full legal protection and respect. In one of our workshops we also discussed the use of colour to produce emotional texture in film. How does it work? Why is it important? What variations may there be for different spectators? We looked at the transition from sepia to Technicolor in *The Wizard of Oz* and also noted the prevailing use of brown in *Rabbit-Proof Fence* and wondered if that colour had an impact on how we understood the film's emotional intentions. A 16-year-old girl remarked that, for her, brown was the colour of humility and decency. She was herself dressed almost entirely in brown tones, a person of quiet aptitude and mature authority in the group. But a 13-year-old boy demurred from her rather calming vision. He told us that, for him, brown was the colour he saw before his eyes and in his head when people couldn't or wouldn't understand him, in terms of what he said and what he felt. He described how he went home to his room after school and lay with his head pressed against the wall to see through the brown. He also said that he wanted to make a 'big movie' one day, about border-crossing bandits and the desert between Peshawar and Kabul. He wanted to get that brown out of his head and onto the screen, to make himself really well understood. We then noted that *Rabbit-Proof Fence* was one of the earliest digitally colour-graded films, and that in a later sequence in the salt flats, 'shots were re-coloured to convey

Figure 2.1 'Molly and her cousins on the whitening plains, early example of digital colour manipulation', *Rabbit-Proof Fence*, image courtesy Australian Film Archive, RMIT Melbourne, permission courtesy Christine Olsen.

a constant passage of time and progressively lightened almost to the point where the image was completely blown out, to convey the extraordinary heat the girls had to endure'[20] (Figures 2.1 and 2.2). It was therefore a clear example of extending time through an engagement with colour.

Furthermore, despite the mix of ages, and perhaps because of the familiarity of family groups, participants revealed some commonalities, which also made this film seem the most appropriate to start the discussion. Also, the group responded well to the opening 'reference grid' exercise in which they were asked to individually match colours with places and emotional states. Subsequent discussions centred on brown and green, both of which are dominant in the *Rabbit-Proof Fence* palette. The group as a whole suggested after seeing *Rabbit-Proof Fence* that the brown of the landscape was also ambivalent. It represented the warmth and traditional space of the Australian landscape which belonged to the girls and their ancestors, but it was nonetheless harsh terrain and dangerous to cross without the support of a tribe or a family. Second, the older members of the group displayed

Figure 2.2 'Molly and her cousins at the fence', *Rabbit-Proof Fence*, courtesy RMIT University Melbourne, Australian Film Archive, and Christine Olsen.

an advanced philosophical and political awareness that they immediately brought to bear in understanding the unjust victimisation of Aboriginal children in twentieth-century Australia. They were particularly outraged that the law was so ineffective in protecting minors but instead was used to imprison them. The connections between contemporary detention of child migrants was not explicit but it is not too much of a stretch to wonder how much they were linking these two experiences or knowledge of the practice and its impacts on members of their peer groups, or what they may have seen on national television news. This brings to mind Ansell's point about the global networks and flattened ontologies of children living as children but in a massive geo-spatial construct of experience and vision.[21]

At the end of the first workshop we also screened an extract from *Jacquot de Nantes* (1991), where colour and monochrome are used, respectively, to indicate the present and the past, but where colour also evokes the strength of feeling in the main protagonist (the young Jacques Demy) towards cinema. The story is about the journey from extreme youth to adolescence in a time of war and from innocence to maturity, expressed through cinema and through Jacques' own journey to become a film-maker. We also looked at a 1949 children's film from China, *Sanmao's Travels*, filmed in black and white shortly after Liberation (1949).²² *Sanmao* concerns the story of a young boy living in the streets of Shanghai. His story resonates with rural-urban migrants around the developing world, but the film is a slapstick comedy, and we used it to think about genre and storytelling. The scene we looked at is where Sanmao salivates over food in the shops and eventually steals a bun, which results in a chaotic chase and a big fight involving lots of boys. The journey in question here was not the circumstances that had brought him to the metropolis, but his everyday journeys through the streets of Shanghai.

The following workshops concentrated on the film-making. The students' brief was to prepare a storyboard of three shots and to tackle the theme of a journey within that very short sequence. Participants were reminded that, given school rules, ethical considerations and the limitations of students coming from all over London, we wouldn't be able to leave the school grounds or work together outside workshop hours, nor would we have much practical control over noise levels, set dressing or timing.²³ This attempt at film-making was always going to be a bit rough and ready but we agreed that we would do whatever we could and have fun. In the event, the group re-convened, presented their storyboards and then split into three smaller production teams to choose a storyboard to work from, allocate roles and start work.

Three films of three shots were duly created. One, *The Wedding*, was a highly comedic account of the theft of a wedding cake by two fat and greedy businessmen, their resulting stomach aches and their rough punishment by the wedding guests. The film was shot in black and white, used costume (fat suits made from cushions) and played with the joint thematic of slapstick humour and retributory violence (punching the cushion-stomach of the 'fat' man). The journey theme emerged through the slapstick as a story of uneven acculturation in a place of arrival and settlement. The story was that two businessmen win the lottery and become too rich too quickly. This makes them greedy and in turn disrespectful of a key family event. The film comments on the disjuncture between family life and the impact of external public worlds which may undermine its principles and security. The second film was a zombie thriller, in which a small brother transforms into a monster and kills his father and sisters. The transition was between one state of being and another, between life and death, and between safety and danger. It may have drawn on devastating memories – or it may simply have been a star vehicle for the boy who could produce a brilliant zombie transformation – but nonetheless the point of the film was to find a visual language in which to communicate change safely. The third film was *Ghost Story*, storyboarded by the 13-year-old boy who viewed brown as the colour of incomprehension. When filmed it was set in the girls' toilet, the idea being that a space that was both private and secluded became uncertain and terrifying. In it, a student asks to go to the bathroom and leaves class. Once in the bathroom she is frightened by an unexplained noise. When she rushes back to class she finds she cannot get back in and the film ends with her pressing her face against the small grated (actually fireproofing wire) window in the classroom door. The ghost was not materialised but manifested as a strange knocking behind a door. Instead of comedy and a spectre with attitude, their film conveyed the transition between security (girls working in a classroom with their teacher) and insecurity (the girl alone in the toilet frightened by the strange noise). One of the three shots panned from the toilet doors, presenting the familiar space as indecipherable and uncanny. The girls asserted their authority through the choice of this film and its main locations – the classroom and the girls' toilets. The teacher was played by the assertive 16-year-old girl (the girl in brown), while its author, by no means one of the more dominant boys in the class, was excluded from a key location (the girls' toilets) where the main action of the film was set. This on-set dynamic was entirely different from *The Wedding*, where the older boys took the best roles and spatially and technically controlled the dynamic of the narrative action, taking also the roles of director and cameraperson. The boys chose relatively open locations outside the classroom – the corridor and landings of the school – and created sequences with fast entries, energetic action in the frame, and noise off-screen. (Indeed, their approach provoked another form of authority as the 'off-screen' noise and general ebullience resulted in our entire project being disciplined by the school's (female) director. We were all confined to the classroom.) *The Wedding* was less disciplined, and of course more comedic, than the serious *Ghost Story*, while the albeit-slapstick violence at the end was necessary but only just under control. However, it proved confronting to the school's director, who requested we film a different ending. We didn't concur but the full edited film could not be shown at the School Open Day because of her qualms about filming masculinity on the edge.

In a one-to-one-feedback interview, Tracey, the research associate, talked with the 13-year-old who had storyboarded *Ghost Story*. He discussed what he felt about the day's filming. He was happy his storyboard had been chosen but felt sad and a bit left out by the decision to make it a film in the girls' toilets (he had set it in a boys' block). He then went on to talk about a film he would like to make. The film is set in a 'deserty place with poor people'. The main protagonist would be a street boy who tries to attack some adults and steal their money. He is caught but they offer him food, education and other (unspecified) advantages. When he does not live up to their expectations they cast him back onto the street. He said he would shoot his film in India although it was set in Afghanistan, because India is safe. He explained that Pakistan would be an option as the army provided some protection, but that Afghanistan was an impossible location as the film-maker might be kidnapped. He was planning a film about the very kind of risk that he has himself escaped, kidnapping, betrayal and random changes in circumstance. In this apparently simple discussion, we get a glimpse of a relationship between sites of global conflict and the safe places identified by children in a school setting – safe places that nonetheless prove haunted and frightening.

The London students helpfully identified three genre films that they felt would be useful to my research, and why. The first, *Twilight* (2008), describes the progress of a young woman who discovers she is destined to be a vampire. Her struggle and her eventual acceptance of her fate as part of her relationship with her vampire boyfriend are the 'journey'. One could see the supernatural in the ghost film made by the predominantly female group, although the romantic element of *Twilight* was not replicated. This was due to the presence of younger brothers in the class. Second, they recommended *I am Legend* (2007), a zombie film. In it the adult protagonist (played by Will Smith) is separated from his family, with whom he is desperate to be re-united. The 'journey' is from despair to hope. He eventually sacrifices himself for the sake of the next generation in the person of a woman and her son. The school zombie film was derived from this kind of inspiration, but the child zombie was at the centre and indeed killed the family. This is clearly not the same as a lost adult searching for his lost children. The ambivalence of the zombie subject has been of immense value in considering films that on the one hand reveal the loss of bodily integrity and security in forced migration and the desire for saviours on the other. Finally, they mentioned *Home Alone 2* (1992). This is a geographical journey and also an internal 'journey' as the protagonist encounters peril, challenges it and overcomes it by triumphing over the bad guys. 'Triumphing over the bad guys' was not obvious in the students' films except perhaps in the punishment of the greedy businessmen. Nonetheless, the obvious connection to children travelling alone and the limits to which a child can trust adults was useful, particularly in relation to *Little Moth* and *Landscape in the Mist* (Chapters 4 and 5) but I also found the children's advice relevant to thinking about comedy overall as a pathway to challenging thematics such as abandonment.

The opening workshop program therefore gave me more films to watch, but also an indication of the value of my co-locutors' insights. Their use of mainstream genre in interpreting a narrative task (the journey), and imagining the challenges as monsters or cartoonish villains, indicates a sensibility that brings together personal and emotional experience with global modalities. This approach both distances the subject from the object of the study (migrant from migration), and reiterates the grounded cosmopolitanism of migrant children within general populations. It makes visible their competent manipulation of global flows of cultural materials and intercultural translation into communicative action. The capacity to see journeying within emotional matrices of despair, hope and destiny suggest a maturity of vision and a depth of comprehension that challenge estimations of youth as pre-subjective and recasts mobility, interruption and settlement as components requiring cosmopolitan endurance. And of course the optimism as well as the frankness of the participants was inspiring.

> We learned that a journey isn't just moving from place to place. It can also be making friends, or starting something new.[24]

Three

A second round of workshops took place in Fairfield, Sydney in 2014, conducted with two research associates, film-maker Enda Murray and social policy expert Inara Walden. The main characteristic of this group was its cultural and ethnic diversity and the speed with which the young people (14–15 years old) had taken on a working multi-ethnic Australian persona. Several of the participants had arrived on the Australian refugee programme over the previous two or three years and were operating in a second or third language.[25] Places of origin included Sri Lanka, Syria, the Pacific Islands, Europe, India, South East Asia, China, Lebanon and Iraq.[26]

The students saw a similar range of film segments and they also completed the colour-emotion-place reference grid and group discussions. The most noteworthy aspect of their responses was their use of black as a colour to designate fear and sadness, and the linking of the colour to a number of places – the road, the station and the city. This was statistically not significant. We were not in any case seeking a quantifiably replicable sample but were rather evoking colour as an elicitation tool for preparing participants for visual expression through film. However, this was the only group in which black figured dominantly as a descriptor of place and as such deserves report. In his book *Notes on an Exodus*, Richard Flanagan recounts a series of meetings with Syrian refugees in camps in Europe and Lebanon. He notices too that children are making drawings in black.

> Like the other children drawing their memories of Syria, he
>   reaches only for black and blue pencils, the darkest colours.
> 'Because of Daesh, everything is black,' Ibrahim explains.
> … 'It was smoky, black, because of the bombing,'
> I ask him what other colours were in Deir ez-Zor.
> 'There were no other colours.'[27]

The reference grids done and discussed, the students familiarised themselves with the equipment through three-way interviews with each other (camera operator, interviewer and interviewee) before sharing those short clips with each other and debating technique. One-on-one interviews were also available for all students as part of the activities, in part for debriefing and in part to ensure that everyone's voice was heard and felt to be heard clearly. As the school had a number of iPads available we used those in place of our own media kits as it made it easier for students to run a dummy edit on their own rushes in the days between workshops. The final films (obeying the rules of three shots on the storyboard) are short but powerful, especially viewed as a collection. Three were made by girls (the gender divide was enforced by the students) and one by a group of boys. Groups were three to four students per film (and per iPad). The films are light in aspect, in part because they are filmed outside in a sunny environment. Fairfield in Western Sydney is a low-rise suburb with wide blue skies, silver-green trees and strong sun. The subject matter of the films is less joyful. All three of the girls' films include a sequence in which a protagonist cries. In *Lost* three girls play together happily sitting on the grass. The camera pans up to a blue sky and then down again to the girls, but now only two are left. Time has passed. The scene shifts to the third girl walking towards a tree and collapsing. Finally, we are in a makeshift hospital scene, the two friends holding the third girl's hand as she dies. They are crying. The first scenes are in colour, the final scene shifts to monochrome. In *New School* a girl is suffering from loneliness and bullying. In scene one she tells her teacher. In scene two her sobbing is interrupted by a third girl who offers to play ball with her. They hug, telling each other that they are friends forever. In the final scene the teacher awards a graduation certificate to the first girl. In *Without You* the soundtrack consists of classical Arabic music. The visuals begin with shots (taken from photographs) of a highly decorative and beautiful Lebanese building in colour (they were unable to tell us what building it was but had cut it out from a magazine at home). This shot cuts to a magazine picture of the Sydney Opera House in monochrome. The next pictures are of aeroplanes, Air Oman and MEA (Middle Eastern Air – Lebanon's national carrier). The latter is a photograph that came from a family scrapbook. The final scenes are live action. Two people sit on the kerb and sob. They walk down a path away from us hand in hand. The final scene is an explanation – the same two people waving goodbye to two others on the steps of a house. The whole is a deft and moving portrait of the swiftness of air travel set against the lingering pain of losing family. The brightness of the first building is contrasted to the dullness of a place that is not yet fully inhabited or emotionally owned by new arrivals.

The boy's film was called *Death of Yasar*. It was less elegiac, but nonetheless disturbing. The boys made good use of pantomime dress ups for their adult characters – a fat dad with an outlandish wig, and a 'psycho' landlord with a long grey cloak and hood. Scene one consists of two boys playing football. There is a shot indicating one boy's prowess as he deals with a ball kicked in from off-screen left. Then they hail their father who has come to watch them play, but immediately shout a warning as the psycho landlord appears in the background and kills the father for non-payment of rent. The film is organised with inter-titles and is stylistically in the realm of silent movies and high melodrama. The adults are present only in their costumed strangeness and an emotional register of indecipherability. *Death of Yasar* does not include the intense and realistic crying and sobbing of the girls' films. It does however portray sudden death and an irrational enemy. In all four films there is a focus on loss, separation and uncertainty. *New School* finds a resolution through a new friendship and a certain trust in an institution to support their progress. The films are nostalgic (*Loss, Without You*), fearful of sudden death (*Death of Yasar, Loss*), and entirely focused on the centrality of youth. Adults are either absent or ineffective, or dangerous. Even the friendly teacher in *New School* does not solve any problems. The girls do that themselves.

A third set of workshops took place in a school in Sydney with a different demographic and category of migrant. A girls' Catholic boarding school offers scholarships to children of Indigenous identity who travel to school from country areas (and elsewhere in the metropolitan region). The students in our workshops were almost all from country New South Wales. The largest number came from socio-economically disadvantaged Aboriginal communities of Walgett, Moree and Bourke, as well as Wagga Wagga, Taree, Tamworth and the Central Coast. Two girls were from Sydney, including one from the coastal area of La Perouse. Not all girls were Catholic. It is fair to say that the films produced by the girls echoed not only a sense of nervousness or suspicion in regards to religious authority, but also a strong indication of the difference between habits of worship and hierarchy encountered through school from those they had been used to (if any) at home. Though we asked the girls to consider the theme of 'leaving' in their story-making, within the environment of the school grounds and given the nature of films the girls chose, which were tending towards comedy and ghost stories, there was less emphasis on the idea that leaving would be associated with leaving home. Characters who had to 'leave' were usually made to leave the school for misdemeanours, or because they were forced out by fear of ghosts.

More reflection from the girls about leaving home and living away from loved ones, animals and familiar places came out in the single and double audio interviews.[28] Many girls spoke of the transition from home to school as difficult, that they yearned for their families, pets and cousins. More time with their mothers was something a number of girls wished they had, others spoke of fond times driving in the car and playing music, and singing together. When asked to bring in items they owned as transitional objects for the film, items they brought along often reminded them of the bond with their mother. One girl brought in a special cuddly dressing gown that she snuggles into as though it were her mother (the same girl quoted at the top of this chapter discussing her choice of music). A number of girls said they would like to cast a family member or pet in a film as they are 'so funny' or would make 'a great character' – brother, mother, little sister, dog. Girls spoke of making a new kind of family at school that included their carers, teachers and other girls. Singing in the shower and playing music together with other boarders was described as a bonding activity. Some girls felt boarding school was always noisy and busy, whilst home in the country is quiet and peaceful. Some were cousins or distant cousins, but others also formed very close attachments with roommates. For the group of cousins, it was important that they had all been given little matching troll dolls by a grandmother and one girl's sister, and this set of dolls formed their own family that lived with them at boarding school, staying with them in their different rooms.[29]

All of the girls were familiar with *The Wizard of Oz* from seeing the film at home and they wanted to watch it again, so this was the most proactively 'Dorothy'-themed workshop.[30] The final group photographs included one with Enda, with a life-size cardboard cut-out of Judy Garland as Dorothy.[31] The cut-out provided a useful elicitation tool for a group who were already so familiar with our background text and instinctively very aware that the film had resonance with discussions about being at home in Australia and being separated from home, despite also being at home in another broader sense within a large and highly differentiated social and physical environment. Their everyday lives necessitated a continued migration between family life and the city school, moving across and between the continuing practices and architectures of a colonial past, Indigenous modernity in rural and urban areas and conflicting religious sensibilities. The girls used the reference grids to indicate very firm ideas about the differences between Sydney-the-city, Sydney-the-school-environment and their homes. There was a notable use of red and orange for rural and regional towns (Moree) and blue and yellow for those who lived closer to the sea (La Perouse). In other words, they found it easy to *describe* home exactly. The city by contrast was either marked with *all* colours or just one – red, blue or white, indicating a shift to impression over description. The girls were also very certain of the 'most important thing you have left behind when you have made a long journey'. The answers were a variation of 'my (extended) family', variously: 'my nan', 'my nan and pop and my dog', 'my brothers and sisters and my dog', 'my mum dad brother and nan'. When asked to name films that used colour well to perform place and emotion they named *Bran Nue Dae* (orange), *The Hunger Games – Catching Fire* (orange, red), *Harry Potter* (black), *Rabbit-Proof Fence* (red – for sadness), *Wild Child* (blue), *The Book Thief* (grey – for a new place), *Red Dog* (red – for dust), *War Horse* (dark colours – for war) and *Frozen* (cold white colours for sad and happy). The value of the elicitation exercise in this group was the introduction of a very differently configured canon of works than those we had seen in London. Gender clearly played a part (*Frozen, Wild Child*) but so did a sense of Australian (especially Indigenous or Indigenous-related) film-making, culture and place (*Red Dog, Bran Nue Dae, Rabbit-Proof Fence*), and there was a profound sense of the difference between places through colour, even though that place might be co-located with non-Indigenous modernity. Kansas is Oz and Oz is Kansas – La Perouse is in Sydney and Sydney started at La Perouse. *The Wizard of Oz* was really *their* film, their text and their conundrum.

The third stage in these workshops was to bring in the beloved or special (transitional) object.[32] The girls brought in teddies and soft toys, a dressing gown (as described above), a phone (which held a cache of photographs) and hard-copy family photos. During the scripting and dressing process, these objects were referred to or used directly. Three groups made three films (with a lot of collaboration in acting, scripting and design). *Ghost Story* was another tale of a ghost in the school lavatory block – which second time around made it seem highly likely that the Harry Potter franchise, in which Hogwarts' girls' toilets are haunted by 'Moaning Myrtle', was impacting global views on toilets in schools. Even without the factor of gender exclusivity, the lavatory block in a school is a special place. Students have some privacy there and they can escape there for a break during class. This element of secrecy and escape makes them (for J.K. Rowling as much as the London and Sydney film groups) an ideal location for the uncanny and the secret to emerge unchallenged by authority.[33] The girls told us that their film was inspired by a story of a nun who died from a fall and who now haunts the older part of the school. The ghost was physicalised in a white sheet stalking the main protagonist on her way through the back corridors to the bathroom. The terror in the film was evinced by the girl's sensation of the creature when the lavatory shakes and disorients her so that she rushes back to her class. The main 'leaving' point of the film seems to come at the end, where the fact of the ghost is used by the students to get back *out of class* as fast as possible with a merry 'bye sir' on their way through the door. *Bullied Teacher* was a story about a teacher (Miss Blueberry in a blue wig) who has a banana thrown at her head and is then mocked by her students. The key character is a diminutive police officer, Sergeant L (played by the youngest girl in the group) with a large plastic microphone and an even larger hat. The performance is funny, mocking the policeman's self-regard but finally allowing him (gendered male by a stick-on moustache) to solve the mystery and lock up the criminal (the head-teacher, who has bribed a student to throw the banana). The 'leaving' in the film is the expulsion from school of an authority figure. The head-teacher was played by a non-Indigenous girl who used a deep-south American accent to emphasise her non-Indigenous identity. Notably, the denouement shifted quite forcibly into the language of a courtroom drama, jail and criminality, with the offending adult placed behind wooden banisters to indicate imprisonment. The indictment was not just about any bullying and any object. Football fans in Australia have been rebuked for throwing bananas at Indigenous players as an overtly and deliberately racist act.[34] The girls' film appropriated the trope of 'throwing a banana', this time at the behest of an authority figure, played by a non-Indigenous girl, at a bullied character, played by an Indigenous student.

The final film *Squirt's Journey* used the objects that had been brought in to elicit a story. Squirt is a soft toy, a tortoise. The film is Squirt's story of travelling and arriving for her first day at school, and her dream about the first day. The opening scene uses other toys (plastic troll dolls owned by the group of cousins) to represent other children who welcome Squirt. This fades to a dream sequence. The dream starts with a journey. Squirt is pulled along on the dressing gown (her train) on the way to the city, and then begins a 'typical' day at school. The girls used the older part of the school buildings that were once part of a convent and which lent a gothic aesthetic to the sequence (it was the same set that afforded the banisters-prison in *Bullied Teacher* and also prompted reminders of the ghostly nun). The dream commences on a dark stairway which serves as a location for a chapel service. The girls used creepy tilted shots of Catholic statues, and the sequence was enacted as though setting the stage for a celebrity preacher: 'please welcome ... the Priest!!' The Priest is dressed up with a mad wig and a sparkling cloak and again speaks with a heavy deep-south American accent, although the character was played by a different girl. The camera pulls back and reveals Squirt on the altar watching the performing priest on the stairway before her. The second part of the dream sequence is a swimming lesson set in the school's beautiful outdoor pool. The soft toys get very wet and a feeling of genuine enjoyment, friendship and happiness is communicated. The dream ends and Squirt's voiceover states she *will have* a good first day at school. Well, maybe. The religious service cannot but be read as a critique of the heaviness of Catholic imagery and hierarchy, and is played effectively for weirdness as well as laughs. In one-to-one interviews, girls mentioned their unease and slight fear of the religious imagery and ceremony of formal worship. *Squirt's Journey* played effectively with tropes learned from *The Wizard of Oz* – dreams, the use of non-human actors, and the creation of a place that is quite exotic and not at all like home. *Squirt's Journey* produced specific and boldly made contrasts between mocking the domination of school hierarchy and acknowledging the pleasures afforded by school life. It is seditious but careful. All the films found some excuse to mock adult, White authority. Whether this was an emotional response of girls in boarding school, or whether this was a direct correlation of girls from Indigenous backgrounds who are well aware of the generations of abuse and the formalised disrespect of settler authority in regards to Indigenous rights and laws in Australia, is difficult to say. However, as we go onto discuss activist critique in film in Chapter 6 we may want to recall these early notes of dissent.

Four

The fourth workshop sessions took place in Guangzhou in southern China. The participants were primary school children (6–12 years) who had moved from other parts of Guangdong and further afield from other provinces, with their parents. They lived in a peripheral area of the city populated by migrant workers. The children all attended a school on the same street most of them lived in. The workshops were organised through an NGO run drop-in centre on the same street, set up for children to use after school so that they could do their homework or be given extra educational resources. Most of them had no space to work at home and many would have had no parental care until late in the evening if they went straight home – migrant parents do not have the childcare resources of grandparents and extended families to draw on. The main security afforded by the residential area was that it lay over about three streets and formed a kind of urban village, so that the children had imaginary boundaries and some sense of home territory.[35]

The facilitation team comprised myself, a Cantonese-speaking, Guangzhou-born colleague from Sydney and a postdoctoral associate from Ningbo Zhejiang University. Two volunteer teachers at the centre also helped, who were both the children of parents who had migrated to cities in the 1980s and well understood the challenges of displacement, separation and prejudice for the children in their care. The children spoke a mixture of dialects although most had a smattering of Mandarin (standard Chinese) as well as southern Chinese dialect. These children were markedly less materially advantaged than our previous groups. Their parents could barely afford school fees and there were no scholarships available to them. Migrant workers do not have the right to remain in the cities nor to access its welfare provisions. These children thus had no access to the cultural systems and State-run opportunities for Guangzhou-born children in the main city, and no contact with children outside their own small urban village network. The area had been built on land previously used for agriculture but was now a high-density urban district rented out by farmers who had been forced off the land by urban development, and who had themselves invested in low-grade property as an alternative livelihood. The farmers passed on the cost of this investment to the migrants through high rents. The NGO's drop-in centre was itself tiny, with only minimum ventilation and heating. That was all they could afford to rent in the street.

In order to show the children films we brought a mini projector and computer which projected across the one metre between the children's work table and a white wall. The film chosen was *The Red Balloon* (1956). The films that the volunteer teachers had collected on VCD and occasionally showed the children on the teacher's computer were mainly titles made by the Children's Film Unit[36] or nature documentaries. *The Red Balloon* was a less didactic choice and it engaged with the children's experience of street life. In the film, a small boy plays with a magically conscious red balloon and together they explore the back streets of Paris. Their friendship is challenged by a gang of other boys seeking to steal the red balloon, which is eventually trapped and popped. A cloud of coloured balloons come from all over Paris to mourn their fellow balloon's passing, and which by take the boy up and away across the city streets and rooftops. It is a moment of absolute solidarity, and escape. We also looked at extracts from *Sanmao's Travels* (1949), the slapstick comedy about the boy living on the streets of Shanghai. Paris in the 1950s and Shanghai in the 1940s are not Guangzhou in 2014, but the narrowness of the streets, the occasional piles of rubble and the attraction of food shops and the possibilities for play to small children provided points of geospatial and emotional reference. *The Red Balloon* is a child-centred film that is close to the kind of flattened ontology, heightened emotional credibility and child's-eye view achievement that Jacqueline Rose and Tian Zhuangzhuang judged impossible. It also features a beloved object – the balloon – that was so central to our filmmaking process. Other benefits of this film were the absence of spoken language, the children's hectic mobility, and the emphasis on colour – this group was young and responded enthusiastically to a film that excelled in visual storytelling.

Their responses were also impressively cogent. The children explained that the film was about true friends (*zhen pengyou*) and false friends (*jia pengyou*). The red balloon was a 'true friend' to the boy and the coloured balloons in the final sequence were in turn 'true friends to the red balloon and the boy'. The boys who chased the boy and balloon were false (*jia*), and not to be trusted. The children's capacity to understand boys and balloons as equivalent subjects and protagonists in the film suggest that they (and the director Lamourisse) were thinking through the film as a field of equivalence in ontological value and subjectivity. It is an example from the perspective of both film-maker and spectators of diversity within a shared (flattened) frame of reference across a global geo-spatial imaginary. The balloon is the boy's friend, not his toy, and the boy is the balloon's friend. The relationship between the two protagonists is crucial and real. We saw echoes of the film in both the interviews and in the final films of this group. These similarities were in part inevitable given that the space available to them in which to film, interview one another and plan their storyboards were the two narrow streets and their tiny NGO library and workroom (Figures 2.3, 2.4, 2.5). The children occupied the streets in parallel with the adults who moved through on their way to and from work or shopping, sat outside shops and homes on plastic crates, or just stood around chatting. These adults were unwitting extras in the resulting films. The children ran around them, played with their ball, and during the workshop with the cameras, as though in a totally different space. Neither group took any notice of the other. This was also a premise of the film – whereby a struggle for safety of both boy and balloon continues through the streets of Paris without any obvious adult interference or interest.

In the second workshop the children brought with them special things from home, which they understood as objects that they felt to be like their own red balloon. One boy brought his tortoise, another brought a packet of colouring pencils, another brought a spinning top and a ball,

The Red Balloon and *Squirt's Journey*

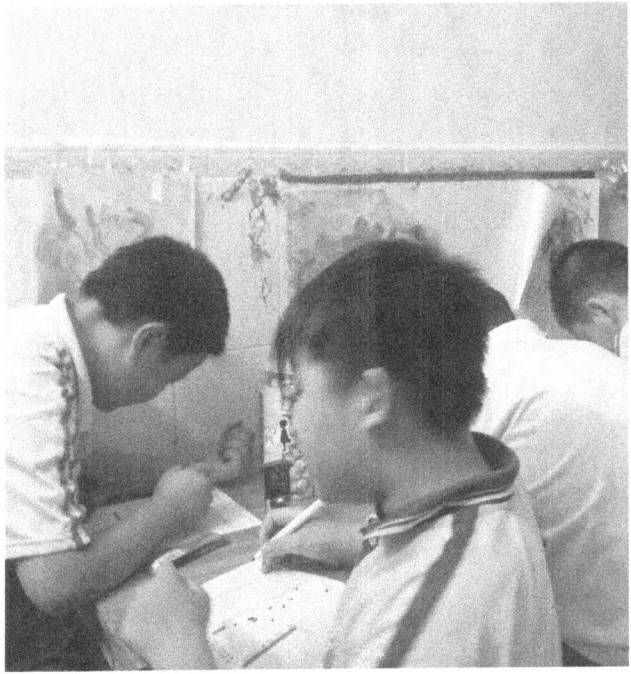

Figure 2.3 'Filling in reference grids, Guangzhou 2014', image courtesy of the author, the children and Ming Liang.

and another a small silver hammer that turned into a knife (which the teacher kept a close eye on as we all nervously suggested that it be kept as a hammer). Two boys didn't bring anything but asked if they could use special things in the drop-in centre instead. The films that resulted were edited and linked up as the 'Red Balloon Collection'. The results were returned to the children on CDs and USB memory sticks so that the teacher could give them a copy each after screening it to them as a group. NGO workers from around southern China also saw them and suggested that the method be rolled out to other teachers and workers in other provinces as the project showed that migrant children were as talented and inventive as any other children and had good stories to tell on their own account.[37] Both adults and children asked that the children be fully acknowledged by name in any write-up of their productions. The

Figure 2.4 'Storyboarding, Guangzhou, 2014', image courtesy of the author, the children and Ming Liang.

final films were therefore named after the nominated scriptwriter. Two friends (Wang Richen and Lu Yifeng) made the 'same' film about a treasure hunt, each finding their treasure after a happy hunt down the street followed by a ransacking of the drop-in centre – 'I'm digging!!' – the treasures were respectively the silver hammer and a teacher's badminton racquet. Tie Hanlong and Lu Weicheng also worked together. They used the coloured pencils to create two simple animated stories. The first is a challenge between two tortoise owners (the 'owners' are drawn figures on paper). Shot one is a mid-shot of Tie's tortoise. The second is an extreme close-up of the same tortoise. The gag is that the second is much bigger than the first so the paper boy with the 'small' tortoise withdraws the challenge. Lu (the artist) made his own story entirely on paper. Three children go to the city to do some shopping on their own to buy toys, clothes and food. They get lost and are relieved when their parents find them and they get home safely. They resolve not to go back into the city again. Lu confided to us that he wanted to be an animator when he grows

The Red Balloon and *Squirt's Journey*

Figure 2.5 'Storyboard for an animation, Guangzhou 2014', image courtesy of the author, the children and Ming Liang.

up. Given the uneven opportunities available to these migrant children it seems unlikely that he will be able to achieve this goal, a realisation which is extremely saddening having watched his careful and determined work on the two animated films. There is a serious lack of educational parity between urban children and migrant children in cities in China. Migrant children 'often face higher tuition fees and exclusion from public schools' and girls suffer most in terms of attendance and attainment.[38] In a study of *Last Train Home* (2009), a film about domestic migration seen from the point of view of the children left behind in the countryside by working parents, Chinese sociologists note of the young female protagonist, 'Whatever she dreams to do, to end up being like her parents is unlikely to be one of the achievements she wants to boast … However, this is to a large degree what the future holds for the majority of Chinese migrant workers.'[39] In other words, she will not achieve the educational excellence that her parents dream of for her. Rather, deracinated by their prolonged absence, she will follow them into migration, unachievable dreams of urban excitement and, most likely, cyclical poverty. All one can hope is that the unlikely occurs for animator Lu.

WZY[40] was the oldest boy in the group (12 years old) and his film was the most ambitious. In scene one the bookseller introduces her selection of books. In scene two a family in the bookshop is disturbed by a man telling them that the bookseller has returned to her hometown and that the shop will close. The son is upset and the parents resolve to buy all the books to protect his education. In scene three the parents admit that they now face disaster as all of their money has been spent. This story draws on the children's experience of financial uncertainty and the instability surrounding undocumented residence. Migrant workers face high levels of prejudice and criticism as incomers, and experience high levels of mental illness and depression.[41] WZY himself exhibited signs of depression and anxiety in the opening workshop, including banging his head on the wall. I asked him to film the proceedings for our record (as well as take part in the usual exercises). With a camera in his hand, and some small control over his life and its representation for a few hours, he was calm, imaginative and powerful. His is a precarious existence and he endeavours to communicate that to us in this film. I would like us to hold that image of a child speaking through film, in his own voice, in mind.

The work with young migrants endeavoured to elicit insights from a wider and ontologically 'flattened' research field through an action-oriented research program of workshops, discussions and feedback opportunities. The children and young people report, through film, seeing themselves in place and out of place, safely at home and yet suspended on the fringes of civility. They ask us to watch zombie films and to think about transformations which are dangerous, horrifying and endlessly repeated by the very nature of a virus that produces death without erasure, and life without breathing. They show us secret places where the imagination can run riot and where fears can rise up without contradiction or denial, like ghosts in the toilet block. To confront the confidence of adult performances, they use the toys, perform as men dressing in extraordinary robes to insist on their authority from God, men with truncheons and teachers with blue hair, or psycho landlords who are capable of killing a man in front of his son. They may not be saying that a psycho landlord is stalking the streets of

Sydney, but they are reminding us that people die for less than unpaid rent. They also tell us stories about restricted opportunities, cities that are too unfriendly to enter alone and greedy societies that rub up against sociocultural behaviours in ways that produce slapstick comedy over the loss of a wedding cake, but also afford us the insights produced by the uncompromising moral scale of childhood judgement. The young film-makers work within a flattened ontology that moves across accelerated cultural decay and the disintegration of family responsibility and security, even as they enact childhood-as-method, portraying worlds in which adults are peripheral to their concerns, and in which slapstick is, rightly, both hilariously funny and intensely serious, and slightly threatening to adult hierarchies looking in.

3

Once My Mother, *Welcome* and *Le Havre*: breath and the child cosmopolitan

One

'If we walk far enough', said Dorothy, 'we shall sometime come to some place, I am sure.'[1]

The first word of *Oz* is 'Dorothy', the last two words are 'home again.'[2]

There is not a country on the planet not touched by human mobility and there are few, if any, examples of human mobility in which children are not moving too. In September 2015, UNICEF reported that 25,000 unaccompanied children had arrived in Europe that year alone. Meanwhile, they noted that up to two million children had left Syria for refuge in the immediate region.[3] In 2012, UNHCR released a report that indicated that 'of the 33.9 million "people of concern" to that organisation around half were under 18 and thus classified as children.'[4] In 2015, Save the Children reported assisting over a million refugee children in Europe.[5] Even in less confronting circumstances, the child migrant has many challenges. She must overcome the vulnerabilities of being both young and foreign, and often without adult assistance. She must have enough of an imagination to hold faith in the idea of a better future, whilst dealing with the long weeks and months (in some cases years) of travel, detention, camps and abuse – without any of the ordinary securities of home, school and community networks to rely on. Thus, the child migrant is the cosmopolitan of the grassroots, a grounded person, a cosmopolitan by necessity, emerging from unintended or inescapable circumstance which may be, as the British cultural and post-colonial theorist Paul Gilroy says, 'uncomfortable' to contemplate[6] – and very difficult to survive. Survival is itself an enterprise of ongoing grounded cosmopolitan endeavour. The child migrant has a whole life to build, she must be 'open'[7] to the world in which she finds herself and thus find ways to subtly contest the powerful fantasies of adult authority that keep children in their place. That is, she must learn how she might create a space of arrival and settlement in which she belongs, where she has claimed both private and public rights, where she is, in short, *at home*. In Salman Rushdie's analysis of *The Wizard of Oz*, Dorothy is a quintessential cinematic migrant child.[8] In my present exploration, she is a signature from which to identify such children across world cinema. This is not because any one film – and certainly not *The Wizard of Oz* – presents a realistic story of all young people moving from one geo-political zone to another, but because the bones of the story have sufficient malleability to capture the sense that change is always hard, that cross-border mobility is a process rather than a smooth movement and that children are constantly moving through versions of the self as a form of maturation and a kind of loss. Dorothy's mobility comments on the different *scales* of the adult world and childhood, the flattened ontology of childhood geography, or simply of childhood encountering adult worlds and surviving them. In filming stories that essay childhood transitions, including actual migrations, the narrative cannot define mobility by distance alone but also by the scaled imaginary power of experience in place and space, especially where that impacts on an accelerated shift from childhood to adulthood. This is I think the point that I am essaying in my own appropriation and development of Rushdie's insight. Cinema at its best asks us to recognise ourselves on screen, singly and collectively. So, for me, the child migrant is an embodiment of human courage and adaptivity and as such she is the quintessential cosmopolitan. Cosmopolitanism does not entail an elite category of borderless, globe-trotting, capital-rich travellers, nor the federated political idealism inexplicably cushioned from the furies and passions of nationalist and ideological community, nor even, or not simply, the general Kantian figure of a peaceful sojourner and traveller in a shared world space who may claim 'the privilege of strangers arriving on foreign soil', a right that underpins a desirable, 'cosmopolitan constitution' between states.[9] Cosmopolitanism is the ordinary, difficult task of remaining a stranger whilst almost 'fitting in'.[10]

The child migrant is also the child who is sent away from home by the state without being consulted and often without the informed consent of parents or carers. This is the stolen child. In film, this specific form of abandonment brings commonality between the Indigenous girls of Philip Noyce's *Rabbit-Proof Fence*, the Catholic, institutionalised forced migrants of the television series *The Leaving of Liverpool* (1992 – see Chapter 6) and the wrecked adult survivors of the same British-Australian child migrant system portrayed in Jim Loach's *Oranges and Sunshine* (2010). The latter film does not work with children directly but with adults carrying their damaged childhoods with them like rocks, a continuation of the forced labour they endured when very young. Stolen children all, they were caught up in a system that could not or would not see children and childhood as valuable, sentient, vulnerable and whole. Ironically, their enforced journeys gave them the insight of the grounded cosmopolitan while the adults who shared the same physical or temporal space refused to embrace or acknowledge that vision and that pain. What, then, distinguishes a grounded cosmopolitan from a traveller who is protected from the impact of displacement, or one who displaces her own unhappiness onto the next generation?

Perhaps we could say that grounded cosmopolitanism is an outcome of *experienced mobility within the condition of migrancy*. Migrancy encompasses the complexities of causation, settlement, pluri-cultural societies and national identities. Migrancy involves mobility, but the condition of being a migrant does not necessarily require constant motion between places of origin and arrival, nor is the term a sufficient descriptor of those who have migrated or of their experience of that process.[11] The migrant is the emigrant, the settler, the grounded, visceral and grassroots cosmopolitan, and that is not a role that everyone can easily inhabit. Experienced mobility is difficult to do – or to cite Paul Gilroy again – uncomfortable to contemplate from the position of one who is always already settled and unproblematically at home.[12]

Empire

This chapter discusses films about children or young people who experience the internal motion of the self. In academic debate it has, in the main, been geographers who have broached the political ramifications of the concept of *mobilities*, its connections to understanding settlement and migration, and the value of historically contextualised, local case studies based on age and class. Such scholars have correctly noted that there are complex relationships between the movement of people in space and the socio-political journeys they take on arrival in a settler or receiving country, and indeed continue to take over decades of settlement and returns.[13] Disciplinary collaborations pursue the relationship between the identity and image of the city, human agency and citizenship and the social politics of place.[14]

> When movement is theorised as a traumatic, enforced experience; or as an elective, opportunistic type of displacement that enables personal growth, exploration or simply an overcoming of ennui; or indeed as a more orchestrated, imperialist kind of territorialisation amounting to conquest rather than quest – when all these types of mobility are accounted for, we are obviously far from an uncritical celebration of the phenomenon.[15]

At the root of these approaches is Henri Lefebvre's seminal work on the 'right to the city' for the working poor. The city is only available to those who can negotiate its pathways and who have the wherewithal to access its affordances. The global city does not display flattened ontology. Its scale is hierarchical and exacting. The arrival of the migrant child in this dynamic develops a flattened set of demands and elaborates Lefebvre's claim that the 'right to the city referred to the right to difference, the right to inhabit, and to participate in the city as a citizen, and was not reserved for the privileged few'[16], with childhood as one point of difference, and childhood migration another.[17]

There are at least two kinds of participation and inhabitation. The child migrant who sees and feels the mutability of place, and senses the imminent possibility of its transformation or disappearance, is not necessarily empowered by that visionary perspective. Indeed, the child may also be the object of post-colonial seeing, and may need an acknowledgment of the liminal fractions of a travelling life. In his assessment of an archive of British colonial cinema, Paul Gilroy is unequivocal on the issue of who defines and inhabits a cosmopolitan outlook and how challenging it might be to adopt it as a form of critical spectatorship,

> we should not underestimate that reckoning with the *uncomfortable* [my italics] material that has been assembled ... demands new interpretative approaches and a novel variety of social, cultural and historical enquiry.[18]

Gilroy proceeds to call for a 'dialogic spirit' and 'a consciousness of a common predicament' in looking squarely at films that see the world from the perspective of a powerful imperial imagination but ignore that of the protagonists. In a prime example of the very opposite of flattened ontology in action, the British Colonial Film Unit created *Springtime in an English Village* (1944), a short film about twin girls, Stephanie and Connie, the daughters of an African seaman, fostered out to a couple in an English village for safety during World War II. The film depicts a May procession and shows one of the twins crowned Queen of the May. The May festival is a manifestation of English village life, a pagan tradition for the start of summer that was appropriated into Christian symbolism from as early as the twelfth century. The children wear white, carry flowers and process in solemn gaiety until the Queen reaches her throne and is crowned with a garland of flowers by her friends. The problem with *Springtime in an English Village* is not the subject matter per se but the use for which it was conceived. The target audience was imperial subjects: 'an extremely pretty little film which we think will have an appeal, not only in Africa, but also in the whole Colonial Empire'.[19] Its self-conscious pastoral version of 'integration' is better than exclusion but, looking together with Gilroy, the film is anachronistic and insulting to the girls rather than the endearing vignette intended. Gilroy asks us to encounter such films through the eyes not only of the oppressed or infantilised colonial subject, but through the unbound eyes of a conjoint, pluri-cultural, contemporary, post-colonial subject.

I borrow Gilroy's twinning of dialogue and consciousness with *a cosmopolitan imagination* as a framework for explaining my interpretative engagement with the cinema of child migration, in which *Springtime* is an early example, although one that lacks a self-critical distance. What is absent is the concept of childhood-as-method and the commitment to a flattened ontology when treating the subject of childhood experience. The remainder of this chapter seeks out films where, in different ways and from a range of subjective positions, film-makers have achieved such unbound eyes. We can start with a welcome contrast to *Springtime*. *Jemima and Johnny* (1966), is a British film by Lionel Ngakane.[20] Jemima is the young daughter (four or five years old) of West Indian immigrants to London who have recently arrived to live in Notting Hill, London. Johnny is the young son of a local white resident who supports racist action against his black neighbours. Indeed, the film was made as a response to the Notting Hill race riots of 1958.[21] Shot in monochrome and focussing on the children's friendship and play in a city still physically scarred by war as well as suffering the tensions of postwar and post-colonial labour migration, Ngakane offers a reconciliatory vision of multicultural existence based on a child's view of the city as an open space accessible not only, but especially, to someone small and happily ignorant of racial boundaries. Despite their parents' mutual suspicion, Jemima and Johnny play together. They play on cleared bombsites and on busy streets. At the end of the day's adventures they become trapped in an unsafe, bombed-out building. Reconciliation is achieved as the children's parents learn to respect each other through their combined efforts to save the children and their subsequent mutual relief at the children's survival.

Ngakane's film was apparently inspired by *The Red Balloon*.[22] Both films are set in postwar European cities and both concentrate on a child's mobility in the city and the relative invisibility of children as they slip through the political and physical boundaries that the city presents. *The Red Balloon*, explained in Chapter 2 by the Guangzhou children as a film about friendship, is also a film about urban space and rising above hierarchies of vision and power. The red balloon that is the boy's companion and the coloured balloons that appear when the balloon is popped float at a different level to the adults (barely visible in the film) and – apart from the fatal moment for the red balloon itself – at a level that eludes the rough boys. The boys (all of them) and the two young children in Notting Hill in turn occupy spaces opened up by the bombings of the 1940s, spaces that present playgrounds that are unmanaged and open to those who can slip through and over fences or walls. In *Jemima and Johnny*, as adults stand on the street listening to racist orators, or distributing pamphlets, the children run between their legs, occupying a different space for unrestricted movement, avoiding the political ill-will brewing above their heads. They create and occupy a new plane of urban space, and scale down the city even as they open it up with a flattened ontology of connection and play-oriented motion. The film complements this vision of freedom with a simple, generous and open ending; the children are rescued and the parents acknowledge one another as fellow humans. *The Red Balloon* takes this stretched ontological vision a little further, as the 'happy ending' here is not a human reconciliation but a show of solidarity by the other multi-coloured balloons and a break for the skies.

Jemima and Johnny is also however surely influenced by the much darker vision of childhood and war, René Clements' *Forbidden Games* (*Les Jeux Interdits*) (1952). In this film, five-year-old Paulette, a beautiful orphaned child carrying her pet, dead, dog (killed on the road as she leaves the chain of refugees fleeing Paris in 1940), discovers sanctuary in her friendship with a farmer's youngest son. Together, Paulette and 11-year-old Michel inter dead animals in a secret cemetery and make or steal crosses to place over the graves. The first animal to be buried is Paulette's dog. The ritual is symptomatic of subjugated grieving for her dead parents, whom she saw bombed on the road out of Paris. Paulette's trauma has been read as a grim tribute to the suffering of children in war, but also as an allegorical critique of France's Vichy regime and the French state's later avoidance of an honest appraisal of that period, its victims and perpetrators.[23] Furthermore *Forbidden Games* can 'be considered a kind of gravesite [read 'ritual memorial'] for the Jews of France'[24] rather as – 50 years later – Michael Haneke's *Caché* (2005) disinterred and reviewed the dead animals and saw, through those small acts of brutality, the pain of colonial children killed or brutalised in the Algerian independence struggle.[25] In *Jemima and*

Johnny the children also play with crosses, on an old bomb site of an old war. It is not entirely clear why they are making crosses. Neither has lost their parents, although Jemima's migration has presumably impacted her family's sense of home and belonging. Nevertheless, in the apparent innocence of this quiet intertextual reference, Ngakane creates a subtle continuity across crises of war damage, exile, displacement and interracial tension. These two children are rescued, but their exposure to the dangers of past conflict runs in parallel with the threat of exposure to new wars of race and ethnicity waged in the public spaces of the inhabited city.

In another film dealing with child friendship threatened by external adult violence and specifically with France's betrayal of French Jews, *Au Revoir les Enfants* (1987), Louis Malle essays an allegory of the creation and destruction of French liberty itself. This was of course precisely what died first in Vichy France. In June 1940, the revolutionary principles of Liberty, Equality and Fraternity were replaced at a stroke of Petain's pen with Work, Family and Fatherland.[26] In Malle's telling, two boys make friends in a secluded boarding school. One (Julien) is the son of bourgeois French Catholic parents, the other (Jean) is the son of bourgeois French Jewish parents. He and two other Jewish boys are being hidden in plain sight by the school's headmaster. Jean and Julien find friendship in one another, particularly through a shared love of music, but they are brutally separated by France's complicity with deportations and the betrayal of the three Jewish students. Jean, who in other circumstances was just a friend who happened to play jazz piano and who wet his bed and kept a prayer book like no other in his locker, is now identified as extraneous, sinfully cosmopolitan; a boy who is marched away to be murdered in a camp somewhere in Poland. As Jean is marched through a door in the wall, he looks back at Julien, standing in line in the relatively safe ranks of the French national subject. Julien raises his hand, then Jean leaves, pushed onward by a soldier. The door in the wall remains open. The backwards look and the open door are both a connection and a moment of severance (between you, me, the Catholic French boys and the forced deportee, the migrant, every child who is pushed out of a door and away from the safety of friendship and kinship and belonging). Malle's film earns that moment of shocked severance not by a continuous emphasis on the horrors of the

1940s,[27] but by the way friendship is created between boys in the coincidences of their imagination – in play, in adventure and in music – and the degrees to which a shared cosmopolitan sense, what we could call decency, preserves the dignity of his child protagonists.

Two

> No child should ever again have that expression on his face.[28]
>
> Time does not heal trauma. A child must be helped to express suffering and to confront bad memories, with the support and guidance of an empathetic and informed adult. The very act of talking or writing about, or even acting out, traumatic events is a way for a child to begin healing and start on the road to recovery.[29]

The trauma of displacement, accelerated entry into adult responsibilities and the witnessing of extraordinary human cruelty results in great damage to the young. Since the end of the World War II and the enactment of the Convention of the Rights of the Child, there has been growing acknowledgment of that harm and its lasting impact on mental health, although the conditions for such harm continue.[30] Presciently, Ian Serraillier's children's novel about child refugees in World War II, *The Silver Sword* (1956), addresses the issue in a manner that is accessible for children who have, one hopes, not been exposed to violence of that scale.

Ruth Balizka is the main protagonist in Serraillier's novel. She is a member of a small group of escapees from Warsaw, where the right to the city has been violently withdrawn by occupying forces. As the eldest child in a family that has been torn apart, Ruth must assume the role of absent parents in caring for her siblings Edek and Bronia and another child, Jan. In the course of their journey she personifies grace under duress, but also experiences the accelerated maturation of growing up in wartime with sudden, extreme responsibility for the survival of others. Her journey produces a traumatic response when she is reunited with her father in Switzerland. Ruth (based on a real-life character) is reported to have withdrawn from human company, formed an infantile level of attachment to home and focused her affection and attention on animals and animal welfare.

Serraillier (1912–94) was a school-teacher, children's author and Quaker who lived in the south of England. After the European war ended in 1944, photographs of displaced people, many of them children, began to be published in magazines and in international reports. He found an image from a UNESCO publication, *Children of Europe*, particularly disturbing.[31] A boy looks past the camera, prematurely aged, despairing, wary and suspicious. His face bears a version of the thousand-yard stare attributed to battle-worn, traumatised soldiers. This boy, maybe eight or nine years old, but maybe older as malnutrition keeps people young in all the wrong ways, has survived a war – or survived it up to the moment that the photograph was taken – but his childhood is lost. Similar images were included in a 2012 exhibition of war photography at the Museum of Contemporary Art in Houston, USA.[32] In this exhibition they chose to show another child of Europe, a girl survivor, with experience in wartime camps or from years of hiding. She stares wildly towards the camera – her eyes more demented even than the thousand-yard stare – from a blackboard where she has scribbled an image of her life to date. It is a mess of chalk, lines crisscrossing, a tornado of despair.

Serraillier wrote *The Silver Sword* as a response to the impact of the war on childhood, and indeed to the direct plea made on behalf of child refugees in *Children of Europe*. The 'letter to a grown up', which acts as a preface to the photographs in the book, recounts the suffering of the war itself but also the frailty of systems to support children looking for a home afterwards. 'We homeless children have our neighbours for a family and you "grown-ups" are our country. We ourselves shall be "grown-ups" in a few years, and if we then see that millions of us have been abandoned, a second time, we shall certainly lose faith in that ideal for which you fought.'[33] Serraillier's book is a remarkable response. First, he noticed that not only were children dying in war, they were also surviving – but that the survival was often at the expense of the idea of childhood itself. Second, he focused his attention on children who travelled alone dealing with inordinate uncertainty and taking responsibility for their own survival. Third, he spoke as an author to his intended readers, children, as though they would understand that children suffer as well as triumph, that real adventures incur real danger, that fantasy is based on fear as well as hope. Thus his contribution to the story of that war, and every war, placed childhood and children at the centre of their own story; a story into which they were thrust by adult failures and aggression. His work is echoed in the reports on children in war researched and published by UNICEF from 1995–2010 that remind us again of the impact of conflict on the young.[34] Every separation creates trauma, each time a child is given an M16 to fight with (light arms have meant that children are increasingly used as warriors in warzones worldwide), each time a child picks up a butterfly mine thinking it may be a toy, something indescribably precious is lost to us all.

The child migrant in the form of a displaced person or refugee is still walking across borders, or roaming in camps, or drawing pictures of despair and hope, or trying to make a new life in a new place with new people. She is also a powerful fantasy structure of escape and infantile freedom, devised by adult storytellers, or framed by documentarists, to embody and aestheticise wish fulfilment, accelerated motion, socio-political displacement and ontological transition – all conditions that generate adult desire, anxiety and fear. The inaccessible or fragile personalities of Dorothy and Ruth are cultural carriers of this enduring child in our midst. Ruth is a Dorothy in a colder world than Frank Baum imagined. Dorothy foreshadows Ruth as a child who takes responsibility for the survival of her companions on the road. And there is Ruth's little sister Bronia, the plucky, funny child who seems to survive with her soul intact, but that might just be the kindness of a children's story where it is vital to offer hope and a point of optimistic connection to the young readers even when talking to them as intelligent co-locutors and inheritors of a damaged society. In other hands, tiny Bronia might easily become the little Paulette from *Forbidden Games*, who finds sanctuary with Michael and buries dead animals in a makeshift graveyard, stealing crosses from the human cemetery to make their world more mimetically acute. Death is the only game in town in a world at war.[35]

Three

The children in the films discussed above are each subjects of a film-maker's cosmopolitan sensibility and gaze. Other film-makers occupy a closer subjective relation to the idea of migration, and how it has impacted their own

Figure 3.1 'Helen, the film-maker's mother', *Once My Mother*, source image, courtesy Sophia Turkiewicz.

lives and their own relationships with family and space. Sophia Turkiewicz's 2014 biographical documentary *Once My Mother* discusses the deportations of Polish adults and children to Siberia, also in the early 1940s. Turkiewicz's docudrama works through the competing childhood memories that interrupt the love between mother and daughter, Helen and Sophia (Figures 3.1 and 3.2). Helen is one of the deportees and several years later she arrives in Australia as a lone mother with her young child, Sophia. Sophia was herself then a child migrant, but in her film she focuses on her mother's tragedies and resilience as a retro-biographical means to understand her mother and herself through their relationship. This powerful documentary comes across as a film made by a child for her parent and for herself, many years after the events that shaped them both but in time for the grown child to retrieve fragments of her past and to make certain memories of childhood whole. The historical tragedy that defines Helen's early life is her part

Figure 3.2 'Refugee camp in southern Africa', *Once My Mother*, source image, courtesy Sophia Turkiewicz.

in the upheavals of Europe in the 1930s and 1940s. She is born in Poland and suffers deportation to a Soviet prison camp, and a subsequent journey across the Soviet Union with travel, arrivals and waiting in camps of one kind and another in the Middle East, Africa and, finally, Australia. Hers is the multiple migration experience of the typical refugee, from one staging post to another, by air or by land or by sea. It is a life event that has the brutal comfort of historical evidence, estimated numbers of survivors, film footage and photographs.[36] Helen's story is part of a national tragedy of Poland. As such, it is a portion of life turned into an historical artefact that can be looked at, dialogically and collectively, by the persecuted and their persecutors. But it is Helen's first eviction from her village home onto the city streets, at about the age of ten, that is so painfully re-enacted in her separation from the seven-year-old Sophia on arrival in Adelaide. She places Sophia in an orphanage for two years while she recovers from a breakdown and sets up house (Figure 3.3). This apparent maternal betrayal is where much of Sophia's childhood pain, confusion and anger reside. Helen's disappearance into dementia during the film-making seems a repetition of that

Figure 3.3 'Sophia, arms crossed, very upset', *Once My Mother*, source image, courtesy Sophia Turkiewicz.

withdrawal. Yet the adult Sophia knows that dealing with a mental breakdown while holding down a job and building a home in a society that did not support single parents could not have been anything but extremely difficult. She asks herself and her audience to recognise that truth is *uncomfortable* but it is also just. The film's patient unwrapping of the causes and sources and repetitions of trauma succeeds in commanding our dialogic and collective gaze onto the long-term impact of a child's forced mobility and her lifelong search for home. That child is both the mother and the daughter. The putative adult confesses her suffering to her child in part by making the child act it out and feel it in her stead, all over again.

Turkiewicz's film draws directly on her remembered childhood and through that lens accesses and unpacks details of her mother's early years. At the time of filming the final stages of the film (Turkiewicz had begun the interview process with Helen two decades earlier but then let it lapse) Helen was suffering dementia.[37] An actress plays Helen for the refugee flashback scenes in the final film. Sophia Turkiewicz provided the images for reproduction here, but notes that the only one of her with her mother (not reproduced here) was reconstructed from two separate photographs as she does not have a photograph of them together when she was in the orphanage. In that sense the film is a composite of many layers of memory and forgetting. Its ontology is flattened by time but elevated by the maturity of the film-maker's protracted engagement with her subject. *Once My Mother* mourns and celebrates her mother's energy, persistence, survival and, belatedly, embraces her heartbreaks and acknowledges her impossible childhood ghosts. *Once My Mother* presents what Nirmal Puwar calls a 'social space in film'.[38] Puwar uses post-colonial cultural theorist Stuart Hall's sympathetic reading of the energy of 'arrival' in the otherwise ordinary lives of migrants from former British colonies to discuss these social spaces in film. In her celebration of South Asian cinema experience in Britain in the 1960s and 1970s, Puwar reinforces a concept of publicness that allows us to relate shared historical and emotional experience within cinematic structures of fantasy. So an otherwise hidden social phenomenon, the 'energy' of new arrivals, becomes visible, legible and validated through film, providing 'the realm of articulation in social life: language culture and mimetic practice'.[39] Puwar is speaking literally of cinemas and spaces where people might commune and enjoy cultural memories in the present. The great achievement of *Once My Mother* is its creation of a social space for any migrant child in the audience, of whatever age, to mutually experience the impossibility of describing the anger of the abandoned child who is also the only one in a position to understand and forgive inexplicably damaging parental decisions made in times of their own hardship.

Michael Winterbottom's docudrama *In This World* (2002) takes on the responsibility of engaging what I am calling the collective cosmopolitan gaze, through telling the story of an Afghani boy travelling to London with an older cousin. Their journey is laborious and dangerous and it is the young protagonists' energy (of journey rather than arrival) against the odds that propels the narrative. The camera follows them, works at their pace and, in so doing, acknowledges the waiting, the uncertainty and the missteps that migration requires. They leave a refugee camp in Peshawar, Pakistan. They undertake several border crossings and survive fraught encounters with police, smugglers and other migrants. The final stage of their journey by sea to the European mainland ends tragically. The younger boy's travel companion dies in an unventilated container on a ship taking them across the Mediterranean to Italy. The boy is a sole survivor. His companions asphyxiated, for the boy it seems that his own energy and optimism are spent. Breathlessness takes over, his energy is muted, his focus constrained, his imagination disciplined, and his potential exhausted. *In This World* explores two complementary themes in the child migrant narrative, the availability and reliability of older companions and supporters, whether they be parents, family members, or strangers on the one hand, and the permission to breathe on the other. The two aspects of survival are explicitly twinned in several films, suggesting that the level of breathlessness is associated with the level of belonging a child can claim in their immediate companionship. There is an understanding that a successful parent not only gives life, but sustains it through good breathable air. The tragedy for a parent who cannot supply the right to the city, the ground beneath one's feet and access to clean, free air is the poisonous undercurrent of these films.

Incidents of suffocation, waiting and suspension illustrate the pervasive condition of uncertainty in forced migration and exile. If you are a migrant but especially if you are a refugee, you must hold your breath until you arrive. Even after arrival, you may be waiting for years to breathe again, keeping any trace of yourself invisible and untraceable from public spaces and public attention until you have the right to the city and a place called home. As Gilroy's thoughts on cosmopolitanism have reminded us, this is a form of silent quiet breathing which is not in this world, but in a suspended, uncomfortable place of cosmopolitan negotiation and observation. These travellers have experience that is much greater than that known by those who don't travel or who only travel by a direct route to an easily accessed destination. The spatial meaning of Winterbottom's *In This World* refers to a border between life and death, a point at which the boy realises that his friend is not here, in this world, but rather in that other world, in death. The phrase also allows us to imagine a world that is beyond the world that has been left and is not quite the world known at the places traversed or at the end point of settlement. It is the sense of being *not* in this world which transforms the child's ongoing relation to an idea of home once the lifelong process of migration has begun. So death – not in this world – is where all breathing has stopped forever, but in this world – life – may still be a place where breathing is suspended, partial and insufficient to provide energy and forward motion.

In *Le Havre*, Ari Kaurismäki's 2011 winsome visual essay on a refugee boy's sojourn in a dour French port on his way to find his mother in London, the adventure turns not so much on the boy's *arrival* (and here I am thinking back to Stuart Hall's essay on arrival in the UK in the 1950s[40]), but on the dangers of simply *waiting* in port for another ship. A boy (Idrissa) escapes from a shipping container, where he and other refugees are waiting to be connected to another ship. The container is discovered by the police, and the boy makes a break for freedom so he can continue his journey. Idrissa becomes the lightning rod by which strange foreign (French) adults measure their worth or their villainy. Who will help the boy to achieve his hopes of reunion with his Mother? Who will try to prevent him from achieving a place like home? The 'good' characters are a man (Marcel Marx, an entertainer turned shoeshine) and his wife (Arletty), who falls sick in the course of the narrative, and their friends, all of whom conspire to assist the child escape the police hunt. These characters are resident within a few back streets of the French port. Kaurismäki separates these streets out from other locations with his habitual recourse to hyper-real colour tones and nostalgically plain set dressings, all here are an unnaturally pastel blue, lending the narration a sense of fairytale. The effect of these intimate streets populated with good people living simple lives is to visualise the 'double occupancy' of *Le Havre*, whereby good characters and migrants live in a moral zone that floats in parallel to the amoral and violent world of the French state, which supports anti-migrant actions and anti-foreign prejudice.[41] The fairytale villain is manifested by a neighbour (played by Jean Claud Léaud) dressed in brown and shot in shadow. He snoops on every identifiable migrant in the town, children not excepted. In Kaurismäki's stylised coding Léaud's persona is both cartoonish and subtle. The character is the personification of a 1940s' wartime collaborator as much as he is a wicked witch, as much as he is the modern nasty neighbour who does not want the foreign boy to stay in a nearby house. Léaud was the child actor in *The Four Blows/Les Quatre Cent Coups* (1959), François Truffaut's breakthrough film concerning a boy running through the city and eventually running away from a corrective school and down to the sea. The self-conscious shift from child to adult and from renegade to collaborator is not a reflection on the actor (except in so far as he adroitly uses his career highlights to make a point about moral inheritance and equivalence) but it is intended as a question for France. His obvious villainy and its association with very dark Vichy history is the pivot around which the film clarifies that this is not a benign drama of kind neighbours and a little boy, but an urgent drama of archetypal evil and good in a modern context of migration and danger for the young. Geoffrey Nowell Smith remarked of Vittorio De Sica's *Bicycle Thieves* (1949) that a film can seem to be about more than one thing at once – 'an account of everyday life and the consequences of mass unemployment in Italy ... [and] ... an evocation of anxiety'.[42] The anxiety in *Le Havre* is focussed on the outcome for the child, but is primarily concerned with what that means as a judgement on the French character, the French capacity to welcome strangers and the degree to which the trope of the collaborator still pertains.

Whereas *Le Havre* eventually opts for an open and 'happy-enough' ending, an earlier film worked more harshly on the same pressures of double occupancy at the French/British soft border, the body of sea between the two European migrant destinations. *Welcome* (2009) evokes the anxiety described by Nowell Smith and takes it through to a terrible conclusion. Another child (Bilal) is waiting – this time in Calais – but he does not survive the Channel crossing to join his girlfriend in London. Bilal is nearly grown; he is a 17-year-old Iraqi-Kurd travelling alone with dreams of school, university and a career in football playing for Manchester United. His dreams are boyish, and his courage boundless. He tries to swim across the Channel in order to avoid an equally perilous illegal crossing in a truck. He is faced not only with the physical threat of travelling without papers and without proper transport but also with a palimpsestic double occupancy of migration and settlement scenarios. London, his destination, is a mirage of fulfilment thwarted not just by the sea and the state, in the person of customs guards, but by the determination of his girlfriend's father to marry her off to an older Iraqi-Kurdish man. The proposed marriage will consolidate a community relationship amongst fellow migrants and provide financial security for the family's eldest daughter. Her gendered, patriarchal family conditions have followed her on her own migration. This is not a situation that would be easily answered in, say, Kaurismäki's characteristic moral zone. In Laura Rascaroli's inspired reading of *Le Havre*, she uses the notion of a 'minor' deployment of language, in a move that is founded on observations of the film's substance and which also speaks to a structure of double occupation, layered residency rights, and a contest between formations of social meaning within a majority landscape of authority (Rascaroli is most interested in the place of European art cinema in world cinema, but her observation holds for the political).

> It does this in its embracing of the minor and of oppositional cultural frameworks, including magical realism, rock music, surreal humour and retro; in its focus on the margins, the outskirts and the provinces; in speaking collectively for a missing people; and in deterritorializing filmic language and generic conventions only to reterritorialize and appropriate them for a contemporary European art film.[43]

For Bilal, there are multiple competing occupancies that must be negotiated and overcome in order to create a space for his own life and his own generation. The magical city, whether it be the Emerald City or contemporary London, is a work of imagination and desire that exceeds and supplants the actualities of the migration experience, both for those who yearn to be there and for those who have already arrived. But do these boys, Idrissa and Bilal, passing through France and passing through French cinema, bear the signature of Dorothy? In a way they do, although the boys' vulnerable reliance on weak men with fundamentally good hearts in a re-territorialising Europe also acts as a critique of American Dorothy's own abundant, colonial White confidence in returning home unscathed. The snooping Léaud, collaborator-witch who seeks to dismantle even the modicum of 'home' the migrants claim, is part of a response to adult anxieties that, as I suggested in Chapter 1, require reiteration of the flattened ontology of childhood, an endless return to the idea that there is 'no place like home'. Léaud's witch-like 'enemy-within' echoes both childhood fears – the sinister Child-catcher in the children's war film from the 1960s *Chitty Chitty Bang Bang* – who in turn echoes the Rat-catcher-Pied Piper of German folklore (see Chapter 6), and adult memories of wartime collaborators.

Welcome and *In This World* and *Le Havre* interrogate the experience of child migration through the prism of unexpected encounters, interrupted mobility and transitory settlement. They make the perturbing and stark observation that the migrant – and, again, especially the refugee – does not even own the air s/he breathes, is literally and metaphorically holding his or her breath. *Welcome* is structured around the dangers of suffocation, as migrants stowing away in trucks learn (or fail) to breathe inside plastic bags to avoid detection by border police testing with probes for carbon dioxide. Many of the film's key events are linked to the idea of breathing and not breathing. Early in Bilal's time in Calais he meets a fellow Afghan Kurd who pays for him to take a place in the back of a lorry to be smuggled to London. All the travellers must cover their heads with a plastic bag to avoid detection. Bilal takes his off in panic and the stowaways are caught. One of their number, another young man, has already asphyxiated. This horror motivates Bilal to find another way over the English Channel. Hence, he decides to learn to swim. In the swimming pool the boy is taught the front crawl, a stroke that requires head movements matched with breathing in and blowing out through the water. He is a determined student, learning how to move smoothly and breathe safely when passing through a soft border (the sea) in order to cross a hard border (the UK Border). One night Bilal and his Afghan friend stay over in the swimming instructor's apartment. The instructor catches Bilal in the bathroom practising 'breathing' with his head in a plastic bag. He is angry, as any parent would be angry, but he also realises the extreme danger to which his protégé is exposed. Yet, several days later, when the instructor discovers that his gold Olympic medal has gone missing (Bilal's Afghan friend has taken it to pay off the debt accrued for the aborted smuggled passage to the UK) he blames Bilal, attacking him by thrusting a plastic bag over his head in a furious reassertion of what he has previously observed Bilal trying to practise in his bathroom. The attack is an act of extreme rejection, displaying the passionate anger – again – of a quasi-paternal relationship. They are reconciled but the form of the attack underlines the unreliability of breathing freely on such a journey, even in a friend's apartment. Eventually, Bilal does swim the English Channel, his strokes strong and his breathing perfect. When he is spotted by a Customs boat he panics again and refuses to wait for them to pick him up. Instead, he plunges under the water, presumably holding his breath. He never resurfaces. He has died in precisely the breathless way he was trying to avoid.[44]

In both films the migrant boy is befriended by a middle-aged white Frenchman at a point in his life where the adult must account for himself to himself. Is he a collaborator or is he a good man? How might he judge his own success? In *Welcome* the Frenchman, Simon Calmat, is Bilal's swimming instructor. His friendship with the boy forces him to confront the limits of his own capacity to take responsibility of the other, for strangers and, thereby, for himself. At the very end of the film, he goes to London to deliver a gift from Bilal to the girlfriend. The gift is one he gave to Bilal earlier in the film: his own mother's diamond ring that he once gave his ex-wife, who lost it in the apartment and which he found after Bilal stayed over on the futon, and eventually re-gifted to Bilal as a gift for his own girlfriend. Thus the ring operates as an object passed between generations as each woman dies, leaves or is herself bereaved. Simon also visits London to pass on the news of Bilal's death at sea. The girlfriend refuses the ring as she will not be able to wear it once married, but also perhaps to enunciate to the French stranger that he remains a stranger and that the multiple layers of occupancy in contemporary Europe persist, despite goodwill. The director Lioret sets this scene in Elephant and Castle, a rundown shopping centre just south of the Thames, which in 2009 had still not been renovated and gentrified. It was what a friend who lives close by once described as a 'shopping centre for poor people'. What he meant, and what the film evokes in the conversation between Simon and Bilal's girlfriend in a busy cafe (with a Manchester United game playing on the big TV screen watched by an enthusiastic group of men), is that this, a 'shopping centre for poor people', is accessible and open to strangers when many other parts of the city are not. This rough and ready place is as close as it gets to a place where simultaneous multiple occupancy is tolerated, if only in passing.

The two French films also indicate that the child is the special case that brings the local population into a close connection with the asylum seekers or, as the French term has it – again bringing us close to breathlessness – 'living dead' (*morts vivants*), in their midst. *Welcome* and *Le Havre* make a case for children but in so doing they create an illusion of affect and special treatment, and risk ignoring the politics of abandonment that many children face on their actual journeys. *In This World* avoids the troubling presence of the paternal adult/friend seeking salvation through his relationship with a lost boy, but that role is replaced by the assumed presence of the film-maker Winterbottom himself. Crucially, all three boys provide an instant focus of affective attention within the diegesis and in the appeal to the spectator. In general, the boys' hunger, need for shelter, capacity for survival and willingness to take adult advice or assistance, renders them separate to the larger body of migrant men and women portrayed in the background of the films. At the same time the boys' accessibility and vulnerability allow a comfortable structure of feeling by which the spectator engages with their status. This renders the films affective but otherwise delinked from the conditions in which child migrants are almost always received or rejected in reality, seen either as metonymic proto-adults, or as transient visitors who will be asked to leave as soon as they reach 18. Much of the political debate in the twenty-first century has centred on the need to care for children travelling alone as children, whereas much of the actual experience of young people has been the converse.[45]

The narrative of a feature film often represents only one stage (in *Welcome*, this turns out to be the final stage) of a journey, of which neither the origins nor other stages are fully essayed. This narrative strategy does however underline that such complexity involves everyone on the journey and not just the migrants themselves. Thus, the films enunciate a mutually responsive form of cosmopolitanism, which the migrant child cannot constitute alone. The fractures of geo-space and social space essential to telling stories of migrancy and mobility must both correspond (or not) to cinematic space and the ways in which this approximates or codes experience, and to its articulation to movement within the frame. In *Le Havre*

Kaurismäki employs formal techniques of set design and lyrical colour coding to define the district where the boy takes refuge. The dominant tone for most locations occupied by the boy or the working-class community is blue and this saturation intensifies in the safest space – the yard and home of the 'good man' Marcel. Along with 'Chang', a Vietnamese settled migrant with a false Chinese name, Marcel makes a living as a shoeshine, his days as an entertainer long gone. The men's social positioning is thereby unequivocally transitory, itinerant or 'low'; both are free to move around during the working day, but both must kneel to their clients in order to perform their task.[46] Idrissa by contrast is more akin to Arletty, Marcel's good wife who is hospitalised with a lung disease that threatens to prove fatal (she is a smoker). Her mobility is therefore compromised but not at the expense of her effect on others, which is uniformly good. Idrissa, despite his youth and outwith those moments when he needs to run, is likewise often held quite still in the frame. Sometimes this is because the other part of running is hiding and, after all, Idrissa is in hiding for his life. He seeks help sitting in Marcel's outshed or in the baker's back rooms, or bobbing in the water at the harbour steps (he too holds his breath under water to hide from the police (Figure 3.4)). At other times he is simply waiting: working quietly at the kitchen sink, asleep, lying down with Marcel and Arletty's

Figure 3.4 Detail from 'Idrissa in the water', *Le Havre*.

dog, listening to adults talk in Marcel's house, cleaning up the kitchen. He is the nominated migrant in the story and he is taking the greatest risks, although one imagines that Chang has done similar in his own time, but it is the adults who move about him pursuing their own lives or acting on his behalf. Idrissa holds the still centre of the cinematic frame and the moral centre of the outside world, while Arletty occupies the equivalent position in Marcel's domestic life. Idrissa and Arletty belong most persuasively in this newly cosmopolitan, folded space of arrival, sanctuary and escape as witnesses to its immoralities as well as its chances for goodness. But we must also acknowledge that Idrissa, young as he is, has learned not to take the space he occupies for granted. Above all, he has learned to breathe carefully.

4

Little Moth and *The Road*: precarity, immobility and inertia

> How long can we stay here, Papa?
> You asked me that.
> I know.
> We'll see.
> That means not very long.
> Probably.[1]

One

Little Moth, directed by film-maker Peng Tao in 2007, is an essay on urban amorality in post-Reform China.[2] The film's Chinese title (*Xue Chan*) is the name of a disease of the blood that causes paralysis. The title refers descriptively to the film's main protagonist, a young girl who has contracted the illness. Another child, a 12-year-old boy, Xiao Chun, is her co-worker once she has been put to work as a beggar (see below) and the closest thing she has to a friend in the film. Chun has one arm missing, possibly from an accident, or possibly removed deliberately to increase his pathos as a street boy. As this may suggest, the film does not present an optimistic view of contemporary China. The title then also captures the metaphorical 'disease of the blood' that has infected and undermined Chinese society in a period of prolonged change and ideological and social destabilisation. The film focuses on the poorest of the poor, for whom uncertainty produces precarity as the prevailing socio-economic state at the bottom of modernity's pile. This same 'disease of the blood' refers to a foreboding sense of the loss of spiritual, ethical and bodily integrity, a loss that is at the core of social disintegration. Nothing is as it should be and no-one is to be trusted. People are quite literally after one's blood. We are not quite in the realm of a zombie film or a vampire movie suggested by my young co-researchers in London but there are connections to be made. Located in small towns with noisy streets and ugly buildings, the dirty, urban *mise en scène* defines and consumes the people who occupy it. The film is set in Hubei, central China. Hubei has some large and important cities; more than 15 have populations of over half-a-million. The great city of Wuhan has a population of 11 million (2016).[3] But the small city, 'He City', that is the main location of *Little Moth* is not listed as a city and is probably much smaller. As such it exemplifies the peri-urban non-place-ness described by Marc Augé[4] of numerous small urban centres with mobile populations, full of displaced rural peasants on their way to find work.

> If a place can be defined as relational, historical and concerned with identity, then a space which cannot be defined as relational, or historical, or concerned with identity, will be a non-place.[5]

As I think my reading of *Little Moth* will show, the children at the heart of this film are travelling in non-place, surrounded by people who are forgetting their humanity. I think about them as proto-zombies. I am not saying this as a flippancy but as a comment on the deterioration of relationships between people that occurs as a result of accelerated capitalisation and the anxieties that result from these processes. The concept has been formulated in several ways, generally associated with America but, as Žižek writes, also as a general commentary on a life without morality but nonetheless possessed by driving, dangerous vitality: 'The living dead are not in-between or undecidable. In fact, they are more living than we the living because they have access to the life substance prior to its symbolic mortification.'[6] That is not to argue that (some of) the people around the children in *Little Moth*, and the children themselves, are not trying to establish, or re-establish, a relational space in which to live as humans. Simply though, this film declares that hope of an identity built on solid relationships and stable historical grounding is almost futile. Chinese modernisation has reached a pitch of chronic acceleration such that the ordinary connections of social trust have atrophied. Peng Tao makes this inertia and atrophy visible through the children's location in a narrative that is inexorably revealed as a kind of banal but terrifying urban horror film. Every adult character, bar one so-called simpleton, is not to be trusted. Dread pervades the non-places of the city of He. Czech philosopher Vilém Flusser has commented of the (im)migrant that the one who enters and observes a new place 'free of the restricted view afforded by always belonging to that place' has a relatively clear view of what is actually happening. 'For the native who is settled, the immigrant is even more alien and strange … because he exposes as banal what the native considers sacred'.[7] Nonetheless, he argues,

> … one must always live somewhere, regardless of where …
> a person will simply perish without a home, a place to live
> … without a place to live … everything that encroaches on one
> is noise – without information – and without information, in a
> chaotic world, one can neither feel, nor think, nor act.[8]

The unrestricted narration that characterises Peng Tao's approach is the closest example I have seen of ontological flattening in the pursuit of a multi-scalar image of homelessness, human suffering and social decay in the context of contemporary China. Technically, he uses simple methods. A mobile camera shifts between protagonists both from scene to scene and within sequences when they are in conversation, and no single protagonist possesses the narrative direction from the camera's perspective. When characters are immobilised by physical incapacity, by drunkenness, by fear, by ignorance, or simply by a cramped means of transport, the camera moves to discover them, and then moves away to discover the conditions and consequences of that immobility.

This is not to say that Peng does not have a central conscience and consciousness within the film. The eponymous little girl provides that. Her name Little Moth (Xiao E'zi) is the English title of the film. Her disease provides the title of the Chinese original, linking her fate to a metaphorical condemnation of China's sickness. She is a migrant in a literal sense as she is being moved, forcibly, from one place to another. She is also a *witness* in Flusser's sense of a migrant observing and learning the 'code' of a place without being in thrall to its hegemony.[9] Her gaze, which is almost entirely silent, suggests an (im)migrant consciousness of banality, here the banality of evil, while her damaged body is required to perform an end point of that evil which is the immobilisation of the weakest in society. Little Moth is incapacitated by her illness of the blood. She cannot walk at all. This physical atrophy reads as composure in the child's demeanour. She appears as if in a reverie throughout the film, a dreamlike state that allows her to survive the demands of adults without complaint while observing everything. She could of course be profoundly depressed. It is not simply that she has a disability, nor that she is a quiet child. Rather, the film presents a social situation where she is rendered inert, a condition created by her physical condition and maintained by the times she lives in and the people she lives with. Her suffering makes manifest the disease of the blood shared by society itself. The philosopher Diana Coote has highlighted Merleau Ponty's comment that there is always a dichotomy in language between the verb and the noun. The first is 'intrinsically and internally dynamic' whilst the second infers 'greater inertia'.[10] I attach this observation to the visual grammar of film, the figure of the child is both the 'verb' deployed to give motion and substance to the matter of adult fears of morbidity; and the ultimate in matter, a 'noun' beyond generative potential.

The film opens with a travelling shot of a couple (Luo and Guihua) on the back of a small open truck. The truck passes along a road in a semi-rural, semi-urban landscape of small concrete farmers' houses and fields. The two travellers are dressed poorly, their faces burned dark by work in the sun. They say nothing to each other along the way. In a Chinese context one easily reads them as peasants. They are visually summed up as those without sufficient quality. That notion of human quality (*suzhi*) and insufficient quality (*suzhi bu gou*) has been widely discussed in relation to migrants moving into larger cities from the rural hinterlands.[11] It is a discriminatory discourse that produces discriminated populations.

The sociologist Loïc Wacquant's assessment of urban fragmentation concerns topographical marginality, the radical dispersion of poverty and disadvantage and stigmatisation.[12] These concepts are highly relevant to understanding the impact of China's urban development and Reform-Era economics on the extremely poor.[13] China-based analyses of these phenomena describe long-held prejudice against country people in general (*nongmin*), and latterly migrant workers (*mingong*). 'Keyword' articles on the topic argue that the discourse on quality (who has it, who doesn't) not only justifies negative discrimination, but also creates a culture of stigmatisation and exceptionalism that enforces a nation-wide, top-down layering of governance and manages down opportunity for major population groups.[14] This stigmatisation of the people who are indispensable to the creation of China's modernisation and reform project has been somewhat mitigated over recent years as well-publicised accidents[15] and the chronic plight of so-called 'left-behind children' has been brought to the attention of relatively well-off urban residents by media, film and social researchers.[16] Nonetheless, the structural impoverishment of those who are already on the margins of hope continues apace. The wonderfully energetic and creative children that I worked with in Guangzhou, where we used the film *Red Balloon* as our text, would quite possibly be stigmatised in such a manner and will have certainly been adversely affected by the political separation of rural and urban residents through a residency or passport system which in turn supports a discourse of unequal potential and quality.

The concept of the country bumpkin, the peasant without quality, has roots in modern Chinese literature where the rural is both a necessary romance for the urban modern imagination, and also a threat of anti-civilisation forces. In his novella *My Old Home*, Lu Xun (1881–1936), a preeminent modernist writer of China's pre-Liberation period, explored the idea of the loss of human distinction in his portrayal of the peasant boy Runtu turning into a grown man. As a boy Runtu is adventurous, full of knowledge about the seashore and animals, and a good friend to the narrator of the story (who approximates Lu Xun himself). When the narrator returns home after years away in the city, he finds Runtu much changed. The healthy boy from a seaside village has turned into a sallow-faced red-eyed man who will only address his former friend as 'Master'.[17] Whilst Lu

Xun is concerned to critique China's rigid social class systems (of 1920), his account of the peasant has stuck in the Chinese lexicon of types. It is revisited by Peng Tao in *Little Moth*. Peng understands, or so it seems, that the behaviour of the men and some women in his film is scripted by circumstance. It is part of a circuit of 'cruel optimism' that Lauren Berlant has warned us against in her analysis of neo-liberal scapegoats and the willingness of the poor to take part in processes that will further impoverish their sector of the population – just in case it will work for them, this time around.[18] Berlant's point is that it never does quite work, and people further cement the despair of their own circumstances by acceding to situations that oppress them. In *Little Moth*, the ugly opportunism of the small man that we first encounter in the back of this little truck reveals that he is caught in a tragedy, the details of which are of his own devising, but of which the genre has been scripted in China through the chaotic processes of accelerated reform and modernisation-without-values that characterise post-socialism. In effect, these peasants have been left behind by history and are not much further down the road than Runtu was almost a century earlier.

Two

The journey in the open truck ends in a laneway. The couple are ushered into a courtyard house where the man Luo sits down to eat with an older man he calls Uncle. The scene appears convivial and family orientated. The film-maker deploys a formal composition in medium-long shot: two men at a table eating, served by women entering from side doors and framed by a large courtyard. They are discussing a business opportunity for the younger man. The combined formality and assumed sociality of the scene is reassuring after the long bumpy tracking shot of the silent journey in the back of a truck. The men appear to enjoy strong ties of *guanxi*, appearances which are maintained both by the affirmation of kinship, the sharing of a meal, and by the longer-term business deal under discussion.[19] *Guanxi* produces and describes ties of mutual responsibility, and produces a formula for intersubjective relationships across generations and within interest groups that form a web of mutuality (*guanxiwang*) and trust (*yiqi*).[20]

The level of affect is greater than self-interest as the connection between the parties is assumed to lead to reciprocity and be based on mutual, lasting responsibility, hence the sharing of food and carefully chosen gifts.[21] *Guanxi* is oil to the wheels of China's society and to the arduous nature of getting things done. It is also however the fuel of corruption where connected individuals and groups operate beyond the law.

> Critics see it as fueling the country's rampant corruption, and as an obstacle to China's becoming a modern society based on the rule of law. Those who see it in a more favorable light contend that *guanxi* adds an element of humanity to otherwise cold transactions, and comes to the rescue in the absence of consistent regulations or guidelines for social conduct.[22]

Guanxi happens in society and in the interstices of institutions. It happens between people, and so it also happens between bad people. It can only be well understood through sifting micro-observations collected in an ethnography, possibly through compiling survey data, making studies of the speech acts of social actors in all walks of life, and applying social science formulae in the analysis of what emerges from that febrile mix. It is subject to great differentiations as society changes, as populations are dispersed through migration and as families are fragmented through the same process. The few comments I have made above are but minute glimpses of complex and mutating social phenomena. In the context of Peng Tao's film, and in this discussion of child migrants as cinematic agents and childhood-as-method, my main goal is to demonstrate how cinema might further elucidate the emotional and social effects of such a deeply entrenched practice and how that impacts the child.

To do so, we need to look carefully at the construction of the narrative, and who is linked to whom. The first convivial eating scene cuts to a very different scenario, in which the couple are led up a mountain track to a hovel in which they find a small girl lying in bed. This is Xiao E'zi, 'Little Moth'. She is framed and central to the shot, in repose and still. She wears pink and is pretty, but not strikingly so. She is above all a little girl devoid of expression. She answers questions – her age (11) and her name – but does not volunteer information unbidden. The formal composition of the shot rests on the framing of the child in bed, which isolates the composure of the child as she lies propped up and uncomplaining. The formal grace that she exhibits is interrupted by the talk of the adults around her and our growing understanding of the dirty nature of their business with her. She is the crucial component of the transactional scene but she is also its object, its perverse gift. Her father, a drunk from the village run by 'Uncle', is selling her, the transaction made possible by a corrupted form of gift giving as Uncle makes the introduction. Her illness has made her a prime commodity in a street begging operation.

So far, we are observing a scene of despair and in circumstances we might ascribe to poverty pure and simple. Yet, we should note that there is a marked difference here between this Reform-Era tragedy of intra-class cruelty and exploitation and revolutionary-era films that indicate class difference as measure of who is subject to whose ill treatment. *Lin Puzi's Shop* (1959) describes the destitution of the poor due to the usury and dishonesty of shop owners and money lenders who are in turn financially destroyed by unscrupulous banks. The film is set in the aftermath of the Treaty of Versailles (1919), and is an attack on bourgeois values prior to Liberation in 1949. Lin's shop is making a lot of money very quickly through selling survival packs (bowls, soap and so on) to the flow of post-war refugees. These desperate souls are close to the bottom of the urban pecking order and are duly fleeced, but lower still is a peasant woman who has deposited her savings with Lin. When credit collapses, and the bills begin to roll in, Lin leaves town. As the woman stands with her baby realising that she has no future, a voiceover recounts an old saying: 'the big fish eat the little fish, the little fish eat the shrimps and the shrimps eat mud'.[23]

Peng Tao modernises this vision with a new variety of urban refugee and a new hierarchy of exploitation, but one which arguably never leaves the working poor or the peasantry. Thus far, *Little Moth* has established a relationship between Luo and his Uncle that is cemented by the exchange of money and the gift of access to the girl whose incapacity will establish Luo's new enterprise on the city streets. The men are related, they eat together and the elder assists the younger in his criminal endeavour of buying a child from another rural man. The child is herself a rural girl, a peasant. What transpires in the rest of the film shows that this bandit relationship does have some grounding in affect and is superficially reliable, but only up to a point. The Uncle is a big man in his local county. He boasts to Luo that he once killed a headman from a neighbouring province in defence of his territory.[24] He does not have as much authority as he once did however. While he helps Luo look for his wife Guihua when she is kidnapped by Chang, a dealer in human organs, he cannot enforce the kind of authority he remembers achieving by dint of earlier bloody struggles. The urbanisation of rural areas disrupts previous regimes of banditry. Just as small industries are removed to industrial zones, and farmers of working age leave for the ever-larger towns and cities to make more money, so the networks of criminality are engaged on differently configured libidinal circuits. They cross borders of clan and county, and their practitioners are contemptuous of the niceties of elaborated human feeling (*renqing*) and brotherly trust (*yiqi*). For this new breed of networkers *guanxi* is strictly functional. Although the skeins of connection and influence might travel for men like Uncle, they are just as likely to attenuate and unravel. This is especially likely for those who are as geo-spatially and historically fixed, and as naïve, as his nephew Luo.

Luo falls foul of a geo-fluid operator, Chang, who has a wider influence than Uncle and whose repertoire of criminality is particularly unpleasant. We meet Luo and Chang sitting together outside, and Luo is easily convinced by Chang that they have a relationship. He has asked for Chang's help in running his begging scam in a new town. They have exchanged cigarettes and Chang has agreed that they are brothers (*gemenr*). Luo has tried to follow etiquette, but this is not a genuine (*zhen*) transaction. It is false (*jia*), just another layer of Chang's set-up sting, in this case to capture Guihua (Luo's wife) and Xiao E'zi for their kidneys. The impact of this betrayal is at the core of Peng's delineation of the breakdown of human relations and China's 'disease of the blood'. If the networks of social relations may no longer be relied on spatially because of migration, urbanisation and regimes of kinship, one must turn to strangers and set up a discourse of trust-in-extremis through familiar *guanxi* patterns of engagement. But strangers prove unreliable and everything, including this fundamental aspect of social relations, is rendered fragile. Most frightening of all is the assault on the integrity of human feeling through a business transaction that so intimately binds those *without quality* into dangerous reliance on those more adept with uncertainty. The simple peasant cannot separate one touchstone of Chinese sociality from another, but the professional criminals can. As Luo puts it to his Uncle after a fruitless day of searching for his missing wife: 'If that scumbag takes her kidneys, he makes a lot of money. She gets nothing from it, and she dies.' In his drunken expostulations he can express neither sorrow nor anger without confusing the matters of bodily integrity, personal feeling for his wife, financial loss on her behalf and unjust transactional relations.

Luo has himself of course been guilty of a disregard of human bodily integrity and human feeling. Xiao E'zi's disability is curable but when Guihua forms a maternal attachment to the girl and attempts to medicate her, he resists strongly. For Luo, the child is a financial opportunity with a specific function, Guihua must feed her and play being her mother during the begging but it must end at the level of the performative. Luo does not have the emotional imagination to extend a sense of empathy to someone unrelated by blood and so specifically allied to his plans. It is his wife, described by the Uncle as simple-minded, who alone amongst the adults displays a capacity for empathy and connection in the non-places and liminal outposts of Reform-Era China.

Three

I have suggested that the rural areas and the small cities springing up in China have reverted to places of shrimps eating mud and fish eating fish, but that the class differences in this cannibalistic hierarchy are increasingly indistinct.[25] I now turn to the child herself and think about how she is used to focus the film's critique of social relations in a Chinese county town, and by extrapolation of China's entire modernisation project since Reform. First of all, we need to characterise her position in society. She is a rural child with one parent and he abandons her for a price. One hundred yuan is about fifteen Australian dollars or seven pounds sterling. She is not a migrant child in the sense that the children in Guangzhou who had travelled with their parents to work are migrants (see Chapter 2). She does not present the challenges to society of children who do not fit and cannot understand the moral and social leadership assumed by those with urban passports, as do migrant children occupying urban spaces but not fulfilling the required metropolitan moral superiority of the city child.[26] Nor is she a left-behind child in the countryside with absent parents working in the city. Rather, she is bought and sold as a slave and forcibly migrated across county borders for economic purposes. Her apparent parents are false (*jia*) parents, and her role as a disabled child is an economic necessity to them (although the balance shifts when Guihua acts maternally and attempts to give her medicine for her condition). Little Moth's labour is sequestered and her rights as a child are contravened. Luo denies her access to medical care when she requires it, and this happens again towards the end of the film when yet another adult lets her down. She is denied access to education and she has no security of housing. Peng Tao has created a protagonist who is literally immobilised by social conditions. In so doing he emphasises the cost of modernisation for China's cultural and social health. Childhood in China and children in China have represented the future of the family, the hopes of revolutionary succession and indicated the state of wellbeing (or not) between the people and their rulers.[27] Conversely, the neglect of children is associated with famine, social breakdown and historical disorder. In folk history, child abandonment is a sign of great trouble under Heaven (*tianxia*), and in imperial times might have suggested the fragmentation of a dynasty and the onset of civil war.

But in the cinematic world, Little Moth's immobility is an omen of misfortune beyond Chinese philosophy. One of the basic things that we know about children in cinema is that they usually move fast or that they move across terrain where adults cannot easily follow. Whatever adventures and deadly escapades await them, the falling boy in the British postwar tragedy *The Yellow Balloon* (1953, J. Lee-Thompson) comes to mind, or the suicidal Edmund in *Germany Year Zero* (1948, Roberto Rossellini);[28] they are still children as long as they are still moving. If not, and if they are dead – Little Moth is eventually abandoned to die – they call up the very worst fears of social collapse. In her superlative essay, 'Lost Angels', on Tim Hunter's *River's Edge* (1986), Vicky Lebeau reminds us that the unmourned dead child onscreen is symptomatic of the deepest malaise in the world of the film, and in the world that produced that film.[29]

The corpse in *River's Edge* is a murdered teenager. She is transforming from the moment of death through the mobile inertia of decay, but she is viewed as a perfectly formed and available body for the young people who go up into the hills to look at her. Based on an actual crime in a town called Milpitas, where the 17-year-old perpetrator left the body in place for his teenage friends to view,[30] Lebeau retells the story of the crime and the film in order to examine the profound social anxiety about youth that the incident articulated. What could be said of teenagers who would not only cover up the murder of one of their friends by another but stare at the dead without horror, without a sense of loss? The exposed corpse enacts the social decay which makes the murder and its aftermath so uncanny. The students' 'failure to mourn a friend' calls up 'psychotic terror, a fear not of one death, not even one's own, but of the death of the world'.[31] There are two strands to this lesson in mourning (loss) and melancholia (failure to recognise the cause of loss). First, the death of a child is always a premature death and as such refers symbolically and emotionally to acute collective loss. Second, if that child is not mourned then the community, the nation, or humanity itself, may have reason for an almost apocalyptic fear of disintegration through a misrecognition of its vulnerability. This dread runs through *Little Moth* like poison.

In a gentler story released a year later than *River's Edge*, Rob Reiner's *Stand By Me* (1987), four boys set out on a journey to see and report (possibly retrieve) the corpse of a boy of their own age. They have heard his death – an accident beside a railway line – discussed by older boys who have a similar plan to 'discover' the body and become famous. They all want to be heroes and, whilst the older boys have a car, the younger boys make a long expedition on foot to be the first at the scene. On arrival, however, they are horrified at the sight of a body that is still recognisably once someone like them. Unlike the teenagers in *River's Edge*, the boys immediately recognise the corpse for what it is and they begin to mourn. The manner of their mourning has a touch of melancholia about it, in that they are sensing the end of all their own boyhoods through the death of a single boy, but it resists the uncanny madness of voyeurism and misrecognition suffered in Milpitas. Reiner's film is a coming of age movie in seemingly ordinary times. The boys are not apocalyptic, they retain decency towards one of their own, as the film's title suggests. There is no current war, or not one that impacts them, so heroism is a matter of sporting prowess or a contrived act of bravery – such as a trek to find a boy's body. As in all coming of age narratives the journey is much longer than the children know at the time. Their walk through the beautiful scenery of Oregon in America's west occurs in 1959. It is an elegy for lost landscapes and lost youth, culminating in an acute *collective* loss of the dead boy, recognised by these four pre-teens as they confront in his body the oxymoronic real-hollowness of their venture. Cinema enunciates their disappointment as the precursor of nostalgia. Innocence dissipates at the moment that melancholy sets in, which we might say is the moment when innocence comes to be desired. The dead child was never more than a child, innocence residing only in the absence of its absence, and the freedom from nostalgia the greatest gift of being young. But the dead child can wreak melancholy in her or his wake. The realisation that death is always real traps the boys into silence by the railway track and then scatters them. One of the extraordinary discoveries of adulthood is that the seemingly indissoluble bonds of child friendship may indeed be broken and that people without whom life appears impossible, leave.

Bohlmann and Moreland suggest, in their analysis of Hitchcock's repeated killing of innocence in his films, that it is those who move beyond innocence and stare it down that are mature and sane, not those who seek to protract it or target it for the maintenance of their own self-delusion.[32] Such empty, disconnected and dissociated characters are the murderer and the teenagers in *Rivers Edge*, but their irresponsible vacancy also characterises almost everyone in *Little Moth*. Even the children, perhaps especially the children, who do nothing to anyone, still understand that they are missing something vital to life. I began my description of Xiao E'zi by suggesting that she seemed calm, but wondering if she might be depressed. One could go further and wonder if she is mourning an innocence that she has never been permitted to enjoy. When Little Moth and her begging companion Xiao Chun have escaped Chang and Luo, but have failed to find 'the man' that Xiao Chun thinks would help them (another promise of *renqing* broken, another dead end), they are scooped up by an unknown woman who says she wants to adopt Little Moth. The boy is briefly tolerated as

Little Moth says he is her brother. He is fed but he is not welcomed. While Little Moth is dressed up like a doll in new clothes, he is left looking down at his dirty ill-fitting shoes. There is something about that look that admits his capitulation to bare life and to both mourning and melancholia. The last shot of Xiao Chun has him walking through the streets at night, the camera prowling beside him with no restriction and no comment. This is just a boy leaving the story with nowhere to go and no-one to trust. Peng's camera does not follow after him as he disappears.

In *Little Moth* the sick child Xiao E'zi is suspended between life and death. This is not a narrative which we can humanely recuperate as a story about a child with a disability that might be remediated. Her immobility is explained diegetically as a disease, but the disease and her resulting inert frame is disconcerting and extra-diegetic in its intention and moral reach. The doctor makes it crystal clear towards the end of the film that, if her disease is not arrested by amputation, the immobility will spread to her entire body and kill her. This could be a comment on her social conundrum. When children are still alive and are yet unusually immobile the implication is that they are somehow in trouble, in pain or enduring an impossible childhood. Hannah Kilduff explains how child actors may even rebel against unnatural stillness in certain scenes.[33] They know instinctively when they would no longer be listening quietly to an adult conversation or when they would have to make some movement to indicate their presence or discomfiture. Children run, they dash and they hurtle. This is particularly true in cities where children run around as though they are literally unable to stop or settle, as though once outside in the street they are compelled to be constantly in motion.[34] And, if the child is an indicator of energy and movement,[35] symptomatic and illustrative of a vibrant, hectic and modern urban environment, then the mobile child is an optimistic trope, obscuring the blockages and interruptions that threaten the ideological teleology of global connectivity and fluid urban systems, but not pursuing those systemic pathways themselves. However, the inert child is a similarly potent figure, no longer a talismanic protection from adult decay and the stench of death, but the epitome of morbid disturbance in the cityscape. She is the unmourned child, a canary in the mine warning of societal collapse. She is also the 'proto-zombie' child who cannot be mourned because she is not physically dead, but also does not embody the regenerative and optimistic energy of childhood. Inert, she is exploited as an object – both a commodity and a doll (a doll which, at that, replaces a dead child). Thus Little Moth is both verb and object in her story and in China's. She is physically transported by adult men, and later by Guihua, carried away by her friend Xiao Chun, who loses her in turn to the woman who wants to replace another lost child 'Lina', about whom we know nothing other than that Little Moth resembles her. The boy is ignored and, as we have seen, wanders away alone. Little Moth is likewise summarily dumped when the new benefactress is informed at the hospital that it is impossible to cure her disease of the blood, and that only the costly amputation of both legs will save her. The woman indicates to her teenage offsider – whose role is doubtful and leads one to wonder if the 'foster parent' is in fact a pimp – that she will not commit to an operation right away. The teenager lifts the child onto her back, the fourth person we have seen carrying Little Moth in the film. The film cuts from the hospital to the threesome crossing a bridge, the woman in front and the teenager with the child on her back in her wake. The bridge seems to be a long way from the hospital, somewhere on the semi-rural outskirts of the town. It is an odd, liminal place and we wonder why they did not take a taxi. Why are they here in this quiet spot? The woman crosses the road to 'have a pee', while the two girls wait. In a painful sequence that gestures to the slow cinema of Tsai Mingliang, the girl stands silently waiting next to Little Moth, and then she too crosses the road and disappears. Little Moth sits like a little pink flower. Her back is against the stone bridge. She says nothing and she can do nothing. She does not call for help. She waits, perhaps for someone new to come and pick her up and move her on. These are small cities so we hope against hope that it is Guihua who finds her and not the villainous Chang. But we know that the first could not afford to save her life and the second wouldn't want to. We also know that happy endings are not Peng Tao's point. China is his subject and that story is not over. So the film ends on the bridge, a child's quiet body being devoured from the inside out by a 'disease of the blood'. This is not so much killing innocence as letting it rot.

The tension between mobility and immobility, or between inertia and motion in *Little Moth* is captured in its mood. *Little Moth* has an overwhelming feeling of dread and foreboding laced into its atmosphere and into the plotting of the rambling but inexorable destruction of a society told through the actual and metaphorical destruction of children. The unrestricted narrative mode that Peng Tao employs is not however a tactic chosen to produce suspense. (Hitchcock, in a conversation with François Truffaut, admitted that killing a child on screen is a mistake for those aiming to produce suspense. The audience will turn against you, or they will simply turn against the suspense, demanding to know what is going on. While Hitchcock is disputing the wisdom of killing children on screen, Peng Tao does not allow us to see the probable death of Little Moth. We must however infer it.)[36] Peng Tao affords us access to all characters and we learn quickly what they are about. He moves us quickly from the purchase of the child to her deployment on the streets. The only possibly suspenseful moment is when two characters discuss stealing Guihua's kidneys, but she overhears and the potential for suspense is changed once more into foreboding. We understand with horror that Chang, who runs beggar children as a business, also delivers bodies to be harvested for their organs, and that the boy and girl would be subject to that attack were they to have remained anywhere near him. As spectators we are not on the edge of our seats, we are instead crushed with despair. The strings of social attachment and human feeling, and the moral duty of society towards its children, all Confucian and Mencian precepts and qualities,[37] are absent. A long and arduous film to watch, it is a road movie that moves in a circle towards itself, finally depositing the dying child on the boundary between Oz and Kansas, the rural and the urban, life and death.

Four

> An hour later they were sitting on the beach and staring out at the well of smog across the horizon. They sat with their heels dug into the sand and watched the bleak sea wash up at their feet. Cold. Desolate. Birdless. They sat there for a long time.[38]

The Road is Cormac McCarthy's apocalyptic masterpiece, in which an unnamed father and son (the Man and the Boy) struggle to survive in a world that is already mostly dead. The father has taught the Boy that they carry the fire of goodness and decency even as the prospect of a future is receding before them down the road to the sea. There is no such thing as childhood without the fire, without the hope. The death of the many adults, reported or observed in the course of the novel and viscerally reproduced in the film, is morbidly distressing, but the plight of every child – and there are very few here – is tragic. McCarthy's child is lonely for the company of other children – for proof of a shared future. He is also alone in the philosopher Bachelard's sense of reverie – he is the child dreamer 'alone, very much alone',[39] able to enter and inhabit a reverie that will later (perhaps) become his adult proof that he was indeed a child, even in this terrible place.[40] Literary critic Kevin Kearney writes of the novel,

> There are far fewer children, the token representatives of futurity, on the road than there are marauders. Worse yet, most young life is either used as food or seen as a potential meal. The most striking manifestation of this is the 'charred human infant headless and gutted and blackening on the spit,' a sight the boy encounters only after his tireless search for other children.[41]

Kearney's point in his analysis (of the novel) is that McCarthy is essaying the 'limits of the human'[42] rather than attempting a realistic scenario of life after an eco-catastrophe or a nuclear holocaust. The Man and Boy are experiencing the empty, grey deadness of life where the only trace of goodness is carried in the idea of a flame that they hold within themselves. In that, they seem to me to be very close to a contemporary refugee whose experience of the road, of seeking shelter, and of waiting, is one in which hope must be internally stoked as it is unlikely to be externally validated. And indeed the protagonists, Man and Boy, describe themselves as refugees, the good guys.

> ... it may just be refugees.
> Like us.
> Yes. Like us.[43]

De Bruyn offers a complementary reading, albeit one that is more concerned with the ecocritical aspects of the writing. He reads the novel through Robert Pogue Harrison's work on landscape, death and mourning,[44] arguing that McCarthy creates the eco-imagery of lost forests and stilled rivers to show humans having wandered away from their own history and culture.[45] Without an environment to which they can refer their memories and their connections to past generations, they cannot understand themselves. In losing their landscape they have lost their lexography, the words we pass on in becoming human, from one generation to another. It is another way of saying that without rivers, forest and grounded memory, they are without words. Lebeau, writing on *River's Edge*, invokes Jacques Derrida's 'loss of the archive' as a way of understanding why it is deadly to forget how to mourn. In *The Road* one can draw on the same work, 'the fundamental threat of the nuclear imagination when no social remainder is left to remember and to mourn'.[46] Without a lex of understanding, with no archive, there are no tools for the imagination. The travellers have no place like home and no way of discovering one.

The film of the book was directed in 2009 by John Hillcoat. Unlike *Little Moth*, the film does not have a local geo-political landscape in its sights when it lays out its dark vision of adult failure, lost origins and the dashed hopes of childhood. This could be America, and probably is America,[47] but it could also be Europe. The elements of two other post-apocalyptic films, *Mad Max* (1979) and *On the Beach* (1959), suggest Australia, perhaps a melancholy version of Oz where Dorothy never existed and the two evil witches won the day. The garbage on the path of the travellers is the litter of capitalism, neo-capitalism and over-consumption, a global phenomenon recalled in Coke and branded hubris (this detritus gives the film one archival source – making humanity's last known home the supermarket). Kearney remarks that the place of the film is unnameable because it is 'devoid of the human'.[48] The roads are peopled by marauders and frightened travellers, fleeing a world without a future and hiding from each other. They are not human in any of the ways which will prompt survival. There is no society, no mutuality, no care. The relationship between man and boy is built on the last shreds of trust and empathy. In *Little Moth* it would be seen as a thread of *ganqing* and *renqing* (human feelings and reciprocity). As if to emphasise that the human has been transformed into quite another kind of creature, the frightening marauders – bands of cannibals – are zombie-like in their indifference to the people they hunt down, torture and eat.

Little Moth and The Road

Children are sought after as though young meat will give strength to those already dying (and morally already dead), introducing vampiric appetites to the monstrous landscape. In a bizarrely domestic sequence, one female cannibal explains to their male companions that she leaves the window open to get rid of the smell (of blood). They reply 'what smell?'.

We may make some sense of the inhumanity of the cannibals through Max Silverman's use of Hannah Arendt's analogy of concentration camp survivors to Lazarus, the man Jesus raised from the dead.[49] As 'living dead' Lazarus is no longer human in the same way that those have never died are human. The logic of the concentration camps was to reduce humans to bare life, to strip physical confidence, moral reality and the essence of hope from victims and, in the process, to remove all sense of moral perspective and scale from the perpetrators. Lazarus survived death because he was resurrected by a living God. But Lazarus is thereby removed from both the living and the dead and is a solitary, unknowable man. Primo Levi has asked 'What is a Man?'. Freed camp inmates escaped death but their resurrection left them with Levi's question personally tattooed on their forearms. In *The Road*, the cannibals have taken on the role of perpetrators and their prey is the inmates – although the analogy is not exact. The cannibals are also victims of the great death that this filmic world has experienced. But, in choosing to survive by violating the ultimate taboo of human ingestion, they have lost all moral perspective and have removed themselves from humanity as such. Only the woman cannibal can still smell the blood and decay in the house they inhabit with their victims.

Despite their professed love of horror, the children in our north London workshops should never see these child-eating quasi-zombies, even though it was they who told me to watch *I am Legend*. They wanted me, I think, to understand an imaginary transformation and the release from fear that a horror movie paradoxically affords by turning ordinary bad people into extraordinary monsters that one can mimic and perform, and by releasing fear into the manageable, closed sphere of genre film. Watching *The Road*, their recommendation of *I am Legend* made sense. The latter ends with the sacrifice of the lead character (and father figure) after he has discovered the cure to the zombie infection and has passed that sacred phial onto to the woman and her son, so that they can save humanity and be saved themselves. Their safety is visualised as an entry through a great black door into a world of Church bells, green fields and sunshine. In *The Road*, transformations are absolute and absolutely terrifying, but persist in the realm of progressively worsening human behaviour rather than noble sacrifice. The sequence dealing with the cannibals 'at home' develops from the man and boy finding a large house which might provide them shelter, only to discover a cellar full of half-mutilated naked people, imprisoned as live meat for the occupants. As they try to escape the clawing entreaties of these doomed people, the Boy sees the cannibals through a window. They are returning to the house, presumably from a hunt. These human monsters troop in single file, moving in an almost processional fashion. They resemble the man-eating zombies of *The Night of the Living Dead* (1968), whose gait shifts between slow to inexorable as they draw close on their prey. Importantly for the deep horror of *The Road*, however, they are not zombies, they are humans who have chosen to survive through brutality and terror, through the deliberate dismemberment of fellow beings. Paul Sheehan notes, brilliantly, that they are even worse than the monsters of capitalist nightmares, 'the loss of civilization, therefore, is signified by a disconcerting compact: the absence of capitalist exploitation, in favor of the horrors and abominations of cannibal consumption.'[50]

Sara Simcha Cohen traces the commencement of *fast-moving* zombie-related humans to 2012 in the British director Danny Boyle's *28 Days Later*, where 'the zombie is updated as fast moving and more physically threatening than merely uncanny',[51] although Boyle himself refused the connection between 'infected' humans suffering from 'rage' and the actually dead zombies of earlier decades of American film. *The Road* was released two years earlier than Boyle's horror. The fearsome hunters in *The Road*, like Boyle's 'infected' humans, are not zombies, but they strongly resemble the zombies that we know in popular culture. They share their reduction to a reflex instinct to eat, and indeed to eat the living as if trying to reclaim – or, like a vampire, revive – life itself. Their violent and repulsively systematic destruction of their prey also leaves their victims not-yet-dead for a time as they devour them piece by piece. The cannibals may not be 'true-dead' (as van Helsing puts it in Bram Stoker's *Dracula*[52]), but they have endured the death of morality, empathy and humanity to be resurrected as monsters who prey on their fellow humans for food. Zombie movies have long been understood as a response to fear, specifically American fear – the 1950s responding to the Cold War, to the threat of nuclear annihilation, the 1980s to AIDS.[53] In the post-9/11 (2001) era the fear of terror at home has created another wave of such films.

The Road draws heavily on images borrowed from apocalyptic visions of the world's eco-death, from end-of-the-world terra nullius fantasies like *Mad Max*, and from images of Hiroshima and Nagasaki after the bombs fell. Certainly the human remnants and their captors are drawn from the concentration camp footage compiled in the aftermath of World War II and subsequent cultural knowledge of what occurred in Europe in the 1940s. Images of bunkers filled with naked prisoners and attenuated limbs awaiting further atrocities to be inflicted upon their person, and photographs of humans piled up in dark pits so disordered and so many together in their death that they lose their corporeal coherence, come straight from the twentieth century's intimate knowledge of man's inhumanity to man.[54] Indeed, Cohen's major thesis is a consideration of the Jew in European thought and literature as occupying a space between life and death. She reminds us that this trope

> of the uncanny Jew, or the Jewish zombie, was intensified after the Holocaust when images of the muselmann, the Nazi concentration camp inmate suffering from a combination of starvation and exhaustion, generally unresponsive, and occupying the space between life and death, saturated the media outlets. The muselmann's inability to speak or walk upright, his exclusion from his surroundings, suggest he has been so divested of his humanity he blurs the boundary between living and dead, serving as a tragic model of the living dead.[55]

These are the images that are recalled by the 'cannibal sequence'. The Man opens a trapdoor that reveals a cavity below the floor. Squinting in the light the shapes and strangely composed beings in the dark reveal themselves to be partially dismembered people, some dead, some alive. It is a pantry. The Man's response when he realises that the cannibals are returning and will kill them too if they are discovered is to hold a gun to the Boy's head. It is the action that we learn from vampire and zombie films: if you are to avoid becoming a monster you must sacrifice yourself and those you love while still a thinking human. A stake in the heart will protect you from transforming into a vampire, fire will prevent your body becoming zombie (and water will dissolve a witch). In the early twenty-first century, you pull out a gun, or you stand firm against the enemy with a hand grenade. As you explode, they burn.

Across this wreckage of humanity and this travesty of a landscape the Boy walks with the Man, his father, seeing things that a child should never see but must if he is to remain alive. For me, in my coming to the film in an era of mass migrations across sea and land, the Boy impersonates all refugee children who ever walked through the hell of war and its aftermath. His loneliness is echoed in online newspaper reports of young boys in makeshift camps in Calais in 2016. Some of the younger children in Calais carry with them a dream of being better than the place in which they find themselves. Some are still recognisably children, 'The most recently arrived still display flashes of humour and childish behaviour; the boys who have been here closer to a year have dulled expressions and say little.'[56] Certainly, McCarthy is not in the business of metaphor or allegory. He is rather offering a literary environment in which to think the unthinkable and then, if we see wraiths and whispers of the unthinkable in the lives we live now, that is for us to recognise and know. So, the boy is not the boys in Calais, nor a concentration camp survivor. He is not a boy walking out from the napalmed forests of Vietnam, or the ruins of Aleppo. As a literary and cinematic child, he performs a recognition of all of those and more.

The Road has a kind of happy ending. The Man dies on the beach having delivered his precious companion to the end of the road and simultaneously the edge of the world. Along the beach walks a family, two parents and two children, who take the orphaned Boy with them. They might be an apparition of the Man's memory of his lost family, but we know that they will not abuse him or sell his son, that they are the non-denominational holy family of goodness against the odds. The family on the beach are still refugees and the beach and horizon are still grey, but they are nonetheless a recognisably human unit. The ending does, after all, locate the Boy in a particularly American nightmare and a peculiarly American dreamscape. Unlike *Little Moth*, where the dread is grounded in a contemporary political manifestation of uncertainty, and where we come to realise that there really is no social trust left in certain parts of China, in *The Road* there remains American optimism that happy endings persist as long as families do. This is not necessarily comforting. Mark M. Anderson has argued that just as the Holocaust in Europe has become the key referent for actual apocalypse in Western culture, so within that construct the child is the key witness to the Holocaust in American life, letters and film. Anderson posits that the child as witness allows America to empathise with the victims of the Holocaust.[57] That is because child witnesses and victims (such as and especially Anne Frank) allowed America to engage in empathy and in a desire to save the children, without confronting their own recent histories of anti-Semitism. It was the innocent childishness rather than the victimised Jewishness of children that became a template for child suffering on film and for recuperation by American sympathy. It also allows a happy ending, although not for Anne Frank. Rather, the optimism is relocated in the continuing possibility of the American family.[58] The father figure dies (in *The Road*, in *I am Legend*) but his legacy continues through the boy he has saved.

The imagery of *The Road* renders the film a cultural inheritor of America's desire to visualise horror without fully considering or accepting the political import of what is revealed or even accepting that death means death. In *Little Moth*, we are left in no doubt that the economic revolution that has been playing out since the Reform Era, in the context of local areas already deeply destabilised by the vandalism and local violence of the Cultural Revolution in the late 1960s, has left a society that is both mobile and insecure, an antisocial network where the strings of human attachment have been unwound and left hanging. Where people seek succour they write false narratives of suffering on sheets of paper and place them in front of child beggars (Figure 4.1) whose own real suffering is much greater than the fiction lying before them, but whose human consequence is minimal. They only matter in so far as fiction will draw a moment's empathy from the crowd, or a stranger will see in them the opportunity for personal profit or emotional gain. In *The Road* the attachment at the centre of the narrative, that between father and son, is strong enough to be passed on through the boy to another set of parents and to a dream of family. The

Figure 4.1 'Little Moth and Guihua begging, with narrative on ground', *Little Moth*.

Figure 4.2 'Little Moth alone on the bridge, final scene', *Little Moth*.

world is a terrible place, the horrors are hyperbolic and extremely violent, but the road leads to the end of that world, on the beach.[59] In *Little Moth*, the prospect of stealing a child's kidneys is a business proposition. In *The Road* it is an act of cannibalism. Brutal criminality returns as monstrous transgression. Nonetheless, the American children are rescued, and the Chinese children just wander away or wait for something worse to happen (Figure 4.2).

5

Landscape in the Mist

One

At the very end of Theo Angelopoulos' *Landscape in the Mist* (Τοπίο στην Ομίχλη, 1988) two children climb from a small boat and run towards a tree on a hill shrouded in mist. We think that they are dead; we've just heard shots and so these must be ghosts, wraithlike personifications of Greece enjoying an endless mythical rebirth through its children. They have crossed the river Styx and are running back to the Tree of Life. Actually, at this point in the film, we don't really want to know that. It is one of those moments when one struggles against the logic of the text to find another ending, to resist the death of a child, to wish for the American family on the beach to scoop them up and take care of them and keep them alive. That is not how Angelopoulos makes history on film, so we must think again. *Landscape in the Mist* meditates on some of the key themes from his larger oeuvre: the repetitions in Greek history, leaving Greece (and staying put), mobility, the revelatory courage of children, the fragility of humankind and the silence of God.[1] It is a valuable, quintessentially European addition to the discussion here, not least because it invokes the relationship between a girl child's maturation and a magical environment, a theme that is so central (albeit coded) to Dorothy's journey to Oz. Angelopoulos' film reminds us that Greece has produced multiple narratives of migration, border crossing, homelessness and migratory returns in classical history and myth, as well as in mid-twentieth to twenty-first-century political history; for example, exile from the dictatorship of the 1930s through to the displacements during and after World War II and then Civil War (1945–9).[2] Now again, at the time of writing, Greece is the frontier point of arrival for refugee children from northern Africa and the Middle East who head for safety across the Mediterranean Sea and sometimes are dead on arrival.[3] It is not surprising that this film should resonate so persuasively over temporal as well as geopoetic borders. As Dan Georgakas explains, 'Angelopoulos' approach to politics ... and aesthetic choices ... (seek) to join history, myth and current events seamlessly and with a healthy disrespect for all things authoritarian.'[4]

The anti-authoritarian mood of *Landscape in the Mist* may originate in the film-maker and speak to regional as well as national politics, but I argue below that it is further hijacked by the girl, Voula, and the actor who plays her, Tania Palaiologou. The film's protagonists are two runaway children, the 11-year-old Voula, and her five-year-old brother Alexander (Michalis Zeke). The third significant party is a young adult, Orestes (Stratos Tzortzoglou), a character that we have met before in previous Angelopoulos films featuring his family *The Travelling Players*.[5] Orestes features both as adult partisan hero and as silent child in that 1975 film-essay on performance and continuity in Greek history. Re-appearing here in the guise of a young man on a motorbike, Orestes is a cinematic 'angel' of history who transcends age and time in Angelopoulos' oeuvre.[6] Voula meanwhile bears the name of Angelopoulos' late sister, producing an emotional proximity and equivalence with the film-maker that supports the argument I wish to pursue in this chapter, namely that Voula is both protagonist and a critical agent within the thinking body of the film. This is in part a question of her diegetic agency. Unlike the children in Chapter 4, all of whom are forced by circumstance to move away from home (and do so in part because they have no home left to leave), Voula makes the decision herself. She leaves home, and her Mother, and starts out on a journey to an imagined land called Germany, far beyond the confines of what manifests as an equally imagined homeland called Greece. If the director's goal for her character is to save Greece from itself even as she witnesses its cannibalistic form of self-historicising (here metaphorical as opposed to the proto-zombie humans of *The Road*), the performance of Palaiologou creates an extra-diegetic resonance in Voula's screen presence that critiques the film's redemptive trajectory even as she presents it through the script. Most crucially for my argument, the rape sequence which supports Angelopoulos' narrative of maturing in a hard world[7] is, through the performance of the actor and by her onscreen friend and angel, Orestes, differently understood from the avowed response of the film-maker himself which is that rape will help her mature. So, when a male critic writes (in an extraordinary and concerning leap of logic) of Voula, who after the rape is an abused child, as 'das zur Frau wurde' ('now a woman')[8], he supports the bizarre but not sadly unusual notion that rape is part of sexual maturation rather than a violent repression of the self which may in fact inhibit the victim's sexual maturation and emotional development. It recalls the real life experience of Ruth Balizka, who managed to save herself and her siblings, but whose own life as an adult was curtailed by what she had endured to achieve that bare survival.[9] This is an important matter for child migrants in the 'real world' where children who have experienced rape and other forms of abuse travel alone and seek asylum. They may therefore indicate premature maturity (as do other sexual abuse victims) and find themselves disbelieved on matters of age. Their abuse can lead to abused and raped girls continuing to be treated as adults rather than children and thereby further psychologically harmed or even denied asylum and returned to the place where they were originally harmed.[10]

Voula's brother, Alexander, shares a name endowed on men and boys throughout Angelopoulos' post-1984 work.[11] What we may draw from this is perhaps that the Greek boy and the Greek man are not always distinct entities, that in fact the boy is already showing the wisdom of age, whilst the aged are already returning to the insights of childhood. Orestes is of course endlessly himself, the ever-heroic, ever-desired soldier, brother and angel.[12] Orestes' appearances as a flesh-and-blood guardian angel inform the spiritual journey of the film and is also perhaps indicative of the effect of Wim Wenders' *Wings of Desire* (*Der Himmel über Berlin*, 1987) on its vision. In *Wings of Desire*, (mainly) male angels look after the people of Berlin, but concentrate on those with a certain stubborn metaphysic(ality) – trapeze artists – finding sympathy with those who can find ways of flying literally or metaphorically across the landscapes of modernity. *Landscape in the Mist* is set in such a mixed landscape: peri-urban industrial dead space, small grubby towns, the great Greek port Thessaloniki (named after the half-sister of Alexander the Great, and we should remember that Voula is named after Angelopoulos' sister; everything connects), and on the road. The landscape of the title includes the non-spaces of the children's journey, the gesture to the past in Alexander's namesake but, over all of this, refers to an occluded, cinematic destination. That hidden misty place is introduced to the protagonists and to us, the spectators, by Orestes. It is printed on a small piece of discarded film stock on which one can discern nothing, but in which Alexander perceives the tree. Invisible to all but the mind's eye of the child, its image is realised in the final frames of the film where the tree emerges through the mist as their final destination, their F(f)ather, and the end point of a hard journey of maturation, sacrifice and (possibly) redemption.

The children's return to a magical centre is also in keeping with the fairytale structure of the narrative. The children are on a quest, they seek one magical answer to all their problems, they receive help from an angel and they transcend mortality. The adult world is dangerous to them, full of beasts. Angelopoulos says that the earth mover (digger) in a scene on an industrial site is supposed to represent a dragon.[13] The film's reliance on the child's mobility within the frame, and its narrative response to their total motivation to find a F(f)ather figure, presents us with a particularly strong case of the child migrant as an agent of history as well as its victim. Although in many films discussed in this book child migrants are physically subjected to conditions made through adult decisions and adult neglect or violence – *Little Moth* being at the other end of a spectrum – it is often still the case that children provide the impetus to travel and to make of history, whether or not we name them Alexander (the Great).

Now, I would contend that the film's progress towards sacrifice is what I am calling a 'pensive collaboration', and partially failed negotiation, between child-protagonists, child-actors and a film-maker. The collaboration entails thinking their way towards a Stygian border, beyond which lies the landscape in the mist. The children leave 'Greece' only to arrive

Landscape in the Mist

Figure 5.1 'Voula at the back of the truck after the rape', *Landscape in the Mist*.

at its heart and soul. The failure (and why the film is saved as a text readable by feminists, which matters to this spectator) is embodied in Voula's on-screen presence. She rushes towards the tree – of life, of death and of salvation – together with Alexander, but other memories of the actor's performance provide stronger afterimages from the film as a whole. I refer to the scene of her exhausted body crawling from the back of the truck after the rape, her hand touching the thread of blood rolling down her hand and leg, (Figure 5.1) and the recollection of her furious, lonely, love-lorn despair and shame on the beach when she realises that her angel Orestes cannot save her soul through pure love, nor refashion her torn body into something more childish, something that can follow a more organic, developmental course to womanhood and, above all, something whole.

Two

Where does this pensivity reside? *Landscape in the Mist* is the final part of a trilogy about silence. The first part, *Voyage to Cythera* (1984), draws on

125

the silence of History, the second part, *The Beekeeper* (1986), on the silence of Love and the third part, *Landscape in the Mist*, considers the silence of God. Angelopoulos thereby presents a semi-mystical and highly religious account of the journey of the two children from Greece towards Germany, seeking their F(f)ather. They do not know that Germany has no border with Greece, but then, one might say that Heaven has no border with Earth. In any case, the film elides that geographical and indeed metaphysical truth. It is more important that Germany, the F(f)ather and the Tree of Life are sought through belief[14] and the strength of the child's need for home. The F(f)ather in the imaginary of the film is both an imagined absent parent and a childish dream of God. He manifests as a voice whispering in the children's heads and through their dreams about their quest northwards. He is not entirely silent, but – if we return to Wim Wenders' conceit – whispers through his angels. Angelopoulos references this conceit in a later film, *Eternity and a Day* (1998), which stars Bruno Ganz (Wender's fallen Angel in *Wings of Desire*) as a dying man named Alexander, befriending a child migrant from Albania.

As *Landscape in the Mist* opens, the children stand undecided on a station platform, unable to board a train. They have done this many times before and again they return home, but the following evening they finally jump aboard and leave. It turns out that the film is not about their indecision but about their courage and their capacity to move, and hence to remain alert and to think about who they are and where they are going, in stark opposition to adult incapacity for mindful action. Angelopoulos poses an adult world that is reactive and venal or simply forgetful and aimless. Adults are shown to be unthinking where the children, and the film itself, think. Mobilising themselves in the face of such monumental adult inertia, it is the children who provide the forward-moving energy for the film's progress. Yet, when the children set out, the geography of their trip is vague. The actual possibility of the children ever leaving Greece is slim, not only because the border they are looking for does not exist, but practically too they have nothing they might normally need for such an enterprise. They do not have tickets, passports or cash. They have no address to aim for and no allies in the adult world. When Orestes appears to help them he is something else, part cinematic magic, part angel. Orestes comes to the children from a deeper ahistorical past, like those child characters in fairytales who slip through fissures of time. Vassilis Rafailidis has noted that '*Landscape in the Mist* is a poetic Biblical parable on the myth of Genesis, or, to put it more clearly, on the myth of the re-genesis of the world through cinema, the only true illusionist'.[15] That sense of cinema is certainly central to the poetic magic that holds the film in thrall to its young protagonists, who in turn hold tight to a strip of film that convinces Alexander at least that they are in the realm of the Creator. Their journey will create a tree and the tree will embody the myth of redemption. The religious force of the film is specifically triggered by the search for the F(f)ather, and is emphasised through descents into hell and visions of glory. But the Father is the Creator, and the Film is that which is created within and outwith his creation.

Voula somewhat undermines this trajectory and forms a complex emotional attachment to Orestes. Diegetically this is not surprising. She is alone, looking for a father figure, and she is on the cusp of girl-womanhood. He is young, handsome and kind and has appeared along the road with his combi-van and his motorbike just as the children are at their most weary, helping them move on once they are thrown off the train. Days later, he takes the children to a nightclub in a cellar and leaves them to wait for him on the stairs. Voula grows anxious and wanders through it, looking for him. She eventually discovers that it is a gay club and she spies Orestes flirting with a young man. The club sequence is shot at child's-eye height. It is dark, confusing and clearly a place exclusively for adults. For Angelopoulos it is a descent into hell, perhaps rather crudely so. But the implied moral criticism of gay men is paradoxically redeemed by Palaiologou's passion, because for Voula this is worse than hell: it is the place where she realises the pain of love. She can only experience this epiphany by seeing that Orestes may be looking for love himself, and that she is excluded from that resolution. In the frustration of desire Voula is vulnerable to despair in a way that she was not when she first boarded the train north. The fiendish agony of adolescent love, a state that should in time develop into the mature love of womanhood, is mutated into something much more sinister and violent by the roadside rape by a truck driver, an assault that short-circuits her journey to maturity. In response, Orestes can offer only a brief vision of platonic fidelity. One morning Voula looks for him in their hostel rooms, and sees he is not in his bed. Frightened that he has left (in this moment Palaiologou becomes a small vivid Electra) she walks outside where he is standing looking out across the harbour, and they stand together, gazing out and over the sea as a great hand from an ancient statue is lifted from the water and borne skyward above the port city by a helicopter. Schütte sees this moment as an illustration of the loss of authority in Greece: 'daß der Hand der Zeigenfinger abgebrochen ist: eine zweifellos drastische Metepher für die orientierungslose Situation, in der alle autoritativen Gesten ihre Macht verloren haben' ('the hand's index finger has broken off, a telling metaphor for a trackless situation in which all gestures of authority have lost their validity').[16] If that is the case, then perhaps we understand why God is silent and must talk through the whispers of angels and the determination of child seers. Schütte's reading does not explain the rapt attention that the two travellers pay to the appearing, disappearing, flying hand. Perhaps this is best understood as another instance of temporal collapse as presence, myth and history combine in Greece's search for a F(f)ather to come home to.

In other moments, the children are truly visionary, seers and martyrs both. They see what others cannot and they move forward as adult others are stilled. On leaving home for the last time Voula and Alexander take a detour to bid farewell to a madman in their town, 'Seagull' (Hlias Logothetis), imprisoned in what seems to be half-migrant camp, half-asylum at the edge of the town. He stands atop the scrubby hillside and calls to them, his arms flapping, over a perimeter fence. To the children he is clearly not a lost soul but an angelic voice that encourages them toward flights which they might take on his behalf. He is an affective but powerless guardian angel or perhaps a wingless Messiah suffering the little children to go from him on the road to ascension. And then there is the final scene, but this scene follows a river crossing that infers their deaths. They have eluded border guards – who knows what border – and found a small boat that they row away from a dark shore. Shots ring out and we think we may have seen Voula slumping in her seat. It is too dark to know exactly what we are supposed to see. As the children are sacrificed, the film reveals more of that disturbingly patriarchal Biblical trajectory. The film ends and the children are left, pinpricks in the mist, hugging the tree and naming it as (the) Father. The tree of life in the Garden of Eden was the site of Eve's corruption by Satan: 'But of the tree of the knowledge of good and evil, thou shalt not eat of it: for in the day that thou eatest thereof thou shalt surely die'.[17] Angelopoulos reclaims Voula's female childishness by making the tree of life a paradoxical proof of salvation: 'Blessed [are] they that do his commandments, that they may have right to the tree of life, and may enter in through the gates into the city'.[18] This is the moment at which one might have to turn one's back on the whole enterprise of the film's journey. If we take on the Biblical narrative of female descent and salvation, then Voula has been used in a way that makes the film mystifying rather than mystical. Some critics understand the film as an 'optimistic and dynamic' treatment of a childish belief in the future,[19] a hopeful embrace of the magical properties of cinema. An abused girl is surely not the best way to achieve cinematic rebirth or to explore the optimism of migration from one state of being to another, nor to rebirth a national history through the sacrifice of children on the hillside.

I have said that the story is structured as a fairytale. The children are on a quest to a destination that turns out to be at the spiritual epicentre of the place they think they are leaving. They escape from Greece only in order to embrace and reveal its soul. Their journey is punctuated by meetings with strangers and their safety is, for a time at least, secured by an angel from Greece's mythological past. It is tempting to make parallels with the journeys of actual child migrants seeking sanctuary, finding that their past can travel alongside them and be waiting for them on arrival. For any girl migrant carrying with her a history of sexual abuse, those memories are embodied and immediate and owned by the child herself. Travel alone will not cure them. Angelopoulos may not grasp Voula's situation as an individual child (and scholars of Angelopoulos will probably remind me that he does not always deal in individual characterisation)[20] but in any case, he knows very well that travel through time and space entrenches rather than disperses collective historical memory. His own travelling players, moving through his history films and now appearing lost and confused in these three songs of silence, end up on the beach hanging up their costumes for sale like discarded washing or the detritus of a sea crossing gone wrong. As the twenty-first century is scarred by the sight of refugee children crossing the Mediterranean Sea and camping on the Greek shoreline, so the film becomes prophetic of a longer desperation.

But in 1988 the soul at stake is Greece's and this is a metaphorical encounter that only pretends to cross borders in order to find a way home – do I need to say 'Oz'?. Pragmatically, the F(f)ather that Voula and Alexander have set out to find is most probably not in Germany, but is/was a man (or two men) who passed through their mother's life, leaving her with children but nothing else. He might be living in their home town. For the children he is real, an audible ghost in their ears who whispers about the future and who comes to rest in the image of a tree. He is a spirit that leaps wherever the children lead him, the idea of his existence persuading the children on a journey into an imaginary utopia. He is both hunter and hunted. Yet, unlike the returned partisan in *The Hunters* (Οι Κυνηγοί, 1977), the utopic gaze that Angelopoulos attributes to this F(f)ather is turned away from the angel of history and towards a nostalgic memory of Greece that is not so easily defined by political history. The absence is much more personal than that. The children's mother is barely seen in the film and is given little credit for her role in the children's lives or sympathy for her likely grief at their departure. Simply, she has no narrative that will sustain them other than the myth of paternity. So, in a decade when Greek labour migration northwards was at last slowing after the rush away from the Junta and civil war,[21] the mother invents a story about Germany. The children's ensuing quest is both less and more than it seems, a pilgrimage from the knee of their mother's fantasy to the borders of their imaginations, couched in the conspiratorial agency of a quixotic body of a film. Various concepts of mobility, 'exile, diaspora and nomadism', raise different spectres of pain, loss or opportunity,[22] explicitly linked to the Biblical wanderings after the expulsion from Eden and the ultimate loss of Paradise. Exile suggests a third party or circumstance enforcing the departure, while diaspora retains the notion of a fixed point from which one is distanced, even if that place is imaginary or inaccessible. In a more political reading of the three terms, nomadism is singularly free of dreams of home.[23] The children's mobility encompasses both the Biblical quest to regain Paradise, and the sense that they are – perhaps in this, closer to the travelling players than I have hitherto imagined – without a way home and in no need of one, other than the myth of paternity held out to them by the film-maker. Theirs is a spiritual and familial migration, part fairytale quest and part indefinite, mortal exile.

The children are also subject to Angelopoulos' understanding of how children encounter 'hard' adulthood; so they are at once courageous travellers, lonely child-migrants and vulnerable spiritual ciphers in an adult tale of innocence lost. Their presence transcends the adult environments through which they pass and subsists on a motivation born of childishness at its most transcendental. Their being in the film is watchful, vigilant and mobile. The children are the thinking subjects in the fabric of the cinematic event, and they imbue the film itself with watchfulness and pensivity, greatly supported by Eleni Karaindrou's score. *Landscape in the Mist* is both a naïvely luminous and parodic version of the sombre journeys of adults in Angelopoulos' other road movies (and so many of them *are* road movies). It also presents an intuitive shift in power, from adult to child and from film-maker to stubborn protagonists and the film in itself. Murphy comments, 'This children's crusade aims to re-consecrate not some literal holy-or father-land, but that breeding-ground of potent dreams, the tabula rasa of the movie screen – screen having replaced stage as the polis' most accessible theater'[24]

If we hold up the religious lens to the children's vagrancy, they take so many parts: Adam and Eve returning to Paradise redeemed; Moses leading the Israelites out of Egypt; the poor, trekking across a wide wilderness towards their own, personal border constructed from opportunity and politics as much as geospatial ordinance; the rich, on a different journey to look for the eye of a needle, but also children as children, suffered to 'come unto me' even when they are sent to wander away on their own. As children travelling alone they are often both invisible and peculiarly subject to abuse, doled out by the systems through which they travel and by individuals they meet along the way. In sum, even as their quest carries the weight of Greek despair and Angelopoulos' belief in impossible redemption through cinema itself, if not through a vague narrative of maturation, the children will notwithstanding be treated like other refugees; extra-territorial, outside the presumed safety of national belonging or geopolitical privilege, vulnerable to exceptional cruelty. For any children, this extraterritoriality is accentuated by being decoupled from a family unit or group, which has prematurely released them from the official state of innocence that has both constrained and endangered them but which serves them even more poorly when they reject its embrace. The sense that even the film-maker believes innocence is something to be lost and found renders them both – and especially Voula – at the edge of bare life, but also, in this film and for this particular journey, sacrificial. There is a contradiction here; surely there always must be when the creator seeks a conclusion but wants to explore redemption. That which was lost is found, that which was dead is alive again.[25] A fairytale transforms into a modern parable of childhood, mobility and betrayal.

As I have already suggested, the cinematic image of children travelling alone usually signifies an environment of national instability or uncertainty. Voula and Alexander's journey north is an anguished eulogy to postwar Greece, a hard world swathed in disappointment, weighed down by a past that seems to have no purchase on the future and little to offer the present – both states exemplified by these deracinated children who simultaneously seek the security of a Father('s) land and exile. The adults that they encounter on the road are disjointed, disorientated, occasionally abrupt and sometimes violent: a sobbing bride, a rapist, policemen frozen to the spot. People stagger in a kind of collective, accelerated dementia. It is a world in drift. The children watch a horse die on a snowy street. Voula strokes the dying horse's head, Alexander sobs out his grief at the animal's distress and death. In the background, a bride rushes out from a wedding party crying. She is taken back into the building and a few moments later the entire party emerges drunkenly singing and weaving out of frame. None of the adults notice the children or the dead animal in the snow.

The problem of children's invisibility is a problem of innocence: 'innocence suggests a state of defencelessness rather than security, and it is as such that it is valued ... the figure of the innocent child – delimits an existence at the extreme of vulnerability, rather than one that is invulnerable to everyday risk'.[26] Childish innocence is an appropriative fantasy, a screen on which adults project their memories and ideals, behind which children move in silhouette unseen and unheard. The analyst Adam Phillips however tells us to be optimistic as well as careful. Yes, the traumatic shades of childhood are where the internal life is built and fortified. But there are many shades of childhood and not all are traumatic. To look for it insistently is to misplace the remarkable wonder of some childhoods. Perhaps something akin to what was once called negative theology might be useful here, so that one could say – and as Gordie finds of his youthful friendships in *Stand By Me* – everything that doesn't return is what is essential from childhood. We may then have no need to go on – or not in quite the same way – plundering our lives and our children, for childhood.[27]

When Voula and Alexander jump on the northbound train, when they refuse the forced return to their mother, they are outside the structures of protection, and simultaneously suspected of being guilty, or not innocent enough. Their innocence, that projection of adults valued as a state of defencelessness rather than security and agency, thus becomes dangerous. This double bind is the trick that catches the child refugee. Refugees see too much, they have earned tragic perspective through their exile as well as a sense of the multiple scales of being and truth in the world. Through their nomadism, they know about going and coming, they have learned the secret of the emperor's new clothes, that the nation is porous and unreliable. They have an end in sight that transcends or at least challenges local determinations of normality and possibility. The children pass through Greece like travelling players, like migrants, like soldiers wandering across a battlefield of strange encounters and casual danger, like children travelling alone. Here adults are disappointing. Angelopoulos' Players, whose whole raison d'être in the earlier eponymous opus *The Travelling Players* has been to perform their play, fail to act. They have retreated to the beach. A man in a café gives five-year-old Alexander work to do in exchange for a bite of food. Rebuffed by a young waitress at a truck stop, a driver rapes 11-year-old Voula in the back of his truck to sate and pass on his humiliation. Soldiers on a border, maybe imaginary or maybe not, shoot at Voula and Alexander in a boat. So perhaps Phillips' argument also supports our concern about appropriation. Children are rendered always vulnerable to harm by the world's strategy of keeping them 'innocent'. That is the point. We ostracise the 'not innocent enough' child travelling alone and perversely expose them to more harm and danger by excluding them from social protections. Where children's subjectivity has been discussed, it is often from the perspective of the needs and fantasies of the adult subject. This is the case to some degree in *Landscape in the Mist*, but not wholly so. As we watch, the children step out of the drifts of adult desire and walk away and through the snow.

Three

One can decide to accept that the combination of the film's beauty, the sustained presence of its child protagonists and the religious intention of the film-maker are powerfully coherent even in their apparent contradictions. Angelopoulos has offered his own internal salvation as a film-maker through certain earlier sequences that, possibly, provoke a viewing that acknowledges the aspects of religious reference within his vision, but at the same time allow that another cinematic and narrative force is at work. It is indeed the agents of the salvation – for cinema, for Greece – the children, both performers and performances, who are enabled to help the film think beyond its own impossible borders. This can be only a suggestive argument, for it is theoretically presumptuous to state that the film thinks against its maker. Nonetheless it is the only way in which the film's power makes sense to this viewer who is not convinced that the children, and especially Voula, are in fact contained by Angelopoulos' religious and political perimeter fence.

I would argue that the children take the film beyond the quest, and into the status of a thinking subject, or a compound thinking subject-ness – children, performances, film. The name of the girl, Voula, admits that the film-maker wants to honour the dead (his sister). The honour shimmers around the intense vivacity of his lead actor Palaiologou. Her performance maintains but also exceeds the religious and political structure of the film's interests. Indeed, she does something quite remarkable, embodying the film-maker's passion for the long shot[28] in a performance that is at once sustained, persistent and grounded in the cinematic intensity and intelligence that must operate at the centre of a pensive film. Jacques Rancière writes of the pensive image, commenting that 'someone who is pensive is "full of thoughts", but this does not mean that she is thinking them'.[29] He also extends Hegel's claim for the active passivity of the gods of Olympus to a wider comment on a new aesthetics of 'immobile motion', echoing the 'radical indifference of the sea's waves'. Rancière is interested in the role of the image in radical and mainstream politics. Nevertheless, his observations address the status of the agents of pensivity that I observe here: the children themselves. The children think throughout the film. Their consistency lends them an air of seclusion from the world they traverse, and from the emotional reach of the audience. At the same time, they deliver energy to both. This again produces the aura of fairytale reality, in which the magical solution is closest to the Real. They think first about their F(f)ather – we hear them on voiceover and we watch their purposeful forward motion and their resistance to those who would take them off their path. But their movement in the film is also a form of positive thinking. The beauty of the film is dependent on the clarity that, without these children moving through the film space, without the sheer will underpinning their performances, without Voula's bright courage and Alexander's gentle certainty – without these crucial elements, the film's beauty would not manifest. The landscape is in the mist, but the set pieces of cinema are sharply in focus. Everything is visible through the children's presence of mind; a bride's inexplicable grief and a dying horse, each picked out like single snowflakes on a child's bedroom window.

The historian Hanneke Grootenboer describes the quality of the pensive image as 'an interiority different from their meaning or narrative through which these images become thoughtful'.[30] Rancière concludes that the pensive image does not signify a 'surplus of plenitude', but enacts a break in narrative that at once halts and extends the possibilities of action. These insights reveal the power of the child actor. The child and the film perform a chiasmic relation of being and thinking. The film's strategy in this interior dialogue with itself is to see itself as through a meteorological veil. The use of snow is a kind of three-dimensional visual joke that remains long after it has stopped falling: a film of snow, snow falling as if on a faulty image, the people as snowmen, snowed under. Snow forces a stillness that is as profound as the silence of snow is dense. The snow sequence starts in a police station, where the children have been taken and from where they would have been returned to their mother but for an unseasonal snow fall. The policemen and women are entranced at the sight and rush down stairs and away from their posts crying 'It's snowing!'. Only an old lady in widow's weeds is unmoved; she sits talking to herself and we realise that she is herself a 'blow-in', a character from Angelopoulos' earlier film *Reconstruction*, (Αναπαράσταση, 1970) an earlier Angelopoulos film about spousal murder and adulterous desire (significantly, the murdered spouse is a returned migrant from Germany). To further the intertextual 'joke', she is already snowed-in in a frozen narrative of return and despair into which she was cast 18 years before. As the children realise that something magical is occurring they slip out of the police station to where all the adults stand rooted, their faces uplifted in wonder. The snow enchants and stills the adult-world while the child-world breaks out and the children run through and past their would-be captors, acknowledging the snowflakes as playmates, but doggedly resuming the quest. The theme 'Father' plays over the silence.[31] There is, if you like, a conspiracy between film and child, the one telling the other that, because they are there, magic is possible and, because magic is there, the snow is possible. So, the film can indeed be filmic and let them escape. Angelopoulos himself said of the sequence: 'The scene with the snow… The snow reflects the kids' desire to go away. The desire is so strong that the imaginary father, or an imaginary sign, produces a miracle: makes people frozen and kids invisible'. And about the scene with the horse:

> The entire trip is a trip in the experience. The kids take the taste of life. Their trip is a trip of initiation. That is what the French call with the specific term 'voyage de initiation'. This is the meaning of the scene in which the boy works to win two sandwiches and by the way he perceives the meaning of work and gain. This is the meaning of the scene with the horse; the kids have their first touch with death.[32]

Angelopoulos' account is provocatively straightforward and, either deliberately or maybe even obtusely, underplays the poetic energy of the children's thinking bodies on screen in relationship with the physical, magical world that he has created and captured for them. The film is a coming of age film, wherein adults reveal their weaknesses and the world makes clear the price of survival (five-year-old Alexander works for food and Voula, the raped girl, tries to seduce a soldier for money). I have already said that the children experience this early initiation into cruelty in part because of their status as travellers, dangerous innocents, child migrants. But perhaps Angelopoulos undersells the revelations inherent in the film's phenomenological substance. The film does not merely instruct its protagonists. Rather, it discovers itself by thinking with the children and through the performances that the film's thinking elicits. The cinematic image is neither diegesis nor personal cinematic history. It is Greece itself allowing itself to be thought differently, to favour childhood over managed innocence, to understand the character of its history as a palimpsest. True, it delivers a pastiche of chance, an unseasonable weather event, to allow the children to escape, but also to emphasise that the children are pensive subjects where adults are defaming objects. As the feminist literary historian Naomi Schor comments (of the French author Henri Balzac), 'To be thoughtful does not signify merely to be contemplative, lost, as it were, in one's thoughts. It also signifies preoccupation and fullness of care'[33]; 'The sober Celeste, so gentle and calm, as equable as reason itself, habitually reflective and thoughtful.'[34] In Balzac the moment of pensivity is a signal that the text is at once at ease and at full alert. The pensivity in *Landscape in the Mist* emerges then from moments of stillness wherein only children and Orestes, the child of actors himself, remain mobile and fully alert to the wonder and tragedy of the world around them: a good madman trying to fly, snow falling, a horse dying, an absent Father whispering in their dreams. It is they who put the film at ease, who persuade through their own gravitas that playfulness is appropriate, that the film may indeed take on its own magical propensity. The adult men and women move or stop without thought or without care, with small motivations and a truncated sense of the possible. When they do look, at snow falling out of season, they are held fast, not alert but temporarily thwarted. They are not the thinking body (bodies) of the film, but the objects of its pity.

The adults in Angelopoulos' first great meditation of 1975 were the Travelling Players. They return here as Orestes' family, employers and as seers of Greece's many lost pasts. Standing on a desolate beach, having been wandering for years before these children took to the road, the now aged Players recite the low points of the twentieth century. They have lost their proactive engagement with historical thought and political confrontation.

The once articulate band of actors and philosophers, who still turn resolutely to camera to assert the detailed trajectories of national disaster, are themselves caught in eddies of repetition and return. With the exception of Orestes the man-angel and Seagull the madman, all adults move as a silenced collective, a chorus staring back up at the beach, out to sea, or at snow falling. Adult actions and inactions alike appear motivated by a capitulation to fate; the bride's brief, tearful escape is an aberration. Perhaps she is suddenly aware that she is about to stop living in thought, that her marriage is the threshold to collective unthinking. Andrew Horton describes Angelopoulos' work as a cinema of contemplation[35] and the contemplation of failure and despair is what is left to adults in *Landscape in the Mist*. Of course, 'contemplation' is also used to refer to the admiration of God. Here, with that spiritual contemplation at work, the object of contemplation is Greece and the mode of contemplation is the tension between mobility and stasis. Travelling players, refugees, conscripts and returning soldiers cross back and forth between the hinterland and the sea, between the past and the present. Greece has had its Gods in plenty, but they are hardly to be seen in these visions. Simply, now and then, fragments of these imperfect overlords rise like shards of conscience from the sea. In a film where Angelopoulos is trying to accommodate an orthodox vision of redemption, the protagonists confront the past rising as a massive, magisterial but broken hand that soars over the city of Alexander the Great's sister. Is this film truly contemplative then, or something more active, more alert, more playful? When Meir Wigoder quotes Barthes and Benjamin on the pensive image he quickly avers: 'Now, we know that he does not mean that the object itself is capable of thinking, just as we know that when Walter Benjamin spoke of the optical unconscious of the photograph no one believed he meant that the object literally stored such hidden thought'.[36] Well, maybe not. But this film is phenomenological. It knows whose side it's on. It connects drift, modernity and mobility. The body of the film, like all film, is 'hazy', 'insubstantial'; like a mist, perhaps, or like drifting snow.

> In the empty moment, what you call identity ceases to be continuous, linear, apparent. It's hazy and insubstantial, a jumbled, fragmented surface. It skips around from one time to another, from one place to another. It refuses to respect the need to keep

one moment consistent and continuous with the ones that precede or follow it. It's a film.[37]

This film does perhaps store 'such hidden thought'. It makes an unruly and disrespectful epiphanic appearance as-itself-as-snow. The children's urgent need to escape forces a rapturous emptiness in which adults are quietened and children run free. The film emboldens itself within its own stab at hexeity. The moment creates an emptiness, a time of drift, in which the film mobilises and prefers its own improbable tale of children escaping the national malaise of disappointment. Their alert belief in angels is essential to stave off one of modernity's more persistent and ugly jokes about time and space. They are travelling along routes of migrant labour to a border that doesn't exist in search of a migrant who has probably already returned, if he ever went away. The mumbling old lady in the police station, numbed by her own cinematic moment decades earlier, has already warned them that a migrant is not welcome when he returns home. He will have been replaced and only his children will wait for him. But this film is on the children's side, it even leaves a scrap, a strip of itself like a director's shadow, for Orestes to find and for Alexander to hold. The snow lays a coating on the film, the tree captured on it is so faint they can barely distinguish it, and the children step across and through the snow. So in the end I find that Voula has been swallowed by the narrative of salvation, but simultaneously she has resisted it. She is a child of Greece and a daughter of the F(f)ather that Angelopoulos provides, but she is also Voula the dangerous innocent, child migrant – and Tania Palaiologou, a child actor who, in performing the impact of rape and the deadening violence of man on child, comes so close to taking her character back from the insult of sacrifice.

6

The Leaving of Liverpool: Empire and religion, poetry and the archive

For all along the highways
Troops of hungry children roamed
And gathered to them others
Who stood by ruined homes
…
A girl of ten was carrying
A little child of four.
All she lacked to be a mother
Was a country without war.
…
In January of that year
Poles caught a hungry dog,
Around his neck a placard hung,
'Twas tied there with a cord.

The words thereon were PLEASE SEND HELP
WE DON'T KNOW WHERE WE ARE.
WE ARE FIVE AND FIFTY,
THE DOG WILL LEAD YOU HERE.[1]

One

In this chapter I turn to one of the drivers of forced child migration in the nineteenth and twentieth centuries, the imperatives of nation building and imperial networks. The children in the following case study are those whose despatch to the colonies, both before and after their Federation (Australia, 1901) and full equal status (Canada, 1931), was in service of a new world and a tacit admission of the failure of the old. The nations and erstwhile Empire that I address most are Britain and certain members of the Commonwealth – particularly Australia and, to a lesser degree, Canada. But, forced child migration also emerges in older tales of children taken away to fight wars, or build new populations in occupied territory. Such stories are related in poetry, in song, in myth, on film and also in the archives that hold these sad histories of childhood gone missing. We have already seen that Baum's Dorothy had an ambivalent status in America – a late nineteenth-century rural girl in a land of westward migration and poverty – but by 1939 she was part of a Hollywood vision of plenitude, an adventurer arriving in other lands seeking happiness. The children in this chapter bare some of these hallmarks. They are the poor and they are the wretched, and the narrative that surrounded their departure from home was, to invoke the title of Ken Loach's film about forced migration, a promise of oranges and sunshine, or at least health and happiness. I quote below a religious poem, found in an archive, written home by a lone child migrant from Canada in the 1890s. The doggerel expresses the formulaic but piercing desperation of long-term family separation and a child's will to communicate shaped by the familiar blessings of home and religious sentiment but voiced with true suffering.

> I wish you length,
> I wish you strength,
> I wish you golden store;
> I wish you Heaven when you die.
> What can I wish you more?[2]

This poem, rather like the quotation from Brecht's Children's Crusade that opens this chapter, is plaintive, its tragedy stark in simple rhyme, and asking to be heard, 'please send help, we don't know where we are.'

The Leaving of Liverpool

The television mini-series, *The Leaving of Liverpool* (1992),[3] the focus of this chapter, is one kind of response to the voices of unheard children. It recounts, in an entertaining and watchable format, the process of forced child migration between the United Kingdom and Australia in the mid-twentieth century in the service of post-imperial nation-building, the management of poor populations and the maintenance of religious power.[4] The mini-series was a success at the time of its release in the early 1990s.[5] As a co-production between two major public television companies (the ABC in Australia and the BBC in the UK) the mini-series had the benefit of high-quality production values and access to large audiences who were suitably shocked at the revelations.[6] Latterly its underpinning story has re-emerged through political activity, scholarly exhibitions and associated events.[7] The television drama was an intervention, with real impacts envisaged for living people, and forms part of a larger, extended relationship between history-making and the archive, archival perspective and witnessing, challenges to the political establishment and survivor pressure.[8] *The Leaving of Liverpool* narrates a history of children who were forcibly migrated without parents or other kin to provide cheap labour and to rid the British state of further responsibility for their care. They are not British or Australian children, but post-imperial subjects on a journey from Liverpool to a destiny which they could not possibly envisage. In Jason Hart's introduction to the contemporary legal definition of forced child migration, he notes that it is striking how the experience of displacement continues to have impacts into later life and even into subsequent generations.[9] He refers to the impact that both inherited trauma from parents or grandparents and first-hand memories of violence wreak on their own imaginations and psyches, and the emotional vulnerability caused by their uncertain relationship to the idea of home.[10] In my discussion of *The Leaving of Liverpool* I suggest that the sense of a continuation of harm contributes to the emotional response that the dramatisation elicits. By continuation I refer not only to the lifelong impact of forced migration on individuals, such as the children portrayed in *The Leaving of Liverpool*, but also to the capacity of societies to repeat behaviours for new groups and in new contexts, despite the truths emerging from archives, and despite national investigations and subsequent apologies for the bad practice, criminal negligence and injustices wreaked by previous generations on the young. The surrounding cultural and activist discourses that historically supported the migration of children without their families help us to identify and explore the ways in which their vulnerability has been abused both in the circumstances of their departure and how they were treated on arrival. They underpin how strategies of care are subjugated to a managerial discourse emanating from quasi-philanthropic enterprises and institutions, with outcomes and rationales closely tied to ecumenical, national, imperial and post-imperial aims. These discourses seem to be as powerful today as the more liberal voices that call for children to be always treated as vulnerable but also and always deserving of respect.

The *Leaving of Liverpool* also raises questions of how to make sense of images and narrative tropes that re-occur across period and genre. It would be naive not to recognise that telling a powerful story on film is usually premised on established ways of seeing a theme or character, on sentiment and on cultural tropes. I acknowledge this issue through taking the long view of history, the traces of which resonate in our responses to child migration today. In the course of my argument I will refer most to specific archives that shed light on the colonial history of child migration and organised religion in the British Empire. I commence however with a history of the Children's Crusade in 1212AD. This story, as explored by Gary Dickson, is fascinating not only because of its global subject – the enlistment of children in war, massive upheaval and mobility and their subsequent disappearance from the face of history – but also because its huge cultural reach indicates that *the fascination it holds for Dickson, every other chronicler of the events, and for the audiences who have read or heard the story through the ages,* the veracity of the tale is extremely difficult to verify.[11] In other words, the fascinated readers – us – are all part of our own problem of miscomprehension and story-telling. The historical journey taken in Dickson's exhaustive account, which he subtitles, 'mediaeval history, modern mythistory', includes the numerous treatments of the tale from the thirteenth century to the twentieth. The bones of the original accounts are fleshed out across the years with each contemporary critic drawing on the fears and concerns of his time. Dickson locates his own study as an investigation into a travelling text rather than a single truth that must be claimed anew. There have been so many versions, incorporations, appropriations and politicisations of the tale that its cultural and political indicators, some which shift from century to century and sometimes with versions echoing across centuries, far exceed the rumours with which it originated. The Children's Crusade was, apparently, an ill-fated mission on the part of thousands of young people to fight in the Christian–Islamic wars of the period. In a wave of religious fervour to recover fragments of the 'true cross', massed bands of mostly boys (or *pueri*) moved through Europe from France and Germany towards Jerusalem to fight. Chronicles of the period recorded that none of these boys reached their destination in the Holy Land and that the vast majority perished on the road or at sea. The French philosopher Voltaire followed this conclusion in his critique of the disastrous events.[12] Dickson comments that the *pueri*'s religious fervour may also have been an escape from poverty and stigmatisation,

> The mass migration of peasants known as the Children's Crusade was hastened by a potent combination of high ideals plus poor material prospects. Nor should a psychological stimulus be ruled out. Mediaeval peasants were subjected to negative stereotypes and literary caricatures. Townsmen sneered at them.[13]

In other words, these were extremely poor children and young people looking for something better than the life they had been born into and the stigmatisation that their people suffered. The reasons for migration and mobilisation are not usually straightforward, but multifaceted with 'push' as well as 'pull' factors. The idea that the children were travelling alone for a shared strategic purpose is reflected in the early chronicles and critical accounts of the Children's Crusade where it appears that, although they were not strictly *refugees* and presumably most of them considered themselves to be *warriors* rather than Christian *migrants* to the Holy Land, they were nonetheless on a journey that deliberately took them away from the settled certainties (and humiliations and poverty) of home. Dickson is most intrigued by the mediaeval connection between the Crusade and the Pied Piper of Hamelin, who may have in fact been a recruiting sergeant for German expansion in the east. Were this true, then the *pueri* were contextually similar (mainly on the grounds of a pre-national form of Empire building) to the nineteenth and twentieth-century child migrants of the British Empire and Commonwealth, albeit they did not expect to return to their homelands and presumably their parents were aware that they had left. In this telling of the Crusade it is those that the children leave behind who draw on other heroic stories of a 'children's crusade' to try to acculturate and live through their own offspring's subsequent disappearance.[14] Dickson does not draw comparison with the millions of child refugees disappearing on their way into and across Europe, attempting escape from wars across the Middle East and presumed drowned, trafficked, or lost. Published in 2007, Dickson's book could not refer to the many instances in the Syrian conflict (2011–) where children have left western Europe to travel to the Middle East for a differently orientated 'anti-Crusader Crusade', aligning themselves with the Caliphate of Daesh but also exploring – sadly in a very dangerous way – the subtle and urgent blandishments of teenage ambition, desire and boredom.[15] Dickson does note that explanations of the fate of the mediaeval children included stories of white slavery to Muslim potentates, and – with peculiar resonance for the present day – an account that claimed that the children had been deliberately led away by corrupt priests who had delivered them as apprentice killers to the 'old man of the mountain', 'the fearsome commander of the fanatical Assassins' who murdered crusaders with knives.[16] It is perhaps too soon to imagine how later chroniclers will retell the stories of the three London girls who went to Syria on a plane in February 2015, but their disappearance from the eye of security cameras in an airport in Turkey was portrayed in the British media of the day as a disappearance from life itself, as though a Pied Piper was leading them, dancing away into the mountain. Meanwhile, children in the Calais Jungle on the sea border between France and the UK, dismantled in early 2017, children caught up in Australia's so-called 'Pacific Solution' detention centres on Nauru and Manus, and children drowning at sea on boats wrecked by smugglers[17] have all been betrayed, traduced and led astray. They have all in their own way met the Rat-catcher of Hamelin.

The idea of a children's crusade was also deployed by Brecht in the context of the European wars of the early and mid-twentieth century. His poem, *The Children's Crusade 1939*, fragments of which are quoted at the top of this chapter, focuses on the ingenuity, collectivity and courage of children and also on their absolute vulnerability in the face of adult war.[18] Brecht's children are not travelling towards the fighting but fleeing from it. Their number includes ex-child soldiers, victims of racial attacks and babies. Its great power as a calling card for considering the fate of the young in conflict is its generally applicable truths and the unflinching desolation and pathos of its address. A girl of 11 carries a four-year-old. The poet comments that this maternal image is in fact the antithesis of maternity. He intimates that in a world without war both children would have parents to carry them, and the girl would grow up to have her own children at an appropriate age for that burden. One is reminded of a scene from *Little Moth* where the boy with one arm carries the girl with her useless legs to try and escape the adults who are exploiting them as beggars. Or consider the dominant image from *Turtles Can Fly* (2004) of the Kurdish girl, about 13 years old, carrying a two-year-old boy on her back. The film posters used this image, and it reads at first as a picture of empathy and resilience between siblings. Yet, he is not her brother but her child, the product of a rape by an Iraqi soldier. She tries to drown the boy, but her elder brother – (in another echo of *Little Moth* he is armless, maimed by a roadside mine explosion) – rescues the toddler, whom he carries out of the water. She tries again and, when she succeeds in drowning her child, she kills herself by jumping from a high cliff. In *The Leaving of Liverpool* the main protagonist, Bert, carries Dave, a small child made deaf by a beating in a Liverpool orphanage, when he finds him drowned in a flash flood at an Australian farm-school. The vulnerability of the drowned boys – Dave and the Kurdish/Iraqi two-year-old – combined with the inappropriate physical responsibility for those who carry them, is a recurring, symptomatic and legible indication of children surviving alone. A child carrying another child indicates a child taking up an adult burden because the adults have turned away, or been killed.

Two

The Leaving of Liverpool presents a harrowing dramatisation of state-sponsored child abuse and forced migration to the British Commonwealth

(Australia in this instance) in the 1950s. This practice had been established longer with Canada but forced migration to that country was on the wane by the late 1920s. The arrangement, and its origins in both colonial and post-imperial expansionism and the export of religious influence, is a complex phenomenon that reflected punitive attitudes to the young poor and also philanthropic attitudes to the same group that had little concept of their needs for emotional support and were coupled with a parallel call for cheap, Christian labour in outposts of Empire, which came and went according to global economic conditions.[19]

The practice of child migration was conditioned through the long-term networking of information, self-interest, organisational continuity and specific behaviours of national governments and peoples. Such connectivities arise from the libidinal circuits of capital, labour and imperial influence that criss-crossed the world in the nineteenth and early twentieth centuries. They have left their traces in contemporary socio-political attitudes as well as on surviving victims and post-memory generations. It is, of course, the point of drama to draw on its internal tropes to fix stories in structures of feeling that will communicate to its audience the certainty of wrongs done, so we should expect a return of places and types that we recognise. It is also the point of activism to draw heightened attention to the errors and perversions of a system or situation in order to encourage change and to demand action. The film is not, therefore, interested in showing a gentler point of view with regard to either forced child migration practices or the institutionalised kidnapping by the British and Australian states, enacted in collaboration with private individuals and religious charities. Given the ongoing harm to child migrants in our own era, it is crucial to apprise ourselves of the return, or normalisation, of state action facilitated by non-state actors.

In the twenty-first century, the desired distinctions between public, private and advocacy are once more confused such that the third space in which minority interests might be aired disappears. Child detention policy in the United Kingdom has again provoked a mobilisation of public-private funding that has resulted in an unethical and possibly dangerous situation. The conflict of interest turns on competition and funding and, again, wider legal issues of responsibility and care are immobilised by the pre-eminence of financial models. Advocacy groups compete for public money with private providers, which are in turn connected to policy delivery – specifically the housing, processing and treatment of young migrants.[20] In short, As social scientists, the authors of the study I quote below do not use cinematic language, but one might well visualise the third space as a form of legal *intervalle*, one that is needed as a safeguard against corruption. The example offered in their research is the case of the Barnardo's Homes charity. They argue that Barnardo's involvement in a government-sponsored, privately run family detention centre, 'CEDARS', is a problematic move into the 'for-profit migrant detention market'.

> While third-sector and private-sector commissioning is commonplace in the delivery of statutory migrant services in the USA and some parts of Europe, tensions around this shift from advocacy to service provision are acute in the UK. This is due in part to a spate of high-profile scandals involving G4S and SERCO, including failures to safe-guard migrants in their care, leading to the deaths of migrants during detention and deportation. Many of our research participants felt that the compromise involved in entering into partnerships with state and/or corporate organisations was fundamentally eroding the capacity of advocacy organisations to effectively protest the deleterious effect of border-control mechanisms on migrants' lives.[21]

Their points are well made and refer us not only to a global problem with state-sponsored monetisation of migration, but to the longer background of child migration *from* Britain and, if we go further back still, to the transport of children via British ports for the slave trade. The slave trade is not my focus here but I think it is it worth recalling that there has been ease with the monetisation of child mobility in and out of Britain, in one way or another, for 400 years. Domestic child convicts were sent to the colonies to work, and children were regularly traded along the African-Atlantic slave routes; indeed 'most of the slaves sold in London were children'.[22] Children were seen as good working stock for both the colonial sugar and cotton industries in southern America and the West Indies, and as domestic labour at home. Despite the outlawing of British involvement in the slave trade from 1807, there is a deeply rooted relationship between British wealth, British overseas power and investors in the main ports – London, Bristol, Glasgow and Liverpool[23] – were often linked to slavery.[24] In that longer view, the capacity of philanthropists to see child emigration as a normal part of imperial business practice, church evangelism and the management of populations is less surprising, although no better for that.

Barnardo's was active in the migration of children to Canada, and later South Africa and Australia, from the 1860s. It was an activity that was attached to fund-raising and in some senses, to profit (both for those who received the children and to the charity) and reputation. Those who ran homes for the poor and desperate were generally motivated by a sense of godliness that they chose to embody by saving the poor, gaining a reputation for social philanthropy in a time when saving the poor (often perceived as from themselves) was a reputable activity for the wealthy.[25] They assumed responsibility for young people and that responsibility shifted towards legal power and absolute authority over young people with little influence over their own lives and little access to family support or authority.[26] Thomas Barnardo articulated his role as service to the Empire and restitution of the needy, 'Barnardo articulated the moral frame drawn on across these schemes by writing that such migration *"supplies Canada's greatest need*: additions to her population of the choicest materials – honest, industrious and piously-trained youth, who, by God's blessing, will grow into the successful citizens of the future".'[27] The historian Gordon Lynch has applied his observation of this 'moral frame'[28] to an Australian/British touring exhibition on child migrants, *On Their Own*.[29] Drawing on the records of organisations such as Barnardo's Homes, the exhibition teases out the processes by which children were selected for transport to Australia, the life they encountered on arrival and the impact of the migration on their lives as adults. Part of Lynch's contribution is to include in the background didactics the declared mission of men and women (including Thomas Barnardo) behind the early migration schemes through video re-enactments, and to note the shift from (broadly speaking) a discourse of 'good works' in the late nineteenth century to the almost exclusively imperial motivations of Kingsley Fairbridge.[30] Fairbridge is a significant figure in the history of child migration to Australia. His insistence on setting up institutional homes for migrants to prepare them for their service to Empire was followed by Barnardo's Homes and the Catholic Emigration Society, among other organisations.[31] Including this motivational history in the exhibition, which otherwise focuses on the memories and material traces of the children themselves, produces a stable vision of the systemic tragedy of religious and state authorities, which conceived of care through the *logic of a camp,* and an inner commitment to the project that defied external critique. The practices of the child migration schemes were to all extents and purposes built on assumed obligations but were, nonetheless, lawless. As Lynch argues, 'the history of the British child migration schemes was one in which organizations running those schemes demonstrated a sustained institutional commitment to the work that resisted any significant self-critical reflection on it.'[32] In his work on witnessing and the concentration and extermination camps (specifically Auschwitz) of the twentieth century, Giorgio Agamben raises problems with the notion of obligation. Obligation, he points out, is originally a legal category not an ethical one. The person with responsibility offers him or herself as a sponsor, a hostage; for, where obligation and a sense of responsibility are elided, the law can also be elided and leave the casus belli unrequited.

> To assume guilt and responsibility – which can at times be necessary – is to leave the territory of ethics and enter that of law. Whoever has made this difficult step cannot presume to return through the door [he] has just closed behind him.[33]

Agamben's insight is very helpful in understanding the lack of legal and ethical regulation in the management of child migration in the twentieth century. It also creates a suggestive and shaming link between the deadly camp culture of the Nazi era and the detention of children in the nations of the British Commonwealth.

The shift from philanthropy to Empire is not the only way to see this history of abuse. One might also declare that the confidence of Empire and the financial demands of overseas trade and growing colonies was always part and parcel of the various drives, religious or political, to remove children and resettle them elsewhere. It was also a way of solving problems at home. In 1864 the first report of the Catholic Reformatory Association in Liverpool noted that reformatory boys were struggling to find work; they had discovered that agricultural farm schools didn't work well for urban lads ('In the history of reformatories how many Liverpool lads have finally settled down to this kind of work?!' ... it is too slow, it does not pay') and they glumly acknowledged that there were a large number of Catholics under 15 years old in gaol. In 1864 there were two figures recorded: February: Catholics (2), Protestants (0); April: Catholics (30), Protestants (4). In response, the Catholic benefactors continued emigration from the Birkdale Farm School,[34] and set up a prison ship on the Mersey, 'The Clarence'.[35] The latter trained boys as seamen, with the assumption that they would leave on merchant ships when they left the school, serving both goals of increased emigration and working for the Empire. 'First of all, it is an advantage to Empire', the relatively unknown advocate of emigration Arthur Chilton Thomas said in 1904.

> Those of other denominations are sending many to our colonies. Surely it is well for us to send those children who might be failures at home, and consequently a weakness to the Catholic Church in England, to a country where they will in all probability become successes and a source of strength for the Church in that country.[36]

The practice of sending children out and away from British cities has thus been underway for a very long time. In the 1750s, most deported convicts were under 18.[37] The motivations for the migrations were various; the removal of vagrants from city streets, the relocation of labour to the colonies, the building of congregations for particular denominations[38] and – more sympathetically – the provision of opportunity for those unlikely to find work at home. The mass removal of children to Australia was a later phenomenon, a response both to a cooling welcome in Canada after the 1930s, especially as Canada felt that they were being sent children who would otherwise be placed in British reform or 'Farm' schools, and to the continuing White Australia policy in John Curtin's wartime and Ben Chifley's post-war Australia.[39] As Lynch has demonstrated through his analysis[40] of the critical Ross report into British assisted migration in 1955 (a report that was largely ignored), the continued migration of children was due to the conspiracy of politicians and the church authorities.[41] The two populations under threat of removal – in Australia Aboriginal children of mixed parentage (as portrayed in *Rabbit-Proof Fence*) and in Britain orphans and children from poor families – were both targeted in schemes that sought to control and manage people according to ethnicity and background, and to do so in the service of a collusive imperial and post-imperial project. If child emigration was important to Britain as a way of controlling the poorest in the population and contributing to the expansion of ex-colonies and trading partners, the practice was valuable to postwar Australia as a source of cheap labour and as a way of supporting population growth with young Britons as well as European refugees. The promised 'British' element soothed the xenophobia of the settled whites. The Minister for Immigration in Australia, Arthur Calwell (1896–1973), heading a new Department in 1945, established the need for increased immigration postwar, but to sell his case he emphasised both British and European sources.[42] Just as the Atlantic slave trade acclimatised British sensibilities towards selling childhoods in a particularly brutal manner, so Australian white migration policy and removal of Aboriginal children from their mothers consolidated a racist version of population expansion that served the state at the expense of children's liberty. Despite the public apology to the 'forgotten Australians' in 2009,[43] the 2015 history of the Department of Immigration does not mention the scandal of forced child migration through the 1920s to 1960s, except in a small textbox that refers to the 'Big Brother Movement', an apparently benign mentoring system for young male migrants, established in 1925.[44]

Returning to Kingsley Fairbridge, if we want to see how his emphasis on the role of white child migrants in the imperial project had been foreshadowed by earlier proponents of emigration, we can go back to Liverpool. Arthur Chilton Thomas gave his speech on 'Wise Imperialism, or the advantage of child emigration within the bounds of Empire' in 1904. Chilton Thomas was a barrister-at-law in Liverpool and an erstwhile manager of the Father Berry Homes for Catholic Friendless Children. His speech on imperialism was part of a fund-raising campaign to support the continued migration of children to Canada. The Father Berry's Homes had been set up in 1890–2 by the St Vincent de Paul Society in Liverpool and originally were intended to extend work opportunities for older Catholic working boys though industrial training and a settled and secure background at low

There's No Place Like Home

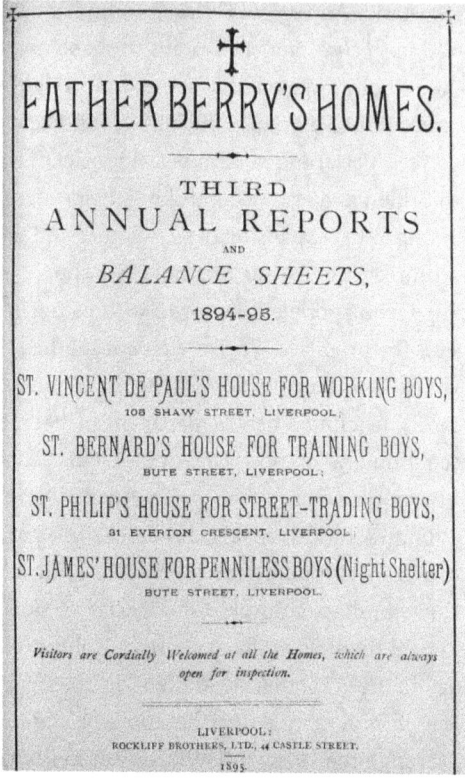

Figure 6.1 Illustration from the Father Berry Homes annual report, 1895, courtesy Nugent Archive, Liverpool Hope University.

cost to them[45] (Figures 6.1 and 6.2). Father Berry took over the leadership of the Homes in 1893, with the overall endeavour still aimed at improving the lives and educational possibilities for young Catholics in a sectarian city full of post-famine Irish migrants and few good jobs for them.[46] The annual reports from the Homes indicate wavering financial support in an environment where only a few of the wealthy industrialists, business owners, and shipping tycoons were Catholic. Those few who were appointed as JPs or were otherwise influential in the city would have been party to the larger narrative of expansionism, especially in the 1890s when Liverpool's own trade was under threat from American competitors. The need to maintain

The Leaving of Liverpool

Figure 6.2 Illustration from the Father Berry Homes annual report, 1895, courtesy Nugent Archive, Liverpool Hope University.

productive relationships with colonial entities was pressing. On 12 June 1897 Chilton Thomas' colleague, the President of the St Vincent de Paul Society and original founder of the House for Working Boys, P.E.J. Hemelryk, along with the Chairman of the Incorporated Chamber of Commerce, F.C. Danson, attended a dinner at the Philharmonic Hall for the Queen's Jubilee at which the Duke of Devonshire and the 'Colonial Premiers' (of Queensland, New South Wales, Victoria and Ontario) were present. It was a grand affair. The burghers of Liverpool were acutely aware of their dependence on these colonial guests for their financial survival.[47] Trading the children of Empire as labour was part of that relationship. Despite the Homes' origins in Catholic welfare at home, seven years after that dinner Chilton Thomas made his argument for child migrants. He ended his oration by reminding his audience and his readers that, as Catholics, there is a 'special advantage that in Canada children are secured in the Faith.'[48] Nonetheless his pitch is to Empire; he places the advantage to Empire as the *first consideration* in funding and arranging more migration out of the city. The supposed advantages to the children themselves are enunciated but are secondary to the opportunity of sending workers to where they were needed, whereby a stronger relationship with the increasingly independent ex-colonies and their trade might be maintained.

Liverpool's (Catholic) Hope University special collections room holds the minutes and accounts of the Catholic Friendless Children Society and the Father Nugent and Father Berry Homes' Committees. The Hope Library is less than a mile from Woolton Heyes, where P.E.J. Hemelryk hosted a party in 1904 after an annual meeting of the St Vincent Brothers (including Monsignor Nugent, who had been the first to take boys to Canada in 1870), and emphasised to his colleagues that 'the poor were to be approached' with 'kindliness, sympathy, consideration and courtesy'.[49] But, these enterprises and some individuals, most obviously Arthur Chilton Thomas, were committed to the emigration of those children whom, he felt, would never make more than a precarious living on the streets around Liverpool docks. Chilton Thomas was active during a boom and bust period in Britain where there were social reasons to send out as well as receive new migrants. Liverpool in the late 1890s experienced fluctuations in the cotton price, and there was a terrible winter in 1896 that killed hundreds if not thousands of poor Liverpudlians, many of them Irish migrants and their descendants. Dock workers did not get day-labour when trade fell, and children's refuges were over-crowded in a harsh winter. The more serious depression hit in the late 1920s and early 1930s, and that too was a period associated with accelerated migration of young paupers, orphans and juvenile offenders. Most had little or no choice in the matter of their 'sending out', and most adults involved seemed to have little comprehension of children's needs for identity and family. Chilton Thomas commented in his address on emigration, 'Walk along the streets … and see the number of lads hanging about out of work. Even St Helens …

glassworks ... has latterly announced that it has more than enough boys of its own for its work.'⁵⁰ Chilton Thomas claims that the children will have a better life away from Britain and away from their past, and especially *away from their families*. His speech prepares the ground for the later strategies of the 1950s when boys like Bert and girls like Lily were emigrated without their families being fully informed (or informed at all), and the children actively misinformed of the status of their parents, even down to the names and whereabouts of their kin or, worse still, being told that they were dead when they were not. The Catholic philanthropists wanted to keep children in the faith and in the Church, and in the Empire, but they did not necessarily want to keep them with their original Catholic families and the class solidarity that that may have afforded. In *The Leaving of Liverpool,* when Bert finally discovers details of his parentage, information which has been suppressed by the Catholic Brothers, he realises his father was Jewish and, even more importantly, was not dead. In case we misread this as dramatic overstatement, Lynch quotes the Ross report in 1956, 'At Clontarf Boys' Town, the Principal said that he had no information about the boy's previous background or previous history, and did not consider there would be any advantage in having such information. He did not think that the boys themselves would ever worry about their parentage.'⁵¹

Reading the transcripts of actual children's experience, even through biased reports and form-written letters, there is varying evidence of the advantage they were promised in the colonies. The following quotations are taken from the diary of a Mrs Lacy whose role was to represent the Liverpool branch of the Catholic Children's Protection Society in visits to Canada, both to deliver new migrants and to visit previously placed children. It appears that she visited about once every five or six years. This handwritten report, submitted in 1892 to the Society, indicates the emphasis on Catholic education over the consideration of placing children within a secure family unit. It also opens serious questions about the appropriate care of girls placed with older men in remote properties. These questions are not addressed in the minutes of the meeting to which Mrs Lacy's report was appended.⁵²

Mary Diamond aged five years Aug '84 placed with Mrs Rice, Morrisburgh. Fr Twomey reported that she used not take the child to Mass lately but was very regular in her attendance at school. Fr Twomey sent for the child; she came accompanied by her adoptive Father; he told the man he was going to take the child because they had not done their duty by her. When the young one heard she was to be taken away, she screamed frightfully and called out, 'Oh Papa take me! oh Papa take me!' The man promised all sorts of things – sending her to Mass and having her prepared for Confession. The Priest would not consent to leave her until he had first seen the Mother. He only consented to leave her on condition that the woman went to her duty, and that the child should regularly attend at the Religious Instructions in the School and on Sundays in the Church.'

Fanny Duggan aged nine, went out in '84, was placed with Mr Philip Ryan, Wolfe Island, was removed whilst I was there to the Sisters of Mercy, Lying-In Hospital. The father of the coming baby said to be an old man and dead.

Meanwhile, also in the appendices of a later report from the Society (1900–01), typed extracts from migrants' letters back to the Homes are collected as evidence of the overall success of the migratory scheme. Given the uniformity of some of the letters, the fact that they are typed up rather than handwritten, and again the emphasis on Catholic worship, one cannot but be more drawn to the expressions of loneliness, of privation from family and of a desire for communication with people from home which erupt – often as the core message – in an otherwise submissive text. There are also points in the letters that indicate the degree to which siblings were not kept in contact, a practice that we have seen continued almost a century later in the Australian system. I quote the first such letter in full (in format).

Ottawa, Ontario, Dec. 18, 1900.

Dear Sister Superior, — I write you these few lines to let you know how I am getting on. I am getting on very well in Canada, and I now have my schooling and am working for myself. It is nearly three years since you have heard from me, and I hope you will not reprove me for not writing sooner than this. I have found my sister, and we are near one another in Ottawa. I write to you to try and find out something, or if you can find any of my relations I would be so glad to hear from them. I have found it very lonesome these last three years, without hearing anything from my parents and relations. If you would be kind enough to try and find out something about my parents; their names are J—— G—— and Mrs, G——; or if you could find out anything about Mr. or Mrs. E——, the bottle-dealers. They used to live at B—— H——. I have written there and they were gone about two years and a half. The people said they did not know where they went to, so you see how lonesome it is to be without hearing from father. I hope, with the help of God, you will be able to find trace of them, and please send me the answer if it be good or bad. But I am sure you will succeed in finding them. I hope everyone is well, and my teacher Sister Mary, is still there. If little J—— C—— is there, tell him I am asking for him. I hope all the Sisters are well, and tell Sister Josephine I have not been sick only once since I have come to Canada. My address is: T—— G——, Albion Hotel, corner Nicholas and Daly Streets, Ottawa, Canada. This is from your loving T—— G——.[53]

Other letters in this report are shorter, but most contain some reference to missing family, missing people from home (including Catholic carers and educators in Liverpool) and needing reassurance:

c/o Mr.C—, St Leonard, Port Maurice
... Dear Sister, I hope I will be able to go and see my little sister soon. She is with my Mistress N— in another country. ... I go to Mass and Vespers every Sunday, and I always see my friend J——D——. he is getting along well and he hopes all Sisters are getting along well too. And I am so glad to tell you that I did see Miss Yates last May. Dear Sister, will you please answer this letter as soon as you can because I am so lonesome. ...
With love. God bless you! Good-bye from T—C——

St. Michel, 14th November, 1900.
Dear Sister, —I write you this letter telling you that I have a very good place with Miss J—. Dear Sister, I was very pleased with your letter and with your medals. Also I ask how is Sister Catherine and Sister Bernard, and all the other Sisters; and now I ask if you can tell me my mother's address, for I wish to write to her. So, good-bye, and God bless you. J—— D——.

These letters vividly and painfully describe the loneliness, the privation of family and the 'terror of solitude' – 'if you can tell me my Mother's address'. Those who cross borders may find themselves the subjects of torture and abuse or they may be simply, terrifyingly lonely like these young people were, deprived of natural connections with their places of origin, or with forms of spoken language that must have characterised their infancy. They may have also been struggling with mental illness, with older grief as well as the anxieties of separation. Steven Taylor has made links between the 'philanthropic abductions' of the late nineteenth century with regard to children being sent to Canada, and the deliberate export of children suffering from mental health conditions.[54] The evidence is not in these particular letters, although we hear nothing more of the story of the girl, Fannie Duggan, sent to live with a single man in a remote area and delivered of a child to 'an old man. Now dead'. To borrow the writing of Hamid Naficy on 'accented' cinema in relation to diasporic and exilic film,[55] the voices that emerge from these diasporic letters have been de-accented, on paper, and it is that flattened sadness that comes through most clearly so many years later.

Three

The Leaving of Liverpool was made just a few years before the fragmentation of television audiences into niche channels and the concomitant rise of internet TV. It predates the long form television series dramas of HBO, Netflix and similar. As such it is of its time, telling its story with a view to a national, domestic, family audience. The child actors are the main source of emotional identification, while adult characters portray types with whom the children come into contact. The storylines are clear and unapologetically written (by Australians John Alsop and Sue Smith) from the children's perspectives. With a focus on two key protagonists, Lily (Christine Tremarco) and Bert (Kevin Jones), the drama spans 1950–5, the years of the children's recruitment from an orphanage in Liverpool, their sea transport to Australia and subsequent lives in rural and remote New South Wales, and latterly in Sydney. In the early 1990s, the writers had archives of historical and emotional information to get across to a transnational audience largely ignorant of the context, and they had to achieve this in two one-hour episodes. The failures of the Catholic church in regards to child abuse, the very fact of twentieth-century forced child migration, the impact of loneliness on the young migrant and the complicity of Australians in child slavery, were all either unacknowledged, or little-known at the time. In that sense the film is a piece of activism as much as a work of entertainment. The writers make explicit the connection between post-colonial forced child migration and Britain's Imperial Commonwealth project through the use of the Union Jack flag, and by book-ending the two long episodes with images of Liverpool as a city of poverty on the one hand and a source of imperial hubris on the other.[56] Liverpool was one of the richest British cities in the imperial era (due both to its early involvement in slavery and its pre-eminence as the hub for the global cotton trade).[57] By situating the story between two nodes of Empire – Sydney and Liverpool – the writers allow the audience in both Britain and Australia to see child migration as part of an intricate pattern of cultural expansion, religious activity, industrial development, economic problem-solving and social opportunism. It might also prepare an Australian and a British audience to make the imaginative leap and see that the phenomenon of forced migration to the colonies was of the same order and scale as other human migrations before, during, and since that era. The setting in Liverpool is especially relevant not only for its historical accuracy per se, but also because it recalls the earlier forced migrations to that city, particularly the land removals of the Irish famine.[58] The contempt for the agency of the poor is ingrained in the city's memory. The impact of traumatic migrations and of the famine resulted in many Irish migrants falling sick and finding themselves incarcerated in lunatic asylums, such that up to 22 per cent of Lancashire asylums were populated with poor Irish from Liverpool. The condition of the Irish poor in the Famine of 1846–8 was also a factor. 'In 1847, three hundred thousand passed through the gateway of Liverpool alone, of whom one hundred thousand were struck down with fever and dysentry, (sic) with a death toll of over eight thousand.'[59] As we see in the contemporary accounts of the Catholic societies, the transit from poverty from ill-health, to mental distress, to criminality, were layered onto an urban landscape already morally scarred by its history of slaving.

There's No Place Like Home

Jim Loach's 2010 film *Oranges and Sunshine*, starring Emily Watson as the campaigner Margaret Humphreys, dramatised Humphrey's social and activist work with adult survivors of the twentieth-century versions of such forced child migrations. The pain of the lost childhoods that her clients suffered is seen through the eyes of damaged adults with fraught relationships to both Australia and the country that exiled them, Britain. Following that revelatory drama, I watched the earlier *The Leaving of Liverpool* in the Australian Centre for the Moving Image (ACMI), the main film archive in Melbourne. In a viewing booth on a warm Australian day, from the perspective of a receiving culture, I was taken into the possible childhoods of Loach's subjects. Watching that film in Melbourne, and the later film in a cinema in Sydney, I was aware of yet more stricken souls, more fellow citizens who may have lost their bearings very young through systemic abuse and through a process of alienation maintained by institutional power and state-sponsored programs of mobile labour. In 1992, in a pre-screening piece in the local press, the journalist opened and closed his review with a comment from John Hennessy, once a child migrant, 'now deputy mayor of Campbelltown, Sydney' ... "The people running those institutions ruined the lives of at least 500 people I know of personally", Hennessy says in a quiet moment to Kevin Jones, the 15-year-old Liverpudlian who plays the male lead.'[60] The notes provided by the National Film and Screen Archives curator about the film's first release on Australian television comment on the deep shock amongst viewers, who had never heard of the British forced migration schemes, or of Australia's part in the tragedies that ensued.[61]

Alford and Smith, the writers of *The Leaving of Liverpool*, make good use of legendary Liverpool charm and wit in the creation of Bert, and of equally legendary Irish-Catholic-Liverpool feistiness in the depiction of Lily[62] (Figure 6.3). The writers do not allow this wit to overcome or underplay the casual loss of children's lives and the degradation of their spirits through actual injuries and continual adult deceit and betrayals. Unlike Dorothy, the children's sheer pluckiness will not prevail against real-life wickedness and trauma.[63] Bert's progress through Australia, from a brutal Farm School in rural New South Wales run by a sadistic priest[64] to life on the Sydney docks, creates an old-head-on-young-shoulders character who is both uniquely conceived by actor and writers and characteristic of

The Leaving of Liverpool

Figure 6.3 'Lily and Bert in Sydney', *The Leaving of Liverpool*, cast shot, image courtesy Australian Film Archive, RMIT Melbourne, permission courtesy ABC Archive.

several protagonists in other child migrant films. After opening sequences in Liverpool and a sector on the ship to Australia, the film divides its attention between the two children after their arrival in Sydney, at which point they are split up. Lily is sent first to a training school for domestic labour and later transferred to a rural property to work as a general help. Despite the stupidities and cruelty of the school, she retains a sense of independent spirit and seems subsequently to manage her role as low-paid servant without losing all her optimism. She is thwarted however by the attentions of the eldest son in the house, which leads to her abrupt dismissal and a necessary escape to precarious city life. As adolescents the two children are reunited due to Lily's efforts at locating and then prising Bert away from the dismal system of institutionalised male bullying offered by the Catholic Farm School and his prospective entry into the priesthood. Lily and Bert spend some time living as a couple in a Sydney rooming house claiming to be brother and sister. She works in a department store (Grace Brothers) where she is rather successful. He finds it harder to find work and especially to de-institutionalise himself. The boy is depressed, self-harms and displays many of the mental health issues associated with forced migration that are explored more deeply in *Oranges and Sunshine* (and which not incidentally are part and parcel of the harm caused to refugee children by Australia's detention centres in the twenty-first century). Bert's involvement with unionised dock workers rekindles his sense of purpose and a newly resurgent awareness of his role on the city streets, but this time with an understanding of international socialist and communist contexts and a developing awareness of his own counter-history in the larger imperial and federated Australian project.[65] From the Australian perspective then the film is less about Liverpool than it is about the rough and ready justice of a 'new' country seeking inward migration and a youthful population at almost any cost, and the ways in which the working class resisted or contested their roles in that process. The children's stories highlight the contradiction between a prevailing Australian national sense of worthlessness, often termed cultural cringe, and the requirement set to all migrants to make the best of one's lot in a doggedly 'lucky country' – lucky or not. From a Melbourne viewing booth, the scenes in Liverpool (notwithstanding some were filmed in the industrial areas of Redfern, Sydney) are curiosities of a bygone working-class England; back streets teeming with ragged boys and girls, children flying the flag on piles of postwar detritus and primly accented bullies caging and caning the poor in Edwardian monstrosities of red brick and iron. It's the fighting working-class boy, the successful upwardly mobile shop-girl and the assault on monarchy that matters.

I revisited the film two years later when living in Liverpool myself. The topography of the streets and the sites of old orphanages and old docks were now the ground beneath my feet. I worked in an archive that has begun to expose how obligations to the poor produced both visionary responses and the ultimate lawlessness of forced migrations, some from the working boys' homes set up by the St Vincent de Paul Society (led by P.E.J. Hemelryk). Not all homes fed the emigration system, but the philanthropic connections between the enterprises were strong. The traces left by Hemelryk are suggestive. He was himself a migrant, leaving the family business in Leiden at the age of 20 in 1860, naturalising as British in 1872 and positioning himself as a philanthropic city businessman, albeit a Catholic and therefore far less eminent than some. Traces of his energetic attempts to be accepted in the largely Anglo-Irish community remain in Catholic and maritime archives as he argues for a Futures market, international business training and multi-literacy for English youth.[66] Relevant to the story of child migration and Empire is his role in the city's atmosphere of commercial and trade competition, in which appeals for children to support imperial and post-imperial relationships by their presence in growing colonies make a certain kind of business sense.[67] His direct interest in child migration did not seem strong, but his commitment to international commercial education segues into that logic of exile. His own sons were expected to travel to South Africa, Brazil and mainland Europe to finish their commercial studies. Hemelryk himself initiated the first full-time, UK-based course at a newly conceived Liverpool School of Commerce (1899).[68] A press report of a speech to the Chamber of Commerce noted, 'It might be well, he urged, to take a leaf out of the book of our competitors, and imitate that part of their system of practical education which is obviously superior to our own.'[69] So, we might see him as a kind of internationalisation activist as well as businessman and philanthropist. Emigration was a natural part of the process of making the Empire pay, so one can imagine a rhetorical question – why wouldn't young Catholic poor boys and girls not want to do the same? One might also consider the efforts of the Catholic business elites to make an impact in Liverpool and on *their* place in *its* place in the imperial network, and increasingly too on its capacity to work with its post-imperial trading partners in the US, while preparing itself for competition in Europe.

The Leaving of Liverpool story is based on child migration schemes to Australia half-a-century later than Hemelryk's intervention, but the Catholic and Protestant hierarchies were still implicated and involved at that time. With Liverpool in the foreground rather than the background of the drama, the emphasis is rebalanced and the children's losses – of family, background and city identity – highlight the connections between place, Empire, nation, religion and childhood that exemplify the story Britain's industrial poor, of mobility in the Empire, and of Liverpool's specific religious and quasi-national character in the Empire migrant narrative. Liverpool and Sydney were two nodes of an imperial system – a libidinal circuit – that spanned a globe, trading capital, goods, people and power back to the Crown and her representatives. Both cities had Irish and English populations that held each other in mutual suspicion.[70] The two cities shared architecture, shipping histories, a tradition of hard dock work and unionism and a substantial population of the poorer citizens of Empire. As we have seen, they even shared their children. Elke Grenzer has described a libidinal circuit as an 'alchemical connection' amongst people in a city, what we might optimistically interpret as a sublimely democratic imagining.[71] Grenzer is also sensible however that our structures of existence are organised by powerful others and that urban dwellers, and specifically the poor – or poorer – are 'hardwired' to 'rigged' systems. The rig in the story here is the capital matrix of Empire and trade, of globalisation and migration, and of childhood and class difference. For eighteen months I walked past the building that housed the Sheltering Home for Boys and Girls, Myrtle Street, Liverpool on my way to work in the building that once housed the Confederate Embassy (and at other times was home to the Bishop of Liverpool) and is now part of a large University that houses many international students – another form of youth migration – studying business and law and paying international fees. That seemed to me a small irony of contemporary Britain. The Sheltering Home was one of the buildings from which children left to serve the Crown. On the doors of the Sheltering Home large stone plaques record the names of ex-residents who served in World War I as soldiers in the Canadian regiments. I walked past streets of gated back alleys in Aigburth, south Liverpool, between my home and the local, very twenty-first-century gym in Brunswick, through the Protestant area of Dingle Vale, where Union Jack flags and the flag of St George regularly hang on lamp-posts. These alleys are now in respectable neighbourhoods, but echo those that feature in the film as a staple location of 1940s childhoods and the geo-ecumenical barriers between Irish-Catholic and Anglo-Protestant. The first episode of *The Leaving of Liverpool* deploys working-class patriotism to trace the disillusion of the seemingly resilient Bert. It is 1950. The opening scene draws on things we know about children in films about postwar Britain. Boys are running and shouting, a standard – the Union Jack – is held aloft by the leader (Bert, of course) the remaining debris of the Liverpool docks blitz flies beneath their boots; they are toy soldiers of the King. The flag held aloft could be a red balloon (or indeed a yellow or white one), it might be a kite or just a trail of bubbles. This flag's metaphorical power goes well beyond childhood games, however. A child may fly a kite to claim transcendence from adult control, and hoist a flag to pretend mastery over the world, but the Union Jack is never innocent and always has its masters elsewhere. Despite the excitement of victory for a band of orphan fighters, it offers no true security to Bert, either from the British state, from which he is already estranged as a Catholic, or from Catholic Church abuse that Bert will face once despatched to Australia, nor from the colonial state which affords him no protection.

The opening scene situates Bert as a passionate young patriot, full of stories and able to sustain the companionship of his fellow orphans. The Union Jack is not only a mixed symbol of wild freedom (the child's fluttering toy), and of class-bound imperial servitude, but also of an imaginary sense of belonging when home itself was absent. Bert leads his platoon of ragged lads, fighting their own war and dreaming of their own place in the romantic world of a victorious Empire. They may not own much but they own their bit of the ruins. We can surmise that these orphans have lost parents in the Liverpool Blitz (May, 1941) when the Catholic area around Scotland Road was all but obliterated. By the end of the film, Bert has seen his best friend abused and die, and he himself has only survived by becoming a non-person, devoid of the irrepressible child whose survival strategies were so tied to a sense of place and a hope of home. He intends to take Holy Orders and submit to the logic of his captors, substituting an idealised version of King and country with the Church. Then, after Lily liberates him and he undergoes his political awakening to his place in British overseas policy and the labour markets that sustain the Commonwealth, he attaches himself passionately to this new sense of belonging. During the first Royal visit to Australia, on 3 February 1954, Bert lobs a missile at the new Queen,[72] thus violently renouncing the flag which he once celebrated. Renunciation brings political understanding, but he loses his connection with an imagined homeland, and he loses his belief in his love for Lily. He also indicates how deeply his grief has been compounded by dissociative institutional regimes of control into a pattern of depression, self-harm and over-identification. The film's plot concludes with Bert in a juvenile prison, reading aloud a stanza from Henry Lawson's 1888 Sydney poem 'Faces on the Street'.

> I wonder would the apathy of wealthy men endure
> Were all their windows level with the faces of the Poor?
> Ah! Mammon's slaves, your knees shall knock, your hearts in terror beat,
> When God demands a reason for the sorrows of the street,
> The wrong things and the bad things
> And the sad things that we meet
> In the filthy lane and alley, and the cruel, heartless street.

Whether this really heralds a new start for Bert, or simply states his bleak understanding of life at the bottom, this early utterance of Australian radical thinking, contesting the lies of a classless society – a bright future – a lucky Empire – could just as easily be another radical poem rising out of the Liverpool streets. Proving the point, the final credits have the ultimate Liverpool poet, John Lennon, responding to Sydney's Henry Lawson. Lennon's *Working Class Hero*[73] rolls like a reprise of the 1960s Liverpool poets, but also echoes the despair and anger of the Liverpool transport strike in 1911, and the ongoing radical edge in a city that has embodied the fault lines between English and Irish, Protestant and Catholic, rich and poor – 'They hate you if you're clever' (Lennon). These are the fault lines through which the working-class children slipped and fell – all the way to Australia[74] (or do I mean Oz?).[75] As the music plays, the credits cut to a new version of the opening sequence. The Union Jack flag fills the screen once more and children rush shouting and excited through a grimy but now ethereal version of Liverpool docks, and down the Scotland Road. Now though, the sequence ends not on Bert crying out 'God Save the King', but on Bert and Lily hand in hand, arms aloft, smiling in triumph – working-class heroes. They are back home, united. It's a romantic ending that sits in parallel to the end of the preceding plot, in which the young people are separated by everyday life and their different responses to living an adult life as child migrants in Australia. Lily working in a shop, thriving and living reunited with her Mother;

Bert pursuing a radical path, probably alone. A boy like Bert may one day talk to a woman like Margaret Humphreys. The credits inform us that the Child Migrant Trust now exists (at the time of the film's release, in 1992) to help the tens of thousands of forced child migrants who need to discover the truth of their backgrounds – 'you can't really function, you're so full of fear' (Lennon). They also state that, while some migration organisations were helping these survivors, many were not and neither the British nor the Australian states were offering practical support. Footnotes to this chapter indicate the improvement in both Australian and British national records and attitudes since the early 1990s. However, given that mass child emigration to Australia was relatively short lived (1938–67), and that it was suspended after yet another poor report in the mid 1950s, it is still remarkable how long it took for the damage to be publicly acknowledged.[76]

Neatly then, the film's locations position the ways in which child labour was utilised by both the United Kingdom and the Commonwealth of Australia. The theme of Empire is firmly positioned in the opening section, in preparation for the demand for the children to 'volunteer' for emigration. These further sequences link Empire, violence and the attack on childhood and play. Lily is left in the orphanage by her mother, herself a migrant from Ireland, apparently just for six months while she finds work; another circuit, the tragedy of *Once My Mother*, where another migrant from another country leaves another child in an institution for safe keeping. A scene in the orphanage shows the Protestant girls practising a showpiece for Empire Day 1951. Lily is there, having pretended on her absent mother's instructions to be a Protestant because 'Paddies always get the worst of it'. The Catholic boys watch with huge amusement from the gallery of the yard, and eventually can no longer contain themselves and invade the pitch. It is a glorious rampage until a small boy, Dave, Bert's best friend, is hit hard round the head by a teacher's cane, and permanently deafened. Lily shows her true allegiance by breaking the cane, while Bert flings himself at the teacher and fights back. But Empire is a serious show and it's one in which the poor may only take part under orders, on pain of violence visited by adults on children. It is little Dave who is later abused and who one night tries to swim in a muddy flash-flood the way he used to swim in the

Liverpool Dock and drowns; another small child seeking safety in an idea of home in a place that is no place like home – like so many other children in this book, in these films and in immediate living memory.

In his essay on the sublime and the avant-garde, the philosopher Lyotard thinks about the terrors of Burke's sublime, principally the terrors of privation: 'privation of light, terror of darkness; privation of others, terror of solitude; privation of language, terror of silence; privation of objects, terror of emptiness; privation of life, terror of death.'[77] This might read as a shopping list for some of the deprivations suffered by the children described in *The Leaving of Liverpool* and in other films described in this book as epitomising the experience of migration from and to different forms of conflict, dehumanisation and imprisonment. In *The Leaving of Liverpool*, the motivation is the relation between a proscriptive ethnic agenda for the labour force, religious organisational culture and nostalgia for Empire. The opening and closing sequences present the visual authority of the Union Jack flag, which the screen even before we see the characters who hold it aloft. The screen is also suffused with red, the colour of war. The flag's sublime power on screen resides in everything we the audience know about the Empire, about state violence and about the betrayal of the poor, and of poor children in particular, at the altar of national sovereignty and imperial advantage. It overrides (even while enlisting) the savagery of the clergy on the Farm. The flag fills the screen and obliterates any other reality, any other subjective resource. Wrapping the stories of Bert, Dave and Lily in the flag present children in thrall to Empire even as the writers attempt to give them the status of working-class heroes.

The justly angry aim of *The Leaving of Liverpool* is to expose the ills of forced migration, abuse and hot nationalism. There is no doubt that the lives of the children fictionalised here are tragically affected by ill treatment, but the structural and systemic conditions of their transport and abuse is not clearly enunciated as a tragedy that exceeds its temporal formulation. One might walk from the film and think that these were deplorable events. Watched in the context of British-Australian colonial, imperial and post-colonial attitudes, the archive that affords a glimpse of the longer background of child migration and the contemporary incarceration of children in refugee camps and detention centres, *The Leaving of Liverpool* reminds us that this is in fact a *continuum* of events, of disastrous responses to immigration in a tragedy of fatal national flaws. The greatest of these is the incapacity to value the young as people. In the nineteenth and early twentieth centuries they were the raw materials for Empire building – chattels and cheap labour. In 1951, child migrants were treated as immoral – or at the most amoral – subjects requiring de-subjectification through excessive management, emotional deprivation and social stigmatisation. In the *Leaving of Liverpool*'s storyline, those who dole out this treatment are to a large degree confined themselves; literally by religious enactment in the case of Catholic priests, nuns and 'housemothers'. All are also confined by punitive narratives of moral order that undermine an ontologically level and just relationship with the children in their care. One might be tempted to think, watching *The Leaving of Liverpool* or reading the histories and archives covering the child emigration of one and two centuries ago that these events were the product of the blunter thinking of a less enlightened past, one which our modern safeguards such as UNHCR and UNICEF have rendered unthinkable. Any attention to the news since 2001 dispels this comforting thought. Forced emigration looks different when precipitated by war rather than policy or philanthropy but, in the end, policy – political, economical, social, legal – is the continuum along which the perpetual dislocation of child migration runs. Power is absolute and those who determine the limits of those borders control the conditions of arrival and survival within them – not the children who cross those borders, no matter how plucky they may be.

7

Diamonds of the Night

For all of us survivors, who are not exactly polyglot, the first days in the Lager have remained impressed in our memory in the form of an out-of-focus and frenzied film, filled with dreadful sound and fury devoid of meaning: a hubbub of persons without names and faces drowned in a continuous, deafening background noise, from which, however, the human word did not surface. *A black and white film, with sound but not a talkie.* [my emphasis][1]

Listen
During any one breath
Make a sound
Breathe
Listen outwardly for a sound
Breathe
Make exactly the sound that someone else has made
Breathe
Listen inwardly
Breathe

Make a new sound that no-one else has made
Breathe
Continue this cycle until there are no more new sounds.[2]

One

The film begins in confusion. Something is happening now. Two teenage boys – perhaps 15 to 17 years old – jump one after another into a ditch filled with water, then out and onwards. They are running for their lives, we know because on the soundtrack there is the sound of gunfire and men shouting 'Halt!' and they are breathing heavily, the way you do when your life depends on the air that fuels you forward. A train is visible in the background for a moment. We suppose that they have escaped from that train. They are scrambling up a hill. Their movements are masculine and determined but also fleeting and boyish. Throughout this sequence the camera stays with them, first moving with the boy in front, then waiting for the other to catch up, not losing focus and not losing step, although the pace slows across the shot. Both boys wear long coats with something written on the back (in chalk or in white paint). The smaller (second) boy takes his coat off and discards it as he scrambles upwards. The camera continues its long track with them – still moving ahead and then hanging back for the other, like a friend that always waits for his friend, even when it is fatally dangerous to do so. But now the camera is zooming in on the boys' faces and, eventually, the editor begins to cut, first on a face, listening in to rasping breath, then settling on one boy's head, and then the other, and finally on the smaller boy's hand as we hear the sound of the train pulling away below. The yells of 'Halt!' cease, and the gunfire recedes. The boys have stopped moving for a moment's respite, or because they cannot move anymore after such exertion. The hand of the smaller boy, or youth, fills the screen. It teems with ants (Figure 7.1). At this point, the film shifts in its axis around four revelations. First, we have seen in close-up the exhaustion on the boy's face and must reconsider our (possible) preliminary judgement of youthful vigour and indestructible freedom as the escapees ascended the hill. Second, the ants on the hand make an intertextual reference to a founding image of surreal cinema, Buñuel's *Un Chien Andalou*, which articulates the

Diamonds of the Night

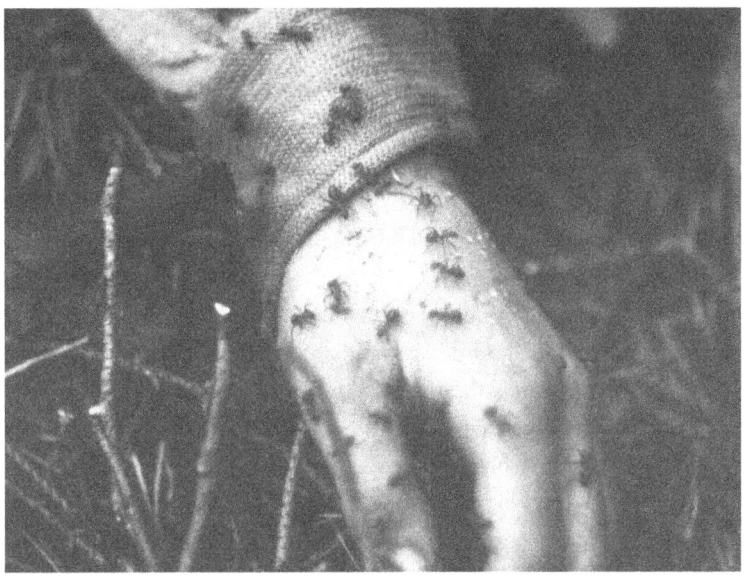

Figure 7.1 'Ants on the boy's hand', *Diamonds of the Night*, image courtesy of TIFF Archive and Czech Republic Film Archive.

darkening visual tone and deadly silent undertow of this film's trajectory.³ Third, the abrupt commencement of the film is now explained aesthetically through its explicit reference to Buñuel's style; Jan Němec's *Diamonds of the Night* (1964) is to be a film marked by interruption and montage. We must expect to see alternatives, contradictions, bizarre turns of events and impossible points of view over the course of the boys' story. Finally, as we are required to listen first to silence in contemplation of the hand and then only to the sound of the boys' strained breathing, we understand that the use of sound will be prioritised over voice, and the use of silence will be prioritised over sound. Virile young men escaping their pursuers have been revealed as victims – as boys too close to the earth to survive, their breath too short to speak. The audience will continue to resist the inevitable end of the film, continue to hope that the boys will get away and get home, while the film-maker continues to insist through his reversals, interruptions and suspensions, that in an era of genocide and total European war, home is only a trick of the mind, and that breath is running on empty.

Buñuel's *Un Chien Andalou* (1928) provided a technical template of inter-diegetic vision that Němec uses to evoke the despair of war and the destruction of youth that it entails. In Buñuel's surreal drama, the hand teeming with ants belongs to a young man who is already dead but who refuses to leave the screen. The ants crawl from a hole in his hand and move in circles on his palm. He looks on in fascination at the confirmation of his decay. A woman moves closer to look with him, an act that he sees as an invitation to rape. Over 17 minutes the man dies, is resurrected, dies again, while the woman walks through time and space to find remnants of another version of life and death on a beach. Life is ephemeral, and so is narrative unity. A young androgyne stands on a street playing with a severed hand, a crowd moving forwards in waves, but kept at bay by policemen. One is not sure whether they want to attack the youth or to steal the hand, or both. The world of the film is riven by uncertainty, it is threatening and ridiculous at once, its temporal and spatial instability revealing a deep malaise at the heart of European youth – or maybe that interpretation is only in retrospect. At the very least Buñuel shows us that if one takes liberties with cinematic space one can make the world shake on its axis and reverse the certainties of cause and effect. The dead can rise up to kill the living and to move between places like ghosts. If one takes liberties with the idea of humanity and the responsibilities of power, one can maim an entire continent and murder a generation – an observation as true now as it was when Buñuel made his film in 1928, at the end of a war a decade earlier, and at the start of another a decade later. After Buñuel then, a hand that teems with bugs might be a perfectly achieved neurotic image about sexual repression, bodily disgust and abjection, or a challenging reference to Christ's crucifixion and the death of God. In Němec's appropriation, the teeming hand is pointedly the fragment of the young European dead who watch their own disintegration from within the very body of the film that bears witness to their demise.

Diamonds of the Night is a Czech film, based on a short story and later novella by Arnošt Lustig (1926–2011). The novella, titled *Darkness Casts No Shadow*, and film are set in the Sudeten-Germanic borderlands in Eastern Europe during World War II. The region was populated by German-speaking peasant-farmers (men and women whose presence takes us back to the theory of the Pied Piper of Hamelin as recruiting sergeant to open up the east to German migrants). The boys are called Manny and Danny in Lustig's novella. They are Czech Jews, from Prague. The book describes their escape from a transport train between camps, their two-day journey through a dark forest, their meeting with a German-speaking peasant woman and her betrayal of them, and their subsequent recapture and execution by a group of elderly German farmers. Lustig himself escaped from a transport when he was 17, and much of the story of the book and film is based on this experience. Lustig was incarcerated in Theresienstadt, Auschwitz and Buchenwald. On a transport to Dachau he escaped when the train came under fire from Allied bombers. The book contains Manny's memories of his father, of conversations with Frank, a fellow inmate, his home in Prague and talk between the boys as they struggle through the forest. Although the fact of the escape and the final encounter with a militia of German peasant farmers is based on Lustig's memory, the book does not give the boys, Manny and Danny, the same 'happy' ending as their author. Lustig turns his story into a witness for those who did not survive rather than for the few who did. Coming close to this film has been dependent on several works of other writers, such as Primo Levi, who also survived concentration camps, and subsequently bore witness.

> They were two small, naked bodies in shoes and rags, one tall, one smaller, hanging on tightly to each other. But they still heard nothing ... They faded into the night, like a slim double shadow. The stillness was not silenced.[4]

In adapting the book into a monochrome film Němec achieves an extraordinary transformation. He takes us back to the strengths of silent film as well as drawing us forward to contemporary attempts to elucidate the worldwide experience of dislocated children and youth, trying and failing to find home. His film is haunted by the boys' memories of home, slipping further away from any indexical reality as the film progresses.[5] In the end, it is sound that guides us. His use of diegetic and non-diegetic sound crafts memory as a fold of time that takes breath as its bass note. I cite the composer Pauline Oliveros (b. 1932) at the top of this chapter, from her exegetical scoring for deep listening. Her own music requires the listener to commit fully to the work, and 'to listen to each and every sound exactly how it is',[6] and thereby to hear sounds anew and in a way that submerges the listener in the sound as she identifies them, one by one and in a continuum of concentration. There is something of this quality in the use of sound in *Diamonds of the Night*, where silence is as poised as a ringing bell or a running boy's breath. Whether the sound, or the silence, is extracted from a dream, or whether it exactly represents the boys' walking or the old men's pursuit, it is imperative to listen 'to each and every sound exactly how it is' as well as look at each shadow exactly how it falls and at every ant walking across a boy's hand, or crowding around his eye.

At the beginning of this book I discussed the relationship between homecoming and maturation and suggested that the Dorothy Complex encompasses the paradox of leaving home and never finding your way back, even if you do eventually return to its physical location. Lustig was born in Prague and emigrated to the US after the war. His obituaries state that he died in Prague. He apparently came home. Manny and Danny tell the petty German mayor who keeps them prisoner and orders their execution by a motley band of peasant militia that they just want to go home. In the novella, they also tell him that they are not Jewish, in the frail hope that he will believe them, or pretend to believe them, and let them free. In the film, the circumstances of their imprisonment are less explicit. They are just boys who are not Germans, and who are not 'polyglots'. Danny does not talk at all in the film. Manny speaks now and then, asking for warmth, for closeness and, to the old German militia who have captured them, he says 'I don't speak German'. As Levi says, they have lived the 'black and white film with sound but not a talkie'.

Diamonds of the Night was Němec's second feature and his second collaboration with Lustig. The film was released in the same year that the Terezin memorial site (the site of the ghetto and the site of the prison) was renamed the Terezin National Memorial, and, unusually, included a temporary exhibit marking the twentieth anniversary of the Warsaw Uprising, as well as new permanent exhibition 'The Whole Town a Concentration Camp'.[7] It is possible that Němec's film is a similarly bold prompt to his fellow Czechs to remember that over two thirds of those Czechs who died in the World War II were Jewish, and 77,296 of those were from Prague.[8]

Diamonds of the Night

Home, Prague, is imagined and visualised through a series of interruptions and repetitions, folding into and out of Manny's consciousness as something between dreams, wish fulfilment and memory. As the film draws to a close (one might say a climax but the boys' last walk into darkness is specifically *not* climactic, although the last sequence renders the boys both shot to death and escaped) the memories become hectic and out of sequence, so that Manny remembers jumping from the train the day before in the same set of flashbacks as an old assignation with a girlfriend in Prague. The memory or dream sequences are increasingly over-exposed so that tableaux and the people within them seem like the ghosts they are, and that the boys will soon become. Each interruption reveals a little more about what he has left and what he wants to find, and what he knows he has already lost. The flashback structure is also reminiscent of Buñuel's surrealism. Here, though, the surreal is deployed as a form of meditation, a fixation on remembering what the past felt like before it disappeared and how the future is already tucked away in its disappearing sounds. It cannot distinguish between diegetic and non-diegetic experience. The only truth of this escape, recapture and annihilation is whatever connections, faces and passages of intent Manny can compile in his mind. Some flashbacks carry sound, others are silent and, in others still, sounds are indeterminately situated between now and then. There is a causal link between some; in one flashback they try and fail to board a moving truck as they run away from the old militiamen. Manny could have done it, but is held back by Danny, whose ill-fitting boots have crippled him. The boots are those which, in another flashback, we see that Danny took from Manny when still on the train. These boots do not take them home but cast them on the ground in front of the old men and their spitting rifles. In another repeated sequence, Manny and Danny march down a Prague street in perfectly fitting black boots. They look delighted, their pain gone. Did they ever own such boots? Is Manny's desire to go home, a place that no longer exists as it did, all about finding a place where they both have boots that fit them? We recall Dorothy's ruby slippers in 1939. In the book they were silver, in the film they are blood red, making her both a magical child traveller and a woman sans-pareil, 'She is more precious than rubies: and all the things thou canst desire are not to be compared unto her'.[9] But the shoes are also the shoes of witches, passed from one to another by murder. Dorothy's womanhood must not only be clasped to her feet, but one day must also be her undoing. It also brings to mind the European fairytale *The Red Shoes*. An orphaned peasant girl is adopted by a kindly old lady, but is corrupted by the gift of a travelling soldier, a pair of red shoes. These shoes seem to save her life, but they are enchanted. Whoever wears them is doomed to dance forever at the expense of all else. As the kind old lady lies dying the girl deserts her in order to wear the fascinating red shoes and dance at a ball. But the shoes – of course – will not leave her feet. They enslave her to the dance of vanity and she wastes away. Eventually a woodman chops off her feet. The shoes dance away into the forest with her feet still inside.[10] Maybe not a conscious decision by director Victor Fleming to introduce surrealism into the (just) pre-war classic, but again, from here, God is dead and the witches are murdering one another one by one.

Manny's memories loop together in stumbling sequence. The camera remains steadfast with the boys every time they run or fall. It traipses behind their heads when they push through the forest. It casts a careful look down at the swollen feet, the ill-fitting boots and the suppurating sores. There is a visual rhetoric here of impossible moral courage, of sticking together and of finally slipping together into the night, film-maker with boys, boy with boy. Even the image of the boys lying dead on the forest path is shot feet-first, so we look again at the boots and the feet wrapped in cloth (Figure 7.2). The singular importance of the damage that forced migration, long distances walked and run, inflicts on feet and courage is exemplified in the testimony of Elie Wiesel, who describes in his memoir the death march from Buna-Monowic to Buchenwald in January 1945 with his father.[11] He was 16. Two considerations drive his narrative. First, will his infected foot hold them back and, second, will he have the moral strength not to abandon his father if the older man's strength fails him? 'Oh God, Master of the Universe, give me the strength not to do what Rabbi Eliahu's son has done'.[12] Later in the journey he witnesses a man withhold bread from his son, and the son kill him for the bread. Elie remains with his father until Buchenwald, where he finds that he too begrudges his now-dying father his soup, 'I gave him what was left of my soup. But my heart was heavy. I was aware that I was doing it grudgingly'.[13] Elie's

Diamonds of the Night

Figure 7.2 'The boys murdered by the old men, their boots and feet wrappings evident', *Diamonds of the Night*, image courtesy TIFF Archive and Czech Republic Film Archive.

self-judgement is extremely harsh. His father died of dysentery and Elie was removed to the children's barracks, which he survived. The spectre of self-judgement is central to Lustig's novella, and is resolved in the film through the reiteration of Manny's trial and his response. The ending of *Diamonds of the Night* is a tragedy but it is also a triumph against the survival logic and dehumanisation of the camps. Manny has not deserted his friend, but Danny's appropriation of shoes that pinch his feet but which actually fitted Manny well has condemned both of them.

In Lustig's novella, Manny remembers the death of his father,

> When they'd ordered Father off the ramp and straight into the gas, Manny had felt more alone than ever. It was the twenty eighth or twenty ninth of September; he couldn't remember exactly ... This loneliness suddenly had a face and a voice which it hadn't had before.'[14]

There's No Place Like Home

In Němec's film Manny is dreaming as he walks, or we are dreaming with him as the film walks with him. He sees a man held by other men at the end of an otherwise empty tram but, despite running toward them, he can't reach them. It's that nightmarish state of suspension in a moment of urgency. In the dream he still wears the coat he discarded when he ran up the hill away from the train. The lettering on the back is now clear, 'KL', the initials of the *Konzentrations Lager* concentration camp. The coat travels with him from the past into the deeper past towards home. He climbs aboard trams that are not moving. He helps a woman down from a tram with her pram and watches helplessly and curiously as the wheel of the pram wobbles off and she pushes on regardless, going nowhere with her child. In the third flashback, where he is by now visible to the people in the last carriage of the tram, he reaches them and finds that they are accusers and fellow victims. His girlfriend smiles nervously, a man in German uniform looks straight ahead, and a man wearing a swastika badge looks round at him and smiles.

In Buñuel's short, the lapse of time is indicated by random intertitles ('*eight years later*', '*au printemps*'). In *Diamonds of the Night* the flashbacks are repetitive, non-linear and shot from different angles, as if intent on communicating something of great personal importance to Manny's own consciousness as well as to our understanding of what we are losing, a whole life wrapped and tucked into tight pleats of forgetting when the boy dies. Manny is going back to Prague but he arrives there as one does when asleep, witness and exile, an existence layered, exposed and smothered in light and sound. Sometimes we look with him at others (a woman at the window with her cats, the SS officers on the sidewalk) and sometimes he is also in the frame and he is looking at himself. Such a multi-locational oneiric edifice is familiar to anyone who dreams. The time that he returns to could be construed as the last day in Prague, with people watching from windows as he and his father are taken to a camp. Or they might be several days and weeks before his arrest. Timing is not the main issue, and memories are inconsistent. The images that persist contradict one another as they repeat – an old woman with a cat looking out of a window, or is it two cats? A pile of laundry on a window sill, but how much washing was there? Two black-uniformed SS officers walking down a sidewalk, talking animatedly to one another. They seem like lovers. They seem like killers. With their dark lips and long black limbs they seem like vampires, over extended creatures of darkness inexplicably walking in the daylight. Their boots are very shiny. Bells toll, silence intrudes, a tram bell rings, silence returns. The memories accompany Manny through the forest, and crowd back in no particular order as he faces the likelihood of death. Simultaneously the images evacuate the past of its substance through an intensity of light and an inconsistency – both level and source – of sound.

Max Silverman's theory of layered or 'palimpsestic' memory elucidates the revelatory structure of Němec's narration. Silverman's thesis considers the cloning of historical points of stress, or indeed periods of extreme violence, across generations and the capacity for one set of actions to resurface in other forms of evil. His argument suggests that traumatic events manifest within the articulation of other similar events, layered across time, space and within the memories of individual personalities, families and whole nations. The pursuit of one kind of violence in one context produces the grounds and the wherewithal, or even theatrical framework, for someone to do something similar subsequently. We learn from our mistakes but not in the way we might hope to. Silverman pursues this theme through French cinematic testimonies and post-testimonies of the Holocaust and the Algerian War, such as Alain Resnais' *Muriel*, which I discuss below.[15] He acknowledges his intellectual debt to Marianne Hirsch and *postmemory*, the transfer of intergenerational shame, pain and anxiety from victim to child,[16] and to Alison Landsberg's idea of *prosthetic memory*, which she summarises as 'public' and 'at the interface between a person and a historical narrative about the past, at an experiential site such as a movie theater or museum'.[17] The term 'prosthetic' refers to the phenomenon of cognitive dissonance where an amputee can still feel pain in a missing limb. Manny looks again and again at his foot and then at Danny's boots as though the boots had been prosthetics of his own but now have attached themselves viciously and ironically to Danny's feet. They do not dance away into the forest however, just stumble. Meanwhile the idea of the palimpsest nuances the image of prosthetics into a notion of animate and malevolent layers, osmotic and multidirectional.[18] The layers are peeled back to reveal, and cover over to conceal, atrocities and horror passed on from generation to generation. Landsberg emphasises that the destruction of family memory – father to son, mother to child and so on – through genocide, slavery and other acts of removal, requires a public response to stand in for the absence of a coherent historical narrative that confounds each new generation. It is the public work of cinema, or literature, or an exhibition that produces a meaningful shift in what is taken to be true. The British and Australian films and exhibitions that share stories of those removed within the British Commonwealth and from indigenous populations could be accounted as just such prosthetic interventions. In *Darkness Casts No Shadow*[19] and its film adaptation *Diamonds of the Night*, Lustig and Němec use interrupted narrative to simultaneously search for the parents that have disappeared and to afford the child his place as witness to a cultural heritage and to affirm a place in the lost world of his family, even as the film, and novella, proceeds towards annihilation.

> Before his eyes, the second boy could see a door with a brass nameplate. The plate was bare. He placed his finger on the doorbell and pushed it. This was the place he always came back to, fearful that nobody would be there.[20]

This passage from the last few pages of the book is almost exactly replicated in the film, in a repeated flashback. The boy runs up some stairs and stops at a door on the first landing. There is a brass plate and door knocker. He pauses. The boy's return to his home and his city now seems like that of an excluded child. He can long for home and he can walk the streets, but he is not able to enter domestic spaces even in his own dreams. Rather, he stands beside doorways, walks down alleyways, and jumps on and off trams, which may or may not be representing the transports to the camps. The excluded child is outside the 'national symbolic',[21] longing for a place called home, but only able to stand witness to his homelessness. Manny inhabits himself as both victim and the child of victims, oneiric encounters which silently remove him from his originary self. The closer he sees, the less he belongs and the man's smile as he turns round at the end of the tram is a smile of refusal from the nation and from his inherited existence.[22] One might say that his own memory steps in to foreshorten and abandon him. Landsberg makes the similar point that that children who were not the primary targets of violence or disinheritance have nowhere to live in their own memory, no corporeal space for themselves.[23] It is this profound lacuna that films and novels may seek to occupy and remediate.

Perpetrators and victims are scarred by the past, and this is where Michael Rothberg's insistence on multidirectional memory is crucial to extending Silverman's framework. The Muriel of Alain Resnais' film is the name of an Algerian woman tortured by a Frenchman, a protagonist in the film, from which Muriel herself is absent. The title of the film is therefore both a question and an answer, and Muriel becomes the eponymous heroine of a mystery created by flashbacks of a family's relationships. The reproach of her absence attaches to the family's consciousness and, through them, to the totality of the French bourgeoisie, hence the layers of guilt are diffused. Bernard, the perpetrator of the crimes against Muriel, is the prime carrier of guilt that infects his direct family, his class and his nation. The matter of this guilt is located not in secrecy but, as Silverman points out, in the interstices of his own records, postcards and photographs of his time in Algeria.[24] The layers of memory are not kept safely locked away in one place, they re-form in correspondence to other histories and in new moments of intense experience. Němec, an admirer of Resnais, is concerned with the layering of one boy's memories as he stands in the eye of history's wrath. The boy, Manny, is not a perpetrator but the prosthetic victim and witness for a generation of dead boys, but the film's layers of revelation are also palimpsestic in Silverman's sense. The cinematic world before the war, and quoted in the film, talked of horror through surreal juxtapositions, indecipherable architectures and vampires. This boy has seen the ants on his hand, and in a subsequent sequence the ants crawl into his eye socket. As a cinematic cipher, as much as a figure in European history, these visual tricks indicate that the boy will die within the logic of the film, or is already dead within the logic of history. The point is not that he is marked by death, just as the point is not that Muriel has already died of torture, but how much we can remember of him, with him, before he disappears back into the forest (how much we can remember of Algeria before it disappears into the silence of the archive and France repeats its mistakes again). That is *our* moral, multidirectional imperative as survivors or spectators, years after the events have retreated into national archives and family history.

Two

The northern and eastern forests of Europe belong to the German and the Russian imaginaries. For the Germans, the forests are the site of frightening fairytales and national nostalgia for a unified German entity; in the nineteenth century forests were the 'only great possession that has yet to be completely given away … every person has a certain right to the forest, even if it only consists in being able to walk around it when the person so desires'.[25] Harrison Robert Pogue comments that, even as Riehl (a contemporary of the great storytellers of the German forest, the Brothers Grimm) was writing those words, the German forest was in fact being sold off, privatised and made inaccessible to every 'person'[26] (and, as the dehumanisation of Jews in World War II, and of the forced emigrants and migrants discussed elsewhere in this book, who exactly constitutes a person and who has sufficient power to determine this is always in question). Nineteenth-century Russians, from peasants to lords, relied on their forests for food, for the decorations of peasant seasonal rituals, for building materials and heating and even the fuel of industry to such an extent that the forest was a site of national anxiety as well as identification.[27] *Diamonds of the Night* is set in the forest of the Bohemian borderlands, a huge, mountainous and wooded area that stretches across the current Czech–German border. The area had been ceded to Germany in the Munich Agreement of September 1938. It returned to Czech sovereign control in 1945–6. A long way from Prague, the boys' capture takes place only a few miles from the Czech spa city of Karlovy Vary (then Karlsbad). The boys walk into the dense darkness of this enemy territory, filmed in dark shadow, but just once struck by light filtering downwards through the trees and once opening out into a stony clearing. The boys are city-bred; they cannot read their direction by the stars, nor recognise what is edible on the forest floor. They have no weapons and probably could not in any case hunt for food. Indeed, it is they who are soon to be hunted down by an armed posse, a decrepit but vicious militia of old, German-speaking peasant men. In other films concerning child migrants during and after World War II, *Ivan's Childhood* (1961), *Lore* (2012), *The Truce* (1998), and *Der Letzte Zug* (2006), the European forest also represents a confusing fairytale space of escape, terror, homeland and contemplation.[28] In the opening sequence of *Ivan's Childhood* the spectator is spellbound by an overexposed image of a very beautiful child, his pale skin and blond hair perfectly youthful and joyfully clean. He climbs a tree and then takes flight, like an angel shining with delight, soaring over the treetops of Russia in peacetime. He flies in a kind of contemplative, delighted trance, surfing a magical dislocation between one place (which we are yet to see for ourselves) and somewhere like home. He lands like a butterfly and finds his mother waiting for him on a dusty path between the trees with a pail of milk for him to drink from. But abruptly his own dream, for such it is, tricks him back into a dark reality with sound and fury. An explosion of mortar fire jolts him back to his solitary life as a war orphan. The boy's mind fashions oneiric sense of the explosion in his waking world by re-witnessing the violent death of his mother. Ivan is not flying above the trees towards his mother but is carrying messages for the partisans, running underneath the trees, or wading through marshlands under dripping branches of dead wood, avoiding enemy fire. Thus the film exposes us to both versions of the Russian forest in a single sequence – a maternal, bountiful homeland and a graveyard of wood and bones.

Ivan's Childhood is a brilliant, delicate, wrenching film that predates *Diamonds of the Night* by three years. The others I mention are less accomplished – although *Lore* is a fine piece of work – but cumulatively reference the forest in ways that are pre-gestured in both the older films. In *The Truce*, based on Primo Levi's account of his return home from Auschwitz after liberation, the character of Primo (John Turturro) has a flashback of the death camps while walking in a forest near a Soviet DP (displaced persons) transitory settlement. The voiceover, of Levi's older self, comments that camp-dwellers view the forest as a place that will give 'the inestimable gift of solitude'. Levi's own text adds, 'Perhaps because it reminded us of other woods, other solitudes of our previous existence; or perhaps, on the contrary, because it was solemn and austere and untouched, like no other scenery known to us.'[29] The sequence prompts the understanding that refugees on their way to a place they can call home (and by extension away from a place that they have called home in the past) may be very lonely in their suffering but that they are also likely to be crowded and huddled in that loneliness. The impression of crowded bodies set against solitary wandering is the central spatial juxtaposition of most films concerning the process of flight, migration and arrival. So, young Primo seeks his solitary respite in a dark forest brightened by sunlight. He comes upon a group of naked children playing in a clearing. They have the same over-exposed beauty and ingenuous laughter as the child Ivan in the dream sequence. In *The Truce*, the adult Primo looks on at the children playing and is jolted back to the memory of children walking towards the camp, 'the children at Auschwitz were like migrating birds ... a few days after they arrived they were swept away to the gas chambers.'[30] Levi's verbal metaphor, of vast flocks of children flying homeward but being detoured towards a brutal death, hits us like the explosion in Ivan's dream. The onscreen, literal juxtaposition between the naked children playing in the clearing in the forest and reconstructed images of children arriving at a camp, cutting to a bleak shot of a chimney stack belching smoke, moves us between two worlds, with the forest as an intermediary space in which European memories of mass murder are traumatically reincarnated in healthy children's bodies. Levi's first foray into the forest is in fact more about his own foreignness. He describes 'no paths, no traces of woodcutters, nothing: only silence, abandonment and tree trunks in every direction ... I learned, to my cost, with surprise and fear, that the danger of "getting lost in the woods" isn't found only in fairy tales.'[31]

Der Letzte Zug (The Last Train), a German-Czech production, recreates a crowded transport of human beings with no water, no food and no space, and posits the escape of a few women and children when the train is stopped by guerrilla partisans from the forest. The film focuses on the last Jewish Berliners in 1943, their physical and mental disintegration in the course of a six-day journey and the escape of a small girl. The escape story is partly based on the experience of an 11-year-old Belgian boy, Simon Gronowski, who was on the 20th transport from Brussels. Gronowski's train was stopped by partisans and many deportees escaped (although far fewer survived).[32] In both *The Last Train* and Gronowski's memoirs, part memoir and part fiction, the children get out through a hole in the floor. *The Last Train* closes on the small girl walking away from the group of escapees and partisans. She finds a clearing in the forest, the sun coming down through the trees, looks up and recites a prayer, *sheme israel*.[33] Her father has told her that through this prayer she will be able to talk to him and express her sorrow. The connection between child and beams of light leading up like shining pathways to the sky above, recalls the flight of migratory birds and the flight of lost angels.

The forest is also a central thematic in *Lore*.[34] Here, the escapees are five German children, whose National Socialist parents have abandoned them at the end of the war. They find their way home across 900 kilometres of forest to their grandmother in the south. During the journey, there is a painful process of moral and ideological maturation for the oldest child, 17-year-old Lore. The journey recalibrates her view of the world, and her understanding of what home means and whether it is in fact worth the journey at all. Lore is a mirror image of the Jewish refugee Ruth Balizka. Both are teenage girls finding their way across Europe with younger siblings to defend, albeit at different stages of the war, and on either side of the conflict. Ruth is fleeing persecution while Lore is – as she discovers en route – a perpetrator by descent. In a small town, she sees Allied posters displaying photographs of the camps, including one of her own father engaged in murder as commander. Further along the path, she meets a terrifying witch-like woman who attempts to buy Lore's baby brother (Peter) in order to get access to his extra rations. Worst of all, one of her younger twin brothers is shot dead by Soviet soldiers when he wanders away into the wrong side of the trees. Lore discovers that her faith in her parents and their ideology has been misplaced and that sacred German forests may be sectioned off to alien forces, their sanctuary divided between different groups of refugees. The children's journey is shared by a young man, Tomas, also about 17 years old. It appears that he is Jewish, a camp survivor trying to find a way home. He carries a pass and identity documents which will ensure his passage out of the Soviet sector. Lore later discovers that he is not the authentic 'Tomas', but it is never clear who he is, whether he is Jewish at all or whether it even matters in the scheme of Lore's great disillusionment with her parents' generation. Shots of the forest include both bird's-eye views of the great expanses of the Black Forest heartlands and quasi-domestic sequences amongst the trees, with the familiar trope of sunlight fading into perilous darkness. The German forest dwellers that the children meet on their journey live on the edges, in farms and small-holdings. There is the witch-like woman who wants to buy the baby, with tar-blackened hands and a dead husband in the barn, his shotgun still pointing at the bloody hole in his face. There are former neighbours to the forest hideaway, where the five children were eventually left alone by their mother. The neighbours are also anxious to distance themselves from the children of hunted war criminals. The fringe-dwellers live close up against the heart of the German imaginary and its moral darkness is pantomimed in their behaviour. The forest encompasses Lore's internalisation of Nazi ideology and her subsequent rejection of it in the face of greater truths. The forest is also where she feels conflicted desire and loathing for 'Jewish' Tomas. Just as the fragmentation of German sovereignty, along invisible territorial lines of the occupying forces, confronts the solid expectation of the irreducible relationship between the forest and homeland – *heimat* – so it introduces, for Lore, the confronting desire for the intimate penetration of the stranger who is also the excluded Jew. While Lore is encountering *heimat*'s moral limits, in what we might call a different part of the woods the Russian forests of *The Truce* and the Polish forests of *The Last Train* provide spiritual shelter to those who would escape the very idea of *heimat*. The old militiamen in *Diamonds of the Night* would have been German-speaking Bohemians, with linguistic and emotional ties to Germany as well as to the lands they farmed. They were likely, had they lived a few more years, to have been amongst the tide of refugees heading back towards Germany in 1945–6, just when Lore was also heading south. One might imagine how pitiable these toothless old men would have seemed travelling to regain *heimat* without the borrowed authority of guns and the war. But unlike Lore, who must struggle to rid herself of the protective and sickening tentacles of *heimat* and her parental legacy, and unlike the old men with their guns, feet crashing through the undergrowth, toothless voices roaring in the pursuit, Manny and Danny have no choice at all. They are homeless, *heimatlos*, and profoundly alone: ' "getting lost in the woods" isn't found only in fairy tales'.[35]

Three

In the 1980s, avant-garde film writer Fred Camper sought to define film sound beyond the binary of silent *or* sound, reminding us of a third version – silence *within* sound.[36] His premises for this are perhaps well-known truisms of film scholarship but still worth repeating and extrapolating from his precepts in order to think through how Pauline Oliveros' own avant-garde proscription to breathe and to listen, and to listen to breath, and to score the listening into the music. First, silent film was/is not in any case *silent* in so far as there was/is an external musical accompaniment to the screening, while the insertion of inter-titles encourages the spectator to create an internal sound-voice, or to sound out one's breath with the film. Second, *sound* film is paradoxically very well suited to highlighting *silence*, either diegetically, or by the obvious removal of a soundtrack where one might normally expect one, or by inserting layers of a soundtrack that insulate and isolate others. Camper refers to the work of Stan Brakhage, Bruce Baillie and others to make the point that 'presented with images drained of life that sound can impart, the viewer is thrust more deeply into a contemplation of their inner mysteries, and of his own state of being as well'.[37]

In that wonderfully elegiac phrase, 'drained of life', Camper refers to images that move with no synched or background noise, although the viewer realises that sound is technically possible and indeed may be straining to hear it before accepting that the silence is essential to the experience. But, *drained of life*? Well, *drained of life that sound can impart*. The figures that move across screens without speech, without a musical theme, without intertitles to indicate their intentions and to confirm their capacity to communicate – these figures are like ghosts. Cinematic ghosts are removed from the spectator's full sensorial reach (of course touch and taste – and usually smell – are already out of range) whilst yet requiring her to contemplate inner mysteries. The mind is not busy sounding out voices, or cathecting with an emotionally fraught vocal timbre, musical score, or location sound. The mind is working to make contact through the impossible refusal to connect – the silence. The ghosts on screen are precisely *not* life*less* but the spectatorial access to their form of life is muted, blanketed, challenging, drained of life. George Kouvaros, in a consideration of Wim Wenders' photography and the passing of time, remarks that we are asked 'to look at something as if it were for the last time, as if the thing looked at were disappearing'.[38] *Diamonds in the Night* does something similar. It offers diverse and interchangeable points of entry to the boys' story, maintaining them as the primary points of identification but without flinching from pushing them towards another ending or another beginning, or just another moment when things might go this way, or that. The further they regress in time and the closer to home that Manny and Danny travel, the more insubstantial they seem. So, in the flashback/dream sequence when both boys walk on the walls of the city in perfect black boots, they might be walking on the moon. Their happiness is real but the conditions of that happiness are not. Wherever it emerges and whatever that image proffers us, there is the sure injunction that we should look at these boys 'as if it were the last time'.

At the very beginning of this discussion I stated that the film commences with the two boys jumping in and out of a stream, or water-filled ditch. I also noted that throughout the film, and in quick succession towards the end, flashbacks filled in what might have happened immediately before that opening sequence. The boys jump from the train. The boys sit on the train, one taking the boots of the other. That image recurs with increasing focus on the boots. The boots do not fit the boy who is taking them off and they do fit the boy who was wearing them before. The boots might be the beginning of death. The boys appear and the boys disappear. A shot of them naked and dead on the road from the mayor's house is superseded by a shot of them still alive and walking away. Time and event are unstable in the narration because death is inevitable. Memory and event are de-temporalised so that causation and longing compose a new dialectic, where the whole of the film is just one moment of realisation. Silverman has pointed out that the word 'flashback' is not appropriate, because it does not describe the way in which time itself is concentrated in another Alain Resnais film, *Night and Fog*, a film about concentration camps and the layers and landscapes of horror. He describes Resnais' 'post-concentrationary aesthetic' as invoking 'multiple connections, continuities and ruptures',[39] as a non-linear history within and between the image. I bring into this description of a revelatory technique of time travel and 'life after death'[40] not only the image but also the *sound* of time collapsing in on itself, *drained of life*. Němec, avowedly influenced by Resnais, deploys, reverses and withholds diegetic sound to underscore the Benjaminian 'constellation' of the boys' escape, recapture and return to the dark, in which 'past and present collide in a flash'.[41]

So, what does come before the jump into the water and the sudden onrush of male energy onto the screen in the opening sequence of *Diamonds of the Night*? The credits. They are simple, white words on black. As the usual information is presented – title, actors' names, director of photography, director of sound, director – the soundtrack is unusual. A tolling bell sounds twice, then silence, then it tolls again more quietly, silence again. Then again, much more loudly, and so on. Only when the credits are done does the conversation between silence and the bells cease, and the boys burst through into the image, jumping into water, the commingled sound of shouts and gunshots accompanying them as they run up the hill. There has been no bleed from the tolling bell to the splashing of boys in water, there is no promise of continuity, there is no explanation of where the bells come from and what they portend. The bells recur in flashback to Prague, church bells and tram bells breaking the silence of Manny's memories and reinforcing it. The walk through the forest is quiet, the sound of silence juxtaposed with cracking twigs, a few words, 'I'll find food', 'No, you won't'; 'Come over to me'; 'She'll have to give us milk', and the sound of breath. The noisiest sequence is in the German clubhouse, where the old men celebrate their successful manhunt with meat and beer, songs and dances, leaving the boys with their faces to the wall. But even these sounds issuing from ancient men with collapsed faces and slobbering jaws and high-pitched singing voices must be heard precisely. Each braying sound assails us. We must listen, note by note, at feet stamping one by one, drooling swallows, a slavering crunch, it is a viscous symphony of ancients creating terror. And at 6 am when the boys are marched out, naked and clinging to each other like the children that they are, onto the path from the club house back towards the forest, they walk into a pall of silence. Shots echo behind them as though someone were shooting in a different part of Manny's mind, some other part of life.

Afterword: where have all the children gone?

> It is only in a land where the spaces of states will have been perforated and topologically deformed, and the citizen will have learned to acknowledge the refugee that he himself is, that man's political survival today is imaginable.[1]

In the 18th Sydney Biennale (2012), two Chinese artists, Yang Jinling and Jin Nü, exhibited works on childhood. Jin's piece used the idea of the ephemeral as a lightning rod to conduct nostalgia. Yang used the same concept to project a transient record of children's daydreaming at school. The installations were located on Cockatoo Island, a small outcrop in Sydney Harbour. Cockatoo Island has been variously used as a prison island and as a shipyard, and is now described as the city's prime location for an aesthetic of post-industrial and post-colonial nostalgia. The place bears traces of misery, both for the shipyard workers and, prior to that, for the prisoners – especially Indigenous men – who were incarcerated there. Substantial quarters were built on the island's highest point for the warden and later for the chief engineer and supervisors when the island was turned over to shipbuilding. Yang and Jin were each allocated a room for their installations in the island's largest such 'historic house' (which is also

There's No Place Like Home

Figure 8.1 Detail, 'Exuviate II: Where have all the children gone?', artist, Jin Nü. Courtesy White Rabbit Gallery, Sydney.

used as an upmarket café and rented out as self-catering accommodation at other times of the year). One presumes that the curator realised the irony of placing installations about the ghosts of childhood on a prison island in a colonial colony and in so-called 'family quarters' placed specifically to overlook and stay apart from the belly of an island swarming with ghosts of Sydney's Indigenous men and boys.

In 'Exuviate II: Where Have All the Children Gone?' (2005) Jin Nü (b. 1984) (Figures 8.1 and 8.2) stages a spectral representation of her lost child-self, a clothes-line hung with girls' dresses. All the clothes are gauzy, pastel or white, and each one is slightly larger than the one before. They recall 'the dresses of five years ago',[2] although here the temporality is indicated by sizing rather than fashion. The dresses do not flutter as they might have done on a clothesline in a courtyard or hanging from a pole outside an apartment window, drying in the breeze, with a busy parent nearby. Rather, they hang still, dry and clean, no longer needed for bodies that have grown. The room of ghostly clothes grieves for these many embodiments of the

Afterword

Figure 8.2 Detail, 'Exuviate II: Where have all the children gone?', artist, Jin Nü, image and permission courtesy White Rabbit Gallery, Sydney.

growing child, for child life that has moved away from its skins. The work declares that change and development come at the cost of the loss of the child's former corporealities, and thus of the child-as-herself. The dresses are like snake skins sloughed off as the snake passes through one embodiment to the next. They are precious and delicate, to be kept in glass cases or children's treasure chests, or lost to the sunlight. Children's clothes are worn, outgrown and passed on to new children, new babies, other families, thrown away, or kept in bottom drawers and handled quietly by parents. Jin Nü's rhetorical question, 'Where have all the Children Gone?' refers to herself, an adult grown from many children, each growth spurt intimating the ephemerality of childhood, at every stage and in every special new dress. Yet, the work also engages with the larger subject of ephemerality, migration and consumption in contemporary China. There are several points of departure. Literally, the child's dress is clean and fresh and useless – as it cannot be handed down to siblings and *worn out*, as there are no siblings in the 1980s and 1990s of the one child policy. Even those precious single children may have been sent overseas for high school or university. They may not have returned home. At the same time, if the dresses have themselves been handed down from parents and their siblings, there is no trace left of those past lives. Then, the dresses are like the skins of Chinese contemporary history. They are the gauze-thin recollections of childhoods that were spent during revolution or reform but which bear little trace of the events of the era or of the times which provoked it: the lost children of Tiananmen, the lost childhoods of their parents' generation during the Great Leap Forward, the Hungry Years of the famine and the Cultural Revolution. They also recall the white material of Claire Denis' critique of colonial refusals, what I described at the beginning of this journey as Maria's particular Dorothy Complex.

Yang Junling (b. 1981) 'Class in a Class' (2011) stages a classroom scene, in which children's schoolbook graffiti is collected and restaged as filmed projections in an empty classroom. The careful reveries and doodles of the daydreaming school child are superimposed on the books and desks they have left behind, ephemera superimposed on more ephemera. The piece therefore engages us in reverie, both with the classroom as a space which children pass through on their way to becoming educated subjects of the state, and with their private graffiti – a specific manifestation of childhood disengagement and rebellion. To dream is to change the course of the present, but it is also to be stuck in a classroom, listening to a version of the past and future (*gongshi gongban*, 公事公办) whilst doodling dreams of the world outside the window. Yang uses projectors to screen the drawings that start small and then expand all over the text and exercise books laid out on each desk. Dreams of enormous, complicated technologies emerge across the page, the desk and the pencil case – the child-inventor imagined at the centre-fold of the open book as a little person with a magic computer, dreaming and drawing. The concept has been seen before in the

Afterword

classic children's story and animation, *Ma Liang and his Magic Paintbrush* (*Magic Brush*) (1955). Ma Liang uses his paintbrush to draw what he needs, and eventually to draw ships that will take the emperor across the seas (a kind of forced migration in reverse). Yang's classroom story ends 'with the teacher throwing chalk at the student's head', but the children's drawings also fight back. The child magician starts out with pencil drawings, but is transformed into a redemptive film-maker. The dreaming doodles collected by Yang are re-inscribed as animated digital films enunciating child rebellion as dreams. Yang's immersive installation in an old Australian colonial house on a grim prison island where many Indigenous men and boys had been incarcerated or drowned (again *this* death) trying to swim home, is an extraordinary experience of sudden connections: the Empire, the child, displacement at home, detention. From the island's peak, the lights of Sydney harbour might look like Gregory Dart's daydream:

> An emporium of endless delights, the big city is also the home of sheer functionality and the notion that time is money. Not since we were children have we been shown so many things and then told not to touch them.[3]

Following Freud and Winnicott, Dart accuses the daydream of trying to console the dreamer who, even if not marginalised as adults marginalise children, is likely to be otherwise liminal or poor, or both. Dart then makes an explicit bridge between Benjamin's Arcades project and the Situationists, specifically Guy Debord's championing of 'the entangled and the eclectic',[4] and thereby imagines the Arcades as wonderlands with a dark edge. Indeed, Benjamin's ruminations speak distinctly across time and space to the modern byways of Chinese modernising culture. The process of Chinese commodification entails a quasi-totalitarian architectural enormity, the twenty-first-century shopping centres of Beijing and Shanghai would dwarf the arcades of nineteenth-century Paris and Berlin (or indeed the contemporary Dublin arcade that Kylie skates through on her ruby heelies in *Kisses*). Nevertheless, these neon-lit passageways of new fortunes and luxurious possession seem related to Europe's illumination by the parallel stories of industrial growth and world influence through the attendant confusions of a youth facing a form of material freedom attached to the accelerated decay of social responsibility and historical recall, and a global footprint that is at once triumphant and hollow.⁵ It is, one might suggest, a global environment of dislocation and forced mobility that seduces one into *daydreaming* rather than the furious and creative *dreaming* of Yang's classroom.

In his essay on children's picture books, Benjamin argues that coloured books are like daydreams. They entrap children in a world with specified entry and exit points for the imagination, whereas black and white images allow for real dreaming and true adventure. 'Children fill them ["black and white woodcuts", but we could add *textbooks*] with a poetry of their own. This is how it comes about that children *in*scribe the pictures with their ideas in a more literal sense: they scribble on them.'⁶ Yang's rebellious classroom doodlers attack their text books as if they were scribbling against both the colourful enticements and the ideological entrapments of education. Benjamin still bases their poetic rebellion on the art of collecting: 'Children know such pictures like their own pockets, they have searched through them in the same way and turned them inside out, without forgetting the smallest thread or piece of cloth'. Yang's doodling child is a daydreamer, slipping away from the classroom into a fantasy world where the teacher could not find him out (like Ma Liang sending the emperor off in a ship to get rid of him, or teenage girls throwing bananas back at authority in Sydney – or Dorothy escaping from Kansas to Oz). Perhaps we should say that the child is dreaming in the Benjaminian sense of making a future out of the present (these textbooks), whilst Yang collects and digitises graffiti, the epitome of ephemeral art, for the installation and makes another dream from the child's efforts.

Yang's installation needs to be seen in a longer context of the Chinese classroom. In the same decade that Yang was born and entering primary school, posters of the ideal child were printed up for use in primary schools as instructive decoration. These became a form of ephemera that linked childhood to the politics of idealism rather than the right to rebel. In the 1980s, when Yang was doodling in school, these posters contributed to a media sphere dominated by public information, ideological advice and national development priorities. The child in these pictures is not the child that we find in reveries, quite the opposite in fact. He is focused, attentive, and indubitably present. Yet these same posters – when they re-emerge on the walls of older buildings, or in old films, or in the markets of modern

China – do indeed invoke the lost idealism of an earlier generation. Yang does not include walls in *Class in a Class*, but those posters would be hanging on them had he done so. But perhaps that would have complicated the message more than offering any clarification of the stultifying environment Yang wants to evade, given that the posters are now the ephemerality of a barely remembered version of early Reform political intensity.

Two

Having begun this book with Dorothy's dream of Oz, I end it with blurred realities and daydreams in China. Along the road we have encountered waking nightmares through which children walk alone. There have been monsters and zombies in the forests and ghosts in the girls' toilets. Children have carried each other on their backs, leaned on one another as they limp away from implacable and violent adults. In the films made by young people there has been dark humour, knowing irony and playful escape. There has also been murder. The films echo real-world categories of extreme vulnerability, disability, children travelling alone, children travelling with a single adult, children to whom actual harm has been done and who are living with trauma, children taken and sent away, children who cannot breathe safely, children whose lives are in real and immediate danger. Most of all, perhaps, we see how the impact of war and the deliberate dislocation of communities and peoples continues for children across the twentieth and twenty-first centuries. It has been said many times in relation to children growing up as refugees that their childhoods have been squandered. The films examined here echo that sentiment, but do so from a longer perspective. In my Introduction, I talked about child life, the ephemeral and precious constituent of hope. In the world of migration today that hope is under siege. Child life is damaged not only by prolonged journeying but by the prolonging of social insignificance for children who have, conversely, been required to grow up fast in order to survive. They get the worst of both worlds. Bonnie Honig has commented that democracy requires magic and wonders 'by what magic are dependent, not yet fully formed followers supposed to become the responsible, active citizens that democracy requires?'[7] She suggests that the figure of Dorothy is the excuse for Oz folk to shirk the responsibility of political maturity and opt instead for a foreign saviour. I agree with her when we see Dorothy re-emerge as the adult French Maria. But I think that we can see Dorothy across a number of less clear-cut incarnations. She is indeed the foreign witch who sometimes saves the day, but at what expense (and whose day?); she is also the child migrant whose body belies her age and whose status is one of indeterminacy and perpetual movement.[8] It is that aspect of the Dorothy signature that we see playing through films where children are on the road, waiting in the ante chamber and used as bait for the political aspirations of others. She is the traveller who must learn where it is safe to breathe and where one may lie down and sleep without fear of death. To return to where Rushdie began, Dorothy is an ambivalent, mobile figure whose maturity must be bound tight and hidden away to maintain an appearance of innocence on the road (Figure 8.3). She is the first person in cinema to say what every migrant discovers, for better or for worse: there's no place like home.

It is not refugees that have to change, but everyone else.

Figure 8.3 'Child adventurer facing the seas before the war, UK, 1939', permission courtesy the author, photographer presumed Fintan Kehoe.

Notes

Introduction

1. Sara Ahmed (2004), 'Collective feelings', *Theory, Culture & Society*, 21/2, p. 28.
2. The research project used media and film practice to investigate the work that children and young people do, as first-generation migrants, in regards to assisting their parents' settlement in a new cultural and political environment with different competencies required for citizenship. The research is reported in Y.C. Chu, Stephanie Hemelryk Donald and Andrea Witcomb (2003), 'Children, media, and the public sphere in Chinese Australia', in G. Rawnsley and M. Rawnsley (eds), *Political Communications in Greater China: The Construction and Reflection of Identity*, original edn., London: Routledge Curzon, pp. 261– 74; and Stephanie Hemelryk Donald (2001), 'History, entertainment, education and *jiaoyu*: a Western Australian perspective on Australian children's media, and some Chinese alternatives', *International Journal of Cultural Studies*, 4, pp. 279–99.
3. Daniela Berghahn (2013), *Far-flung Families in Film: The Diasporic Family in Contemporary European Cinema*, Edinburgh: Edinburgh University Press, pp. 1–5, 26–8 and ff.
4. Our first port of call, Malta, was under emergency direct rule from April 1958 until mid-1961. It achieved an interim Government in February 1962 and full independence in September 1964. Our family had been re-posted back to Hayling Island by the end of 1961. The Suez Crisis (1958) accelerated decolonisation overall as British overseas policy looked weak. We were sent to Singapore and Malaya in 1963, the latter became independent Malaysia in 1963 along with Singapore. There were later splits (1968–71) between the two former colonies, one with a predominantly Chinese leadership under Lee Kwan-Yu, and Malaysia led strongly away from Chinese and British influence by radicals such as Mahathir Mohamad. Simon C. Smith, (2007), 'Integration and disintegration: the attempted incorporation of Malta into the United Kingdom in the 1950s', *The Journal of Imperial and Commonwealth History*, 35/1, pp. 64–5, and Karl Hack (1991), 'Decolonisation and the Pergau Dam affair', *History Today*, 44/11, p. 10.
5. See: Australian Government (2009) 'Apology to the forgotten Australians and former child migrants,' Canberra, 16 November. Online: https://www.dss.gov.

au/our-responsibilities/families-and-children/programs-services/apology-to-the-forgotten-australians-and-former-child-migrants, accessed 1 October 2016; see also Isabelle Auguste (2009), 'On the significance of saying "Sorry" – politics of memory and Aboriginal reconciliation in Australia', *Coolabah*, 3, pp. 43–50.
6. In brief, a boatload of asylum seekers was rescued by a Norwegian tanker, *Tampa*, in Australian waters. Contrary to international maritime law, the Australian Government made every effort not to receive them. The general election was fought on an anti-migration ticket and the Government of the day was re-elected. The impact of *Tampa* has reverberated through Australian politics and debates on the rights of the refugees to seek asylum, and on the national character. Suvendrini Perera (2002), 'A line in the sea: the Tampa, boat stories and the border', *Cultural Studies Review*, 8/1, May: pp. 11–27. Dennis Del Favero's meditation on the *Tampa* incident, 'Tampa 2001', was shown at FACT Liverpool as the key exhibit in the Libidinal Circuits exhibition and conference, 2015. Online: http://www.fact.co.uk/projects/libidinal-circuits-scenes-of-urban-innovation-iii/dennis-del-favero-tampa-2001-2015.aspx, accessed 1 April 2017.
7. Karen Lury (2010), *The Child in Film: Tears, Fears, and Fairytales*, Brunswick, NJ: Rutgers University Press, p. 10.
8. Chu, Donald and Witcomb, 'Children, media, and the public sphere in Chinese Australia'.
9. See child-created chapter images (throughout book) in Stephanie Hemelryk Donald (2005), *Little Friends: Children's Film and Media Culture in China*, Lanham: Rowman and Littlefield.
10. Giorgio Agamben (1998), *Homo Sacer: Sovereign Power and Bare Life*, Stanford, CA: Stanford University. See also Lury, *The Child in Film*, p. 6, who turns to Agamben's *Remnants of Auschwitz* for her war-focussed analyses of *Ivan's Childhood* and *Diamonds of the Night*, both of which films I also discuss.
11. Paul Ricoeur (2004), *Memory, History, Forgetting*, Chicago: University of Chicago Press, p. 415.
12. Ahmed, 'Collective feelings'.
13. Andrei Makine (1995), *Le Testament Français*, Paris: Mercure de France, pp. 125–6.
14. Susan Buck-Morss (1989), *The Dialectics of Seeing: Walter Benjamin and the Arcades Project*, Cambridge, MA: MIT, p. 275.
15. Walter Benjamin (1999), *The Arcades Project*, Cambridge, MA: The Belknap Press, H4a, 2, p. 211.
16. Adam Phillips (2007), *Side Effects*, London: Penguin Books. Source used: Phillips, Adam (2005), 'The forgetting museum', *Index on Censorship*, Volume 2. Online

Eurozine, http://www.eurozine.com/articles/2005-06-24-phillips-en.html, accessed 30 October 2016.
17. Anne Friedberg (2002), 'Urban mobility and cinematic visuality: the screens of Los Angeles – endless cinema or private telematics', *Journal of Visual Culture*, 1, pp. 184–5.
18. The notion of urban complexity is manifest in Chris Doyle's award-winning cinematography for the Hong Kong-based film-maker Wong Kar-wai. In Doyle's work, the city is paradoxically afforded emotional substance through the ephemerality of light shows and carefully edited disconnections.
19. Ricoeur, *Memory*, p. 445.
20. Andreas Koefoed (2015), *At Home in the World*, Sonntag Films. Online: http://www.athomeintheworldfilm.com/#a-home-in-the-world, accessed 19 November 2016.
21. Merrick Burrow (2004), 'Dialectical fairyland, cosmic advertising and the mimetic faculty in the Arcades Project', *New Formations*, 54, p. 122.
22. Buck-Morss, *The Dialectics of Seeing*, p. 274.
23. Maeve Pearson (2004), 'Arcadian children: Benjamin, Fourier and the child of the Arcades', *New Formations*, 54, p. 128.
24. Maeve Pearson (2007), 'Re-exposing the Jamesian Child: the paradox of children's privacy', *The Henry James Review*, 28/2 (Spring), p. 115.
25. Benjamin, *The Arcades* (Convolute H *The Collector*), p. 205.
26. Gregory Dart (2010), 'Daydreaming', in Matthew Beaumont and Gregory Dart (eds), *Restless Cities*, London: Verso, p. 85.
27. Susan Buck-Morss (2011), 'Communism and ethics', in *Communism, A New Beginning*, Conference paper, Cooper Union, New York: online: http://www.versobooks.com/blogs/706-communism-a-new-beginning-alain-badiou-and-slavoj-zizek-with-verso-books-at-cooper-union-new-york-october-14th-16th-2011, accessed 6 May 2016.
28. Italo Calvino (1954/2011), *Into the War*, London: Picador, p. 54.
29. Ibid., p. 49.
30. Ibid., p. 55.
31. Eliza Carthy, 'The Big Machine', by Eliza Carthy & The Wayward Band, The Music Room, Liverpool Philharmonic, 18 November 2016.
32. Ahmed, 'Collective feelings', p. 30.

Chapter 1: The Dorothy Complex

1. Emma Wilson (2003), *Cinema's Missing Children*, London: Wallflower Press, p. 332.
2. L. Frank Baum (1900/1960), *The Wonderful Wizard of Oz*, New York: Dover Books.

3. Salman Rushdie (1992/2002), *The Wizard of Oz: An Appreciation* (BFI Film Classics), London: BFI Publishing, p. 57.
4. For discussions of the period in which Baum witnessed poverty and populism in the American context, please see: Alexander D. Noyes (1998), 'The banks and the panic of 1893', *Political Science Quarterly*, 9/1 (March 1894), pp. 12–30. John H. Hamer (1998), 'Money and the moral order in late nineteenth and early twentieth century American capitalism,' *Anthropological Quarterly*, 71/3 (July), pp. 138–49. James R. Barret (1992), 'Americanization from the bottom-up, immigration and the remaking of the working class in the United States: 1880–1930,' *Discovering America*, 79/3 (December), pp. 996–1020. For studies on American cultures of class, home and dispossession, conducted through the prism of the Oz paradigm, please see: Richard F. Selcer (1990), 'From Tara to Oz and back again: home sweet movies', *Journal of Popular Film and Television*, 18/2, pp. 52–63. Kathleen P. Barsalou (2008), *The Age of William A. Dunning: The Realm of Myth Meets the Yellow Brick Road*, unpublished PhD thesis, Florida Atlantic University, UMI Number: 3339601, pp. 25–44.
5. Henry M. Littlefield (1964), '*The Wizard of Oz*: parable on populism,' *American Quarterly*, 16/1 (Spring), p. 50.
6. Ibid., pp. 52–4.
7. There are numerous interpretations of Dorothy as queer icon. Two notable starting points: Alexander Doty (2000), *Flaming Classics: Queering the Film Canon*, London: Routledge, p. 65 and throughout. Todd S. Gilman (2003), '"Aunty Em, Hate You! Hate Kansas! Taking the Dog, Dorothy," conscious and unconscious desire in *The Wizard of Oz*', in Suzanne Rahn (ed.), *L. Frank Baum's World of Oz, A Classic Series at 100*, Lanham, MD: Children's Literature Association and Scarecrow Press, pp. 127–45.
8. Rushdie, *The Wizard of Oz*, p. 57.
9. Giorgio Agamben (2009), trans. Luc D'Isanto and Kevin Attell, *The Signature of All Things: A Note on Method*, Cambridge, MA: MIT Press, pp. 41–4. For a superb analysis of the full work, see William Watkin (2014), 'The signature of all things: Agamben's philosophical archaeology', *MLN*, 129/1 (January), p. 144.
10. Agamben, *The Signature*, p. 64, quoted in Watkin, 'The signature', p. 150.
11. Andrew Plaks suggests these bipolarities in his analysis of the vernacular classic *Dream of the Red Chamber (Hong lou meng)*. Andrew H. Plaks (1976), *Archetype and Allegory in the Dream of the Red Chamber*, Princeton: Princeton University Press, p. 55.
12. *Ju Dou* concerns the marriage of a young woman to a much older man, who abuses her. She has an affair with a younger man, her husband's nephew. However, her young son turns against the couple, causing the lover's death.

13. Baum's own attempts to film the Oz series is described in Anne Morey (1995), '"A whole book for a nickel?" L. Frank Baum as film-maker', *Children's Literature Association Quarterly*, 20/4 (Winter), pp. 155–60.
14. Chen Kuan-hsing (2010), *Asia as Method: Toward Deimperialization*, Durham, NC: Duke University Press.
15. Nicola Ansell (2009), 'Childhood and the politics of scale: descaling children's geographies', *Progress in Human Geography*, 33/2, pp. 190–209.
16. Nicholas Lee (2001), *Childhood and Society: Growing up in an Age of Uncertainty*, Buckingham: Open University Press, p. 19, quoted in E. Kay M. Tisdall and Samantha Punch (2012), 'Not so "new", looking critically at childhood studies,' *Children's Geographies*, 10/3, p. 254 (pp. 249–64).
17. A relevant and cogent discussion of the concept available in Karen Lury (2012), 'A high wind in Jamaica: blank looks and missing voices', *Screen*, 53/4, pp. 447–52.
18. Laura U. Marks (2000), *The Skin of the Film: Intercultural Cinema, Embodiment and the Senses*, Durham, NC: Duke University Press, p. 24.
19. Marks: *The Skin of the Film*, p. 24. Meanwhile Lury's essay on 'dirty little white girls', cites films where the desires of older men are served by the 'complicity' of female actors and child subjects, arguing that 'our response to children on screen is a form of anthropomorphism'. The child cannot be 'read' but she may be a screen within a screen for the projection of whatever the adult film-maker, or adult audience member, needs to locate in a non-active combatant in the war of adult emotions. Karen Lury (2010), *The Child in Film: Tears, Fears and Fairy Tales*, London, New York: I.B.Tauris, p. 106.
20. See Chapter 5.
21. Amal Treacher (2006), 'Children's imaginings and narratives: inhabiting complexity,' *Feminist Review*, 82, pp. 96–113.
22. In a later discussion of Vicky Lebeau's work on *River's Edge* (Chapter 4 of this volume) we encounter the question of the dead child or the inert child (*Little Moth*). I am extremely reluctant to discuss the death of Alan Kurdi, a three-year-old boy washed ashore in Turkey in 2015, as his lifeless form is fast becoming a film trope rather than a document of an individual child's death. However, the public sympathy for a dead child, as opposed to an ongoing outcry for complex, needy living children requiring resettlement might be seen as part of the overall social discourse of preferring children to be sweet, innocent and non-challenging, whatever their experience.
23. The position of national governments and national moralities toward children are often compromised by the compulsion to criminalise strangers. For asylum seekers this can result in children being wrongly classified as adults and sent back to the place they have sought to escape. For a philosophical analysis

see Joanne Faulkner (2010), *The Importance of Being Innocent: Why We Worry about Children*, Cambridge: Cambridge University Press, pp. 46–8.
24. Annalisa Furia (2012), 'Victims or Criminals? The Vulnerability of Separated Children in the Context of Migration in the United Kingdom and Italy', Working Paper 69, Farnham: Sussex Centre for Migration Research. Mary Crock (2006), *Seeking Asylum Alone: A Study of Australian Law, Policy and Practice Regarding Unaccompanied and Separated Children*, Sydney: Themis Press and several publications by Heaven Crawley whose work is important for both gender and child/girlhood experiences in migration and settlement determinations. See Heaven Crawley (2001), *Refugees and Gender: Law and Process*, Bristol: Jordan Publishing; also, 'Gender-related persecution and women's claims to asylum,' (online information tool) online: http://www.refugeelegalaidinformation.org/gender-related-persecution-and-women's-claims-asylum, accessed 2 August 2016. Heaven Crawley (2000), 'Gender, persecution and the concept of politics in the asylum determination process,' *Forced Migration Review*, 9, pp. 17–20. An introductory essay is available in Jason Hart (2014), 'Children and forced migration', in Elena Fiddian-Qasmiyeh, Gil Loescher, Katy Long and Nando Sigona (eds), *The Oxford Handbook of Refugee and Forced Migration Studies*, Oxford: University of Oxford Press, pp. 383–94.
25. John Funchion (2010), 'When Dorothy became history: L. Frank Baum's enduring fantasy of cosmopolitan nostalgia', *Modern Language Quarterly*, 71/4, December, pp. 429–51.
26. Ibid., p. 432.
27. That is somewhat unfair given Baum's own commitment to the populist social activism of the 1880s and 1890s. Yet, we should also note Baum's anti-Native American writings which do support Funchion's critical stance. (see for example: Mary Pierpoint (2000), 'Was Frank Baum a racist or just the creator of Oz?', Indian Country: today media network.com 25 October 2000. Online: https://indiancountrytodaymedianetwork.com/news/was-frank-baum-a-racist-or-just-the-creator-of-oz/, accessed 1 April 2017.
28. Faulkner, *The Importance of Being Innocent*, pp. 46–7.
29. The deployment of child soldiers in civil war is analysed in Myriam Denov's ethnographic study. She makes the important distinction between structure and agency and insists that whilst children may be tricked, threatened or abused into fighting but that they may also have ideological alliances with rebels in their homelands. Myriam Denov (2010), *Child Soldiers: Sierra Leone's Revolutionary United Front*, Cambridge: Cambridge University Press, pp. 39–43.
30. Background to the longer history of Xinjiang: James A. Millward (2007), *Eurasian Crossroads: A History of* Xinjiang, New York: Columbia University Press.

31. Nicholas Bequelin (2004), 'Staged development in Xinjiang,' *China Quarterly*, clxxviii, pp. 358–78; See also in the same issue, David S.G. Goodman (2004), 'The campaign to "open up the west": national, provincial and local perspectives', clxxviii, pp. 317–34.
32. The riots and multiple deaths are variously explained as due to economic inequities and religious intolerance and repression, but with increasing focus on historical tensions on the borders of China. Angel Ryono and Matthew Galway (2015), 'Xinjiang under China: reflections on the multiple dimensions of the 2009 Urumqi uprising', *Asian Ethnicity*, 16/2, pp. 235–55; and (note the convolutions of the title), Hao Yufan, and Liu Weihua (2012), 'Xinjiang: increasing pain in the heart of China's borderland,' *Journal of Contemporary China*, 21/74, pp. 205–25.
33. Plaks, *Archetype and Allegory*, p. 55.
34. Chin, Ann Ping (1988), *Children of China: Voices from Recent Years*. New York: Cornell University Press, p. 18.
35. Ye Jingzhong and Lu Pan (2011), 'Differentiated childhoods: impacts of rural labor migration on left-behind children in China,' *Journal of Peasant Studies*, 38/2, pp. 355–77. Li Na, Wei-hsin Lin and Wang Xiaobing (2012), 'From rural poverty to urban deprivation? The plight of rural-urban migrants through the lens of *Last Train Home*,' *East Asia*, 29, pp. 173–86. Zitong Qiu and Maria Elena Indelicato (2017), 'Beiqing, kuqing and national sentimentality in Liu Junyi's *Left Behind Children*', in Donald, Wilson and Wright (eds), *Childhood and Nation in Contemporary World Cinema: Borders and Encounters*, New York: Bloomsbury, pp. 215–24.
36. Tom Cliff has worked with Han Chinese migrants in the oilfields of Xinjiang. The quote is related to another anonymous child (Cover Image) (private correspondence with the author). A selection of Cliff's series of photographs of Han migrants and settlers is explored in: Tom Cliff (2016), *Oil and Water, Being Han in Xinjiang*, Chicago: University of Chicago Press.
37. The Treaty of Accession, 2003, began a period of labour migration across the region. Online:http://europa.eu/european-union/about-eu/history/2000–2009/2003_en, accessed 1 April 2017. The European Union Schengen Agreement 2004, and further modifications in 2007 and 2013, form the basis of free movement in the European Union. Only Ireland and the UK did not ratify full Schengen rights to their own and other EU citizens. However, even without this full ratification there was mutual agreement to increased EU migration for these two outlying parties. Online: http://ec.europa.eu/dgs/home-affairs/what-we-do/policies/borders-and-visas/schengen/index_en.htm, accessed 6 September 2016.
38. Thomas Elsaesser (2005), 'Double occupancy and small adjustments: Space, place and policy in the New European Cinema since the 1990s', in *European*

Cinema: Face to Face with Hollywood, Amsterdam: Amsterdam University Press, pp. 108–30.

39. This theme is explored in more detail in Chapter 6. The key document is the report into the dispossession and removal of Indigenous children, Lavarch, Michael (1997), *Bringing Them Home: Report of the National Enquiry into the Separation of Aboriginal and Torres Strait Islander children from their Families*, Canberra: Commonwealth of Australia; and on the Commissioner to that inquiry: Antonio Buti (2007), *Sir Ronald Wilson: A Matter of Conscience*, Crawley, WA: University of Western Australia Publishing, pp. 301–29. The enquiry into forced adoption is also relevant, Community Affairs References Committee (29 February 2012), http://www.aph.gov.au/About_Parliament/Senate/Committees/Community_Affairs/Commonwealth_contribution_to_former_forced_adoption_policies_and_practices. Canberra: Australian Senate, accessed 1 April 2017.

40. The role of protectors in Australian state laws underpinned the legal removal of children from their mothers. The legacy of institutionalisation is ongoing in 2016 with high rates of imprisonment and family breakdown in Indigenous contexts. Child removal was legalised in 1865 (*The Industrial and Reformatory Schools Act of 1865*): 'any child born of an Aboriginal or half caste mother' was deemed automatically neglected, and the approach was reinforced in 1897 (*The Aboriginal Protection and Distribution of the Sale of Opium Act of 1897*). The practice of child removal continued into the late 1960s. See Ian O'Connor (1993), 'Aboriginal child welfare law, policies and practices in Queensland: 1865–1989', *Australian Social Work*, 46/3, p. 12. See also Shirleene Robinson (2013), 'Regulating the Race: Aboriginal children in private European homes in colonial Australia', *Journal of Australian Studies*, 37/3, pp. 303–305.

41. Aboriginal women fought for the return of their children, sometimes with the support of white feminists. The Chief Protector of the Aborigines was seen as an 'oppressor' complicit in the 'systematic theft of Aboriginal land and children', quoted in Marilyn Lake (1999), 'Childbearers as rights-bearers: feminist discourse on the rights of Aboriginal and non-Aboriginal mothers in Australia, 1920–1950', *Women's History Review*, 8/2, p. 349.

42. Despite the sentimentalism of Luhrmann's portrayal, European home boarding and fostering generally led to subtle and not-so-subtle enslavement, bullying and loss of identity for the children involved. Robinson, 'Regulating the race', p. 311.

43. Adam Muller (2007), 'Notes towards a theory of nostalgia: childhood and the evocation of the past in two European "heritage" films,' *New Literary History*, 37, p. 741.

44. The work of Max Silverman on palimpsestic memory has prompted this thought. Max Silverman (2015), *Palimpsestic Memory: The Holocaust and Colonialism in French and Francophone Fiction and Film*, Oxford: Berghahn.
45. Henri Lefebvre (1968/1996), *Writings on Cities* (eds/trans. Eleonore Kofman and Elisabeth Lebas), Oxford: Blackwell, p. 174.

Chapter 2: *The Red Balloon* and *Squirt's Journey*: story-telling with child migrants

1. Interview, 2014: M, 16, Indigenous background, high school student. NSW.
2. 'Like the United States, Oz is a country never captured holistically or homogenously but instead presented as shifting, segmented space, a series of complex routes that also acknowledge the organizing principle of region.' Katherine Simons Slater (2013), *Little Geographies: Children's Literature and Local Place*, University of California, San Diego. Unpublished PhD thesis. UMI Number: 3601902, p. 42.
3. Jacqueline Rose (1984), *The Case of Peter Pan: Or, the Impossibility of Children's Fiction*, London: Macmillan, pp. 1–2. A short version is available in Henry Jenkins (1998), *The Children's Culture Reader*, New York: NYU Press.
4. Stephanie Hemelryk Donald (2000), *Public Secrets, Public Spaces: Cinema and Civility in China*, Lanham: Rowman and Littlefield, p. 49.
5. Parts of this discussion have been previously published in Stephanie Hemelryk Donald (2015), 'Cosmopolitan endurance: migrant children and film spectatorship', in K. Beeler and S. Beeler (eds), *Children's Film in the Digital Age: Essays on Audience, Adaption and Consumer Culture*, London: McFarland and Company.
6. Alan Prout (2005), *The Future of Childhood*, Abingdon/Falmer: Routledge.
7. Louise Ackers and Helen Stalford (2004), *A Community for Children? Children, Citizenship and Internal Migration in the EU*, Aldershot: Ashgate Publishing; Terry E. Woronov (2004), 'In the eye of the chicken: hierarchy and marginality among Beijing's migrant school children,' *Ethnography*, 5/3, pp. 289–313. John Comaroff (2006), 'Reflections on youth, from the past to the post-colony,' in G. Downey and M.S. Fisher (eds), *Frontiers of Capital: Ethnographic Reflections on the New Economy*, Durham, NC: Duke University Press; David Buckingham (2007), 'Selling childhood? children and consumer culture,' *Journal of Children and Media*, 1/1, pp. 15–24.
8. Ulrich Beck (2009), 'Critical theory of world risk society: a cosmopolitan vision,' *Constellations*, 16/1, pp. 3–22.
9. Arjun Appadurai (2006), *Fear of Small Numbers: An Essay on the Geography of Anger*, Durham, NC: Duke University Press; Seyla Benhabib with

Jeremy Waldron, Bonnie Koenig and William Kymlicka (2006), *Another Cosmopolitanism*, Oxford: Oxford University Press; Amartya Sen (2006), *Identity and Violence: The Illusion of Destiny*, New York: Allen and Lane. The phrase 'human flourishing' is used by Martha Nussbaum, arguably not a post-colonial thinker but one focussed on human rights discourse; Martha Nussbaum (1997), 'Capabilities and human rights', *Fordham Law Review*, 6/2, 197, p. 297.

10. Jens Qvortrup (2007), 'Editorial: a reminder', *Childhood*, 14/4, p. 395.
11. Claudia Castañeda (2002), *Figurations: Child, Bodies, Worlds*, Durham, NC: Duke University Press, p. 152.
12. Kathrin Hörschelmann and Lorraine van Blerk (2012), *Children, Youth and the City*, London: Routledge, p. 159 ff.
13. Sara Ahmed (2004), 'Collective feelings', *Theory, Culture & Society*, 21/2, p. 27.
14. The workshops were conducted on different timescales depending on the participants' availability and the capacity of host institutions and organisations. In London the participants were all attendees at an Afghani Saturday morning school.
15. The challenges of facilitating 'authentic' participation is discussed in Tracey Skelton (2007), 'Children, young people, UNICEF and participation', *Children's Geographies*, 5/1, pp. 174–5.
16. Georgia Donà and Angela Veale (2011), 'Divergent discourses, children and forced migration', *Journal of Ethnic and Migration Studies*, 37/8 (September), pp. 1273–89. See also the point that migration inserts children into complex global networks such that subjectivity may be multi-scalar. Ansell, 'Childhood and the politics of scale', p. 10 ff.
17. Eleonore Kofman (2005), 'Migration, citizenship and the reassertion of the nation-state in Europe', *Citizenship Studies*, special issue on Spaces, Places and Scales of Citizenship, 9/6, pp. 453–67; Christiane Brosius and Nicolas Yazgi (2007), 'Is there no place like home?: contesting cinematographic constructions of Indian diasporic experiences', *Contributions to Indian Sociology*, 41, pp. 355–86. Mica Nava (2007), *Visceral Cosmopolitanism: Gender, Culture and the Normalization of Difference*, Oxford: Berg; Lydia Morris (2010), *Asylum, Welfare and the Cosmopolitan Ideal: A Sociology of Rights*, Oxford: Routledge.
18. This film was chosen 'on the spot', in an iterative response, from a number of possible texts that were prepared for screening in advance. This decision was based on observations made in the first hour of the workshop.
19. The Moore River settlement also contained adults usually kept separate from the children, especially when one or more of the child's immediate kin were non-Aboriginal. The film is based on the biography of one child, Grace,

recounted by her daughter, Doris Pilkington /Nugi Garimara (1996), *Follow the Rabbit-Proof Fence*, University of Queensland Press. Background documents include Christine Graf (2013), 'Childhood lost: Australia's stolen generation', *Faces*, 29; Michael Lavarch (1997), *Bringing Them Home: Report of the National Enquiry into the Separation of Aboriginal and Torres Strait Islander Children from their Families*, Canberra: Commonwealth of Australia; and the text of the official apology to the Stolen Generations, made on behalf of the Australian nation by then Prime Minister Kevin Rudd, which may be read online at http://www.australia.gov.au/about-australia/our-country/our-people/apology-to-australias-Indigenous-peoples, accessed 17 September 2016.

20. Trish Nicol and Dominic Case (2001), 'Rabbit Proof Fence', *Metro*, 131/132, pp. 286–9.(quote, p. 288).
21. 'If research into children's geographies is to be relevant to the transformation of children's lives, however, it is crucial to consider not only children's encounters with the world, but also the processes, decisions and events that shape the world they perceive, interpret and act upon.' Ansell: 'Childhood and the politics of scale', p. 15.
22. Liberation (*jiefang*) is the term used to describe the victory of the Chinese Communist Party, led by Mao Zedong, over the Nationalists (led by Jiang Kaishek) and the subsequent founding of the People's Republic of China.
23. There was strong discipline for both the research team and the students from the director of the Saturday school, a young English woman who was concerned at too much disruption of routine. This contrasted with other contexts where we were able to work more flexibly and the participants had more freedom to choose locations even in a constrained area.
24. UK-Afghani workshop participant, 2014, aged ten.
25. In 2014 (and subsequently) Australia had a dual immigration policy, the 'migration programme for skilled and family migrants' and the 'humanitarian programme for refugees and others in refugee like situations', https://www.border.gov.au/about/corporate/information/fact-sheets/60refugee, accessed 5 September 2016. Discussion of the contentious offshore processing programme may be found in Chapter 6 of this book.
26. In Sydney my colleagues were an activist film-maker and a social scientist who was working closely with Indigenous families in her own research. One was a migrant to Australia, the other was the daughter of postwar migrants from Europe. Moreover, the Sydney feedback took place in the context of a University-based conference so that the students could show their films to visiting specialists and discuss the cinematic qualities of the work with them, as well as take part in specialist seminar-workshops on other films with child protagonists.

27. Richard Flanagan (2016), *Notes on an Exodus*, Sydney: Vintage, pp. 4–5.
28. I am indebted to the note-taking and interview skills of research associate Dr Inara Walden, Social Policy Research Centre, UNSW.
29. Interview notes on site, Inara Walden.
30. The trailer for the 2017 Australian short film festival FlickerFest headlined an all-Indigenous cast in a remix of *The Wizard of Oz*, http://www.sbs.com.au/nitv/article/2017/01/09/watch-official-flickerfest-trailer-all-Indigenous-cast-playing-wizard-oz, accessed 2 March 2017
31. Thanks due to Dr Enda Murray, research associate and an award-winning film-maker and educator with 30 years of experience in the media industry in Ireland, England and Australia.
32. This stage was used in all workshops and brought significant impact in this instance, mainly because the participants were living away from their families. It was also partly logistical because all the girls lived onsite and so remembered to bring their object along – or could run back to their rooms and collect it. (It was similarly effective in the Chinese workshop where the children lived near where we worked and where they did not possess a large number of personal items.)
33. For the opposite outcome see Marciniak on toilets, abjection and migrant women: Katarzyna Marciniak (2008), 'Foreign women and toilets', *Feminist Media Studies*, 8/4, pp. 337–56.
34. 'Football fan banned after banana thrown at Indigenous AFL star Eddie Betts', *ABC News*, 21 August 2016. http://www.abc.net.au/news/2016-08-21/fan-banned-banana-thrown-at-eddie-betts-port/7769766, accessed 29 August 2016. The incident is reminiscent of similar behaviour in Europe and Brazil, and was the focal point of anti-racism on the pitch action in England in the 1980s, with leadership from the Liverpool star John Barnes. Richard Evans (2016), 'Throwing bananas at black sportsmen has been recognised as racism across Europe for decades'. *The Advertiser* online. 2 August. Online http://www.adelaidenow.com.au/news/opinion/richard-evans-throwing-bananas-at-black-sportsmen-has-been-recognised-as-racism-across-europe-for-decades/news-story/afcb5d4a634119b327507e7616755e0b, accessed 1 September 2016.
35. Our link to the NGO came through an educational contact in Guangzhou. The senior director of the resource network held a PhD in education and was ambitious for the children. Nevertheless, the NGO had religious affiliations and, due to government clampdowns in subsequent years on religion and religious-affiliated organisations, only the barest of identifying information will be reproduced here. There was no sign of religious indoctrination or interference with the children's parental belief systems in our observations.

36. For more information on the Children's Film Unit and Film Course, see Stephanie Hemelryk Donald (2005), *Little Friends: Children's Film and Media Culture in China*, Lanham: Rowman and Littlefield, pp. 84–90.
37. Lina Tao explores the problem of representation in print and online for migrant children in China: Lina Tao (2014), 'Media representation of internal migrant children in China between 1990 and 2012', Masters Dissertation, UNSW.
38. Orna Naftali (2016), *Children in China*, London: Polity Press, p. 157.
39. Na Li, Wei-hsin Lin, Xiaobing Wang (2012), 'From rural poverty to urban deprivation? The plight of Chinese rural-urban migrants through the lens of *Last Train Home*', *East Asia*, 29, p. 187.
40. I have anonymised this boy due to the vulnerability his behaviours suggested.
41. Naftali, *Children in China*, p. 173.

Chapter 3: *Once My Mother, Welcome* and *Le Havre:* breath and the child cosmopolitan

1. L. Frank Baum (1900/1960), *The Wonderful Wizard of Oz*, New York: Dover Books, p. 138.
2. Katherine Simons Slater (2013), *Little Geographies: Children's Literature and Local Place*, University of California, San Diego. Unpublished PhD thesis. UMI Number: 3601902, p. 98.
3. UNICEF (2015), 'Refugee and Migrant Children in Europe'. Online, http://www.unicef.org/publicpartnerships/files/Refugee_and_migrant_children_in_Europe-Sept.2015.pdf, accessed 13 July 2016 (UNICEF re-organisation of web pages underway 2017).
4. UNHCR figures quoted in Jason Hart (2014), 'Children and forced migration', in Elena Fiddian-Qasmiyeh, Gil Loescher, Katy Long and Nando Sigona (eds), *The Oxford Handbook of Refugee and Forced Migration Studies*, Oxford: OUP, p. 383. See also http://www.unhcr.org/children-49c3646c1e8.html, accessed 13 July 2016.
5. *Save the Children Annual Report*, 2015, p. 30.
6. Paul Gilroy (2011), 'Great games: film, history and working-through Britain's colonial legacy,' in Lee Grieveson and Colin MacCabe, *Film and the End of Empire*, London: BFI/Palgrave, p. 13 (pp. 13–32).
7. 'In what sense does cosmopolitanism need to be grounded in an open, experimental, inclusive, normative consciousness of the world, which calls for "perpetual" peace and the end of cultural intolerance and hostility? Such a consciousness would need to include elements of self-doubt and reflexivity, an awareness of the existence and equal validity of other cultural practices and

values.' Pnina Werbner (2006), 'Understanding vernacular cosmopolitanism', *Anthropology News* 47/5, p. 11.
8. Salman Rushdie (1992), *The Wizard of Oz: An Appreciation*, BFI Film Classics, London: BFI Publishing, p. 23.
9. The third definitive article of perpetual peace between states (1902 translation), section of Immanuel Kant (1986), 'Perpetual Peace', in Ernst Behler (ed), *Immanuel Kant: Philosophical Writings*, New York: Continuum, third definitive article: pp. 284–6; whole section: pp. 270–311.
10. Stephanie Hemelryk Donald, Eleonore Kofman and Catherine Kevin (2012), 'Processes of Cosmopolitanism and Parochialism,' in Donald et al. (eds), *Branding Cities: Cosmopolitanism, Parochialism and Social Change*, 2nd edn., New York: Routledge Academic, p. 12.
11. Excellent summaries and explanations: Alison Blunt (2007), 'Cultural geographies of migration: mobility, transnationality, and diaspora, *Progress in Human Geography*, 31/5, p. 685. Tim Cresswell (2010), 'Towards a politics of mobility,' *Environment and Planning D: Society and Space*, 28, pp. 17–31.
12. Gilroy, 'Great games', p. 13.
13. See note 3. Also, Eleonore Kofman (2005), 'Migration, citizenship and the reassertion of the nation-state in Europe', *Citizenship Studies*, 9/6, p. 453 ff.
14. Jacqueline Bhabha (2009), '"The mere fortuity of birth"? children, mothers, borders and the meaning of citizenship,' in S. Behnabib and J. Resnik (eds), *Migrations and Mobilities: Citizenship, Borders and Gender*, New York: New York University Press, pp. 187–227.
15. Polona Petek (2010), 'Highways, byways, and dead ends: towards a non-Eurocentric cosmopolitanism through Yugonostalgia and Slovenian cinema', *New Review of Film and Television Studies*, 8/2, p. 219.
16. Henri Lefebvre (1968/1996), *Writings on Cities*, (eds/trans. Eleonore Kofman and Elisabeth Lebas), Oxford: Blackwell, p. 174.
17. Donald, Kofman and Kevin, 'Processes of cosmopolitanism', p. 11.
18. Gilroy: 'Great games', p. 13.
19. *Colonial Cinema*, July 1944, p. 27, accessed BFI Archive.
20. For background on Ngakane's life after he arrived in Britain from South Africa (1950), see Stephen Bourne (2001/2005), *Black in the British Frame: The Black Experience in British Film and Television*, London: Bloomsbury, pp. 127–9. Also Sarita Malik (2002), *Representing Black Britain: Black and Asian Images on Television*, London: Sage, p. 159.
21. The riots took place in late August and early September in Notting Hill. Businesses and families were targeted in the violence. 'The most disturbing [absorbing] feature of the conversation was that the Jamaicans did not believe that if they stayed at home they would be left in peace, since a bomb had been thrown through the window of the Calypso Club in Notting Hill last Tuesday

(a further incident of this kind was reported in the press on Friday), nor did they believe that the police could or would give them adequate protection. They said that police had used foul language to them particularly in the Harrow Road Police Station.' Extract from a Trade Unions Congress Memorandum, 5 September 1958. Held in the University of Warwick Archive, Trade Unions Congress, Doc ref. 292/805.7/3/212. Online: https://www2.warwick.ac.uk/services/library/mrc/studying/docs/racism/riots/, accessed 12 August 2016. The Notting Hill Carnival was a positive response initiated in January 1959 to celebrate Black culture in London.

22. Bourne, *Black in the British Frame*, p. 130.
23. Esther Rashkin (2009), 'Psychoanalysis, cinema, history: personal and national loss in René Clément's *Forbidden Games*', *Projections*, 3/1, pp. 55–6.
24. Rashkin, 'Psychoanalysis', p. 72.
25. Haneke's film tells the story of a Parisian family man, Georges, forced to revisit memories of the Paris Massacre of 1961, a long-denied State attack on Algerian protesters during the Algerian War. In it, Georges reveals that he tricked Majid, an orphan of parents killed in the massacre living with his family, into cutting off the head of the family's chicken, telling his parents that he did it to frighten him. Majid is then sent away to an orphanage; in the climax of the film the adult Majid slits his own throat in front of Georges.
26. Rashkin, 'Psychoanalysis', p. 62. In a book that claims the French have worked hard but not always productively on the memory politics of the Vichy period, Conan and Rousso offer an unusually frank/revisionist perspective on how this generation reads the violence of the mid-twentieth century. Rashkin's psychoanalytic framework strikes me as a careful analysis that does not seek to punish France so much as to understand the filmmaker's subtlety. See Conan, Éric and Henri Rousso (1998), *Vichy: An Ever-Present Past*, Hanover: Dartmouth College, University of New England Press, pp. 203–11.
27. Malle's context was the deportation of Jewish children from Paris in 1942 to Drancy and thence to Auschwitz, Madianek. Attempts to hide them were mainly short-lived.
28. Ian Serraillier (1956/2012), *The Silver Sword*, London: Jonathan Cape, p. 194.
29. UNICEF (1996), 'The Trauma of War'. Online: http://www.unicef.org/sowc96/7trauma.htm, accessed 7 September 2016 (UNICEF re-organisation of web pages underway 2017).
30. McAdam, Jane and Fiona Chong (2014), *Refugees: Why Seeking Asylum is Legal and Australia's Policies Are Not*, Sydney: UNSW Press, pp. 24, 101.
31. David Seymour/UNESCO (1949), *Children of Europe*, Paris: UNESCO, publication 403, p. 30. Online: http://unesdoc.unesco.org/images/0013/001332/133216eb.pdf, accessed 7 September 2016.

32. Anne Wilkes Tucker, Will Michaels and Natalie Zelt, *War Photography: Images of Armed Conflict and its Aftermath* (2012), Museum of Contemporary Art, Houston, New Haven: Yale University Press, p. 464.
33. Seymour/UNESCO: *Children of Europe*, p. 12, for further context see also Boaz Cohen and Rita Horvath (2010), 'Young witnesses in the DP camps: children's Holocaust testimony in context', *Journal of Modern Jewish Studies*, 11/1, pp. 103–25.
34. See notes 4 and 32.
35. 'The increasing number of child victims is primarily explained by the higher proportion of civilian deaths in recent conflicts. In the wars of the 18th, 19th and early 20th centuries, only about half the victims were civilians', UNICEF (1996) 'Children in War'. Online: http://www.unicef.org/sowc96/1cinwar.htm, accessed 7 September 2016 (UNICEF re-organisation of web pages underway 2017).
36. Gensburger uses photographic evidence to elucidate the removal of objects (theft) from Jewish French citizens as a crucial stage in the destruction of their human status by Vichy and the Reich. Sarah Gensburger (2014), 'Witnessing the looting of Jewish belongings during the Holocaust: what can history do with images?', *Dapim: Studies on the Holocaust*, 28/2, pp. 80, 89, 95. The rescue of children and other French Jews is discussed in Reneé Poznanski (2014), 'Anti-semitism and the rescue of Jews in France', in Jacques Semelin, Claire Andrieu and Sarah Gensburger (eds), *Resisting Genocide: The Multiple Forms of Rescue*, Oxford Scholarship Online, p. 2 ff.
37. Conversations with the film-maker in UNSW in 2014 and 2016 as part of the 'Dorothy Project'. See also the film's website http://oncemymother.com.au, accessed 16 September 2016.
38. Nirmal Puwar (2007), 'Social cinema scenes,' *Space and Culture*, 10, p. 254.
39. Stephanie Hemelryk Donald (2000), *Public Secrets, Public Spaces: Cinema and Civility in China*, Lanham Rowman and Littlefield, p. 117.
40. Stuart Hall (2004), *Calypso Kings*, in Michael Bull and Les Back (eds), *The Auditory Culture Reader*, Oxford: Berg, pp. 419–26. (Originally published in the *Guardian*, 27 June 2002.)
41. Elsaesser's theory of 'double occupancy' – a Europe where there is spatial (and Nestingen adds, temporal) dissonance between populations – is well interpreted in Nestingen's longer work on Kaurismäki's oeuvre, and in particular in his use of nostalgia for political comment. Andrew Nestingen (2013), *The Cinema of Ari Kaurismäki; Contrarian Stories*, New York: Bloomsbury, pp. 94–7. Another approach to the question of space and arrival is offered in McAllister's discussion of what she calls 'home territory asylum films', here contrasting local struggles with the macro-narratives of globalisation. Kirsten

Emiko McAllister (2011), 'Asylum in the margins of contemporary Britain: the spatial practices of desire in *Gypo*,' *Space and Culture*, 14/2, p. 166 ff.

42. Geoffrey Nowell Smith (2012), 'From realism to neo-realism,' in Lúcia Nagib, Chris Perriam and Rajinder Dudrah (eds), *Theorizing World Cinema*, New York: I.B.Tauris, p. 148.
43. Laura Rascaroli (2013), 'Becoming-minor in a sustainable Europe: the contemporary European art film and Aki Kaurismäki's *Le Havre*,' *Screen*, 54/3, p. 328.
44. Davina Quinlivan describes the suffocated child 'a little girl – lying down on the harbour' in her discussion of Lars von Trier, arguing that the missing child, deprived of breath, is fundamental to his work. Quinlivan (2012), *The Place of Breath in Cinema*, Edinburgh: Edinburgh University Press, p. 127 ff.
45. Mary Crock (2006), *Seeking Asylum Alone: A Study of Australian Law, Policy and Practice Regarding Unaccompanied and Separated Children*, Sydney: Themis Press.
46. Chang and Marcel's occupation references Vittorio de Sica's film, *Shoeshine* (1946), a neo-realist Italian drama about life on the edge of society (the shoeshines in de Sica are boys, and Kaurismäki by inference suggests the childlikeness of the principal adults in *Le Havre*).

Chapter 4: *Little Moth* and *The Road:* precarity, immobility and inertia

1. Cormac McCarthy (2006), *The Road*, London: Picador, p. 260.
2. For introductions to Chinese independent film in the twenty-first century see: Paul G. Pickowicz (2011), 'Independent Chinese film: seeing the not-usually-visible in rural China,' in C. Lynch, R.B. Marks and P.G. Pickowicz (eds), *Radicalism, Revolution, and Reform in Modern China*, Plymouth: Lexington, pp. 180–1; Yingjin Zhang (2012), 'Directors, aesthetics, genres: Chinese postsocialist cinema, 1979–2010', in Y. Wang (ed.), *A Companion to Chinese Cinema*, Oxford: Oxford University Press, p. 61; and on contemporary documentary: Luke Robinson (2013), *Independent Chinese Documentary: From the Studio to the Street*, London: Palgrave. In her analysis of the post-classical art film in Taiwan, Jean Ma points to the repetition of a motif of water (human, bodily and external) in the poetics of loneliness. Her insights serve to underline the contrastive dry, almost emotionless inertia of the mainland indie film as represented by *Peng Tao*. Jean Ma (2010), *Melancholy Drift: Marking Time in Chinese Cinema*, Hong Kong: Hong Kong University Press, pp. 86–7.

3. See the *Chinese Statistical Yearbook*, produced annually by provincial and national statisticians and state officers, for annual reports: http://www.stats.gov.cn/tjsj/ndsj/2014/indexeh.htm, accessed 10 January 2016.
4. See Marc Augé's fine thesis on non-place, Marc Augé (1995), *Non-Places: Introduction to an Anthropology of Super-Modernity* (trans. John Howe), London: Verso. Also, Dai Jinhua on visibility and disappearance for the working poor, 'Invisible writing: the politics of Chinese mass culture in the 1990s', in T.E. Barlow and J. Wang (trans.) (2002), *Cinema and Desire: Feminist Marxism and Cultural Politics in the Work of Dai Jinhua*, London: Verso, pp. 213–34; See also Stephanie Hemelryk Donald, 'Global Beijing: *The World* is a violent place', in C.P. Lindner (ed.) (2010), *Globalization, Violence and the Visual Culture of Cities*. London: Routledge, p. 123.
5. Augé, *Non-Places*, pp. 77–8.
6. Slavoj Žižek (2007), *Enjoy Your Symptom!: Jacques Lacan in Hollywood and Out*, London: Routledge Routledge Classics Edition, p. 131. Also '…the modern zombie is always connected to anxieties about enclosed spaces as well as the collapse of boundaries between interior and exterior in the context of modern urbanization … In every permutation of the zombie trope, the primary thematic concern has been the reestablishment of clear enclosures, the safeguarding of private property, and the raising of barriers that unambiguously resolve economic and social tensions'. Dan Hassler-Forest (2014), 'Zombie Spaces', in E.P. Comentale and A. Jaffe (eds), *The Year's Work at the Zombie Research Centre*, Bloomington: Indiana University Press, pp. 119–120. Or again, 'What the zombie outbreak narrative really reveals – as do all epidemics – is the shape of our networks and risky attachments, our sense of an incredibly fragile global ecology', Roger Luckhurst (2015), *Zombies: A Cultural History*, London: Reaktion Books, p. 183.
7. Vilém Flusser (2013), *The Freedom of the Migrant: Objections to Nationalism*, trans. Kenneth Kronenberg, Champaign, IL: University of Illinois Press, p. 6.
8. Ibid., p. 12.
9. Flusser, *The Freedom of the Migrant*.
10. Diana Coote (2010), 'The inertia of matter and the generativity of flesh,' in Diana Coote and S. Frost (eds), *'New Materialisms' Ontology, Agency and Politics*, Durham, NC: Duke University Press, p. 99 ff. (See also as quoted in Stephanie Hemelryk Donald (2014), 'Inertia and ethical urban relations: the living, the dying and the dead', in S.H. Donald and C.P. Lindner (eds), *Inert Cities: Globalization, Mobility and Suspension in Visual Culture*, London: I.B.Tauris, pp. 19–20.)
11. Ann Anagnost (2004), 'The corporeal politics of quality (*suzhi*)', *Public Culture*, 16/2, pp. 189–208; Terry E. Woronov (2009), 'Governing China's children: governmentality and "Education for Quality"', *Positions: East Asia*

Cultures Critique,17/3, pp. 567–89; Orna Naftali (2016), *Children in China*, London: Polity Press, pp. 75–6; Luigi Tomba (2009), 'Of quality, harmony, and community: civilisaion and the middle class in urban China', *positions*, 17/3, Andrew B. Kipnis (2006), '*Suzhi*: A keyword approach', *China Quarterly*, 186, pp. 295–313.

12. Loïc Wacquant (2008), *Urban Outcasts: A Comparative Sociology of Urban Marginality*, London: Polity, p. 163 ff.
13. Reform Era refers broadly to the decades following Mao's death (1976) and Deng Xiaoping's re-accession to power and the establishment of his economic model (1978–).
14. Tamara Jacka introduces the topic most effectively in an introduction to a special edition on suzhi as keyword: Tamara Jacka (2009), 'Cultivating citizens: *suzhi* (quality) discourse in the PRC', *positions*, 17/3, pp. 523–35; see also Yan Hairong (2003), 'Spectralization of the rural: reinterpreting the labor mobility of rural young women in post-Mao China', *American Ethnologist*, 30/4, pp. 1–19; and the useful shorthand: 'In popular usage, the notion of "lacking quality" is used to discriminate against rural migrants, litterbugs, the short, the nearsighted and the poorly dressed,' Kipnis: *Suzhi*, p. 296; also, Ann Anagnost (1997), 'Children and national transcendence in China,' in K.G. Lieberthal, SF. Lin, and E.P. Young (eds), *Constructing China: The Interaction of Culture and Economics*, Ann Arbor: University of Michigan Press, pp. 195–222.
15. I refer to an underground construction accident in March 2007 during preparations for the Beijing Olympics. Donald: 'Global Beijing', pp. 22–3; see also online news archives. Online: http://www.asianews.it/news-en/Beijing:-six-workers-condemned-to-death-to-cover-up-an-accident-8877.html, accessed 2 September 2016; and on the response to another subway collapse in Hangzhou 18 months later, Jing Xiaolei (2008), 'Tragedy prompts action, *Beijing Review* online, 48 (25 November). Online: http://www.bjreview.com.cn/nation/txt/2008-11/25/content_166482.htm, accessed 2 September 2016.
16. Social studies include: Jingzhong Ye and Lu, Pan (2011), 'Differentiated childhoods: impacts of rural labor migration on left-behind children in China', *Journal of Peasant Studies*, 38/ 2, pp. 355–77; Xiang Biao (2007), 'How far are the left-behind left behind? A preliminary study in rural China', *Population, Space and Place*, 13, pp. 179–91. Film studies are relatively new: Zitong Qiu and Maria Elena Indelicato (2017), 'Beiqing, kuqing and national sentimentality in Liu Junyi's *Left Behind Children*', in Stephanie Hemelryk Donald, Emma Wilson and Sarah Wright (eds), *Childhood and Nation in Contemporary World Cinema: Borders and Encounters*, New York: Bloomsbury.
17. Lu Xun (Hsun) (1921/1960/1972), 'My old home', *Selected Stories of Lu Hsun*, Beijing (Peking): Foreign Languages Press. *My Old Home* is a poignant and literal exposition of the rural-urban class divide, and it is semi auto-biographical

in content and tone. Readers are also pointed to *The True Story of Ah Q*, a key modernist work in contemporary Chinese fiction, and as described by Zhang Xudong, a work of exemplary stature to which *Little Moth* might rightly be said to aspire, 'No other works in modern Chinese literary history even come close to Ah Q's literary and political intensity and popularity, which seem to have crystallized into a monad, a pure thought-image capable of confronting History – both in the ahistorical sense as tradition, culture, and morality and in the historicist sense as process, scheme, and the new as the next – by means of its allegorical complexity and simplicity in one'. Zhang Xudong (2012), 'The will to allegory and the origin of Chinese modernism: rereading Lu Xun's Ah Q – the real story', in M. Wolleager and M. Eatough, *The Oxford Handbook of Global Modernisms*, Oxford: Oxford University Press, p. 2 (online version). Online: http://www.oxfordhandbooks.com/view/10.1093/oxfordhb/9780195338904.001.0001/oxfordhb-9780195338904-e-7?print=pdf, accessed 16 September 2016. For Lu Xun, the rural type and historical context, see Andrew F. Jones (2002), 'The child as history in republican China: a discourse on development', *positions: east asia cultures critique*, 10/3, p. 696.

18. Lauren Berlant (2011), *Cruel Optimism*, Durham, NC: Duke University Press, p. 31. I would like to thank Toronto colleagues at The Culture of Cities Center, Alan Blum and Elke Grenzer and their students and colleagues, for early comments on this discussion, Toronto, July 2013.

19. The literature on *guanxi* is extensive. Suggested readings for those addressing the term for the first time: Mayfair Mei-hui Yang (1994), *Gifts, Favors and Banquets: The Art of Social Relationships in China*, Ithaca, NY: Cornell. A collection, published a decade later than Yang's work, pays particular heed to the impact of reform policies and economics on older networks of exchange: Thomas Gold, Doug Guthrie, and David Wank (eds) (2004), *Social Connections in China: Institutions, Culture and the Changing Nature of Guanxi*, Cambridge: Cambridge University Press. An essay which discusses how much *guanxi* is reliant on socio-somatic integrity (and conversely how it can fall foul of social trauma) is presciently relevant for *Little Moth*: Arthur Kleinman and Joan Kleinman (1994), 'How bodies remember: social memory and bodily experience of criticism, resistance, and delegitimisation following China's Cultural Revolution', *New Literary History*, 25/3/1, p. 713.

20. On brotherhood and lasting trust, see Yang: *Gifts*, pp. 119–20.

21. As a film researcher in the late 1990s I gave an Australian leather cowboy hat to an aged actor/director who liked cowboy films. He wore it for the rest of the day and extended our interview from one hour to six (plus lunch and dinner). We had made a connection. Had I ever had the power to do anything more for him I would have done it. I had (happily) signed up for that responsibility by researching, choosing and gifting the hat, listening to his talk all day,

meeting his sick wife and eating his food. My commitment was soon tested when a Party official telephoned and required my research assistant to attend a meeting that the official had arranged unexpectedly. I couldn't go at that point, and she didn't go. We were both in trouble with the Party authority figure and with my assistant's well-placed uncle, who had of course used his own *guanxiwang* to get the unexpected meeting scheduled. I give an example of a foreign researcher making a strong contact with an interviewee, not because this is an example of strong *guanxi* (I would be leaving the country only a few weeks later) but because it indicates the sophistication of the gift culture, the importance of performing *guanxi* in the enactment of social relations and the links between transactional arrangements and human feeling (*renqing*). Andrew Kipnis (2004), 'Practices of *guanxi* production and practices of *ganqing* avoidance', in Gold, Guthrie and Wank, *Social Connections*, p. 24 and passim.

22. Gold, Guthrie and Wank, *Social Connections*, p. 3.
23. Wolfgang Mieder (2016), *Tradition and Innovation in Folk Literature*, Oxford: Routledge, p. 179.
24. These struggles also refer back to the anarchy of the Cultural Revolution period. For an account of clan warfare and its role in the Cultural Revolution (based on older traditions of inter-clan rural warfare) see Su Yang (2011), *Collective Killings in Rural China during the Cultural Revolution*, Cambridge: Cambridge University Press, pp. 86–9; see also chapter three of Jonathan Unger (2002), *The Transformation of Rural China*, New York: M.E. Sharpe, pp. 49–56.
25. As with work on *guanxi* and *suzhi* the literature on contemporary class emergence in China post Reform is immense: David S.G. Goodman (2008), 'Why China has no new middle class: cadres, managers and entrepreneurs,' in David S.G. Goodman (ed), *The New Rich in China: Future Rulers, Present Lives*, London: Routledge, pp. 23–37; the middle class being a grouping that Goodman essentially critiques as a construct of Party discourse: see also David S.G. Goodman, *Class in Contemporary China*, Cambridge: Polity, p. 106; Luigi Tomba's work on middle-class aspirations and quality, Tomba, 'Of quality, harmony and community' (ff. 12), pp. 591–616; and Liu Xinyu's film-based discussion of the ruination of the industrial working class through reforms to state industry, Liu Xinyu (2005), 'Ruins of the future: class and history in Wang Bing's Tiexi district', *New Left Review*, 31, pp. 125–36.
26. Terry E. Woronov (2004), 'In the eye of the chicken: hierarchy and marginality among Beijing's migrant schoolchildren', *Ethnography*, 5/3, p. 290.
27. Limin Bai (2008), 'Children as the youthful hope of an old Empire: race, nationalism, and elementary education in China 1895–1915,' *The Journal of the History of Childhood and Youth*, 1/2, pp. 210–31; a full collection and historical range of perspectives on childhood and filial and imperial duty presented in the now classic, Behnke Kinney, Anne (1995), *Chinese Views of Childhood*,

Honolulu: Hawaii University Press. On the continuation of childhood responsibility to the nation, Terry E. Woronov (2007), 'Performing the nation, China's children as Little Red Pioneers,' *Anthropological Quarterly*, 80/3, pp. 65–71.

28. *The Yellow Balloon* is discussed in Karen Lury's keynote address 'Children, objects and motion ... balloons, bikes, kites and tethered flight', at Royal Holloway London, 19 April 2016. Audiofile available online at http://childnationcinema.org/events/international-conference/, accessed 10 June 2016. The key scene shows two boys playing with a balloon in bombed-out buildings in London. One boy falls from the building and is killed, abruptly altering the mood of the film.
29. Vicky Lebeau (1995), *Lost Angels: Psychoanalysis and Cinema*, London: Routledge, pp. 120–51.
30. Ibid., pp. 12–22.
31. Ibid., p. 134.
32. Markus P.J. Bohland and Sean Moreland (2014), '"If you rip the fronts off houses": killing innocence in Alfred Hitchcock's *Shadow of a Doubt* (1943)', in D. Olsen (ed.), *Children in the Films of Alfred Hitchcock*, New York: Palgrave, pp. 92–3.
33. Hannah Kilduff (2017), 'The child as hyphen: Yamina Benguigui's *Inch'allah Dimanche*', in Stephanie Hemelryk Donald, Emma Wilson and Sarah Wright (eds), *Childhood and Nation*, London: Bloomsbury, p. 209.
34. Karen Lury has suggested there is a link between the toy that moves the child along (a balloon) and the kind of breathless suspended energy that propels their physical motion. Lury, 'Children, objects and motion ...'.
35. In Chinese films (from *The Kite*, 1950s, to *The Yellow Kite*, 1980s, and *The Blue Kite*, 1993) the kite – a toy that requires us to run if it is to fly – exemplifies childhood and the loss of childhood as a heterospectic return.
36. Bohland and Moreland: 'Killing innocence', pp. 87–8.
37. Anne Behnke Kinney (1995), 'Dyed silk, Han notions of the moral development of children,' in Behnke Kinney, *Chinese Views of Childhood*, pp. 30–3.
38. McCarthy, *The Road*, p. 230.
39. Gaston Bachelard (1960), *The Poetics of Reverie: Childhood, Language and the Cosmos*, (trans. David Russell, 1971), Boston, MA: Beacon Press, p. 108.
40. Bachelard's attempt to place an adult within reach of the child self, through reverie, is nicely captured in the work of a human geographer, Chris Philo (2003), '"To go back up the side hill", memories, imaginations and reveries of childhood,' *Children's Geographies*, 1/1, pp. 11–12.
41. Kevin Kearney (2012), 'Cormac McCarthy's *The Road* and the frontier of the human,' *Lit: Literature Interpretation Theory*, 23/2, p. 161 (quoting McCarthy, *The Road*, p. 198).
42. Ibid., p. 166.

43. McCarthy, *The Road*, p. 82.
44. Ben De Bruyn (2010), 'Borrowed time, borrowed world and borrowed eyes: care, ruin and vision in McCarthy's *The Road* and Harrison's Ecocriticism', *English Studies*, 91/7 (November 2010).
45. Ibid., p. 780.
46. Lebeau, *Lost Angels*, p. 134.
47. Kearney, 'Cormac McCarthy's *The Road*', p. 161.
48. Ibid., p. 166.
49. The Gospel according to John, 11:1–43, The New Testament; Max Silverman (2015), *Palimpsestic Memory: The Holocaust and Colonialism in French and Francophone Fiction and Film*, Oxford: Berghahn, pp. 40–1, 58.
50. Paul Sheehan (2012), 'Road, fire, trees: Cormac McCarthy's post-America,' in Julian Murphet and Mark Steven (eds), *Styles of Extinction: Cormac McCarthy's The Road*, London: Continuum), p. 95.
51. Sara Simcha Cohen (2013), *Hearth of Darkness: the Familiar, the Familial, and the Zombie*, PhD Diss. Submitted to University of California, p. 6. Accessed via Proquest.
52. Bram Stoker (1993/1897), *Dracula*. London: Wordsworth Editions, p. 124.
53. Mark C. Anderson (2014), 'Zombies and cowboys: how to win the apocalypse', *European Scientific Journal*, 2 (September), pp. 207–15.
54. Jean-Michel Frodon (2010), 'Referent images', in Frodon J.M. (ed.), *Cinema and the Shoah: An Art Confronts the Tragedy of the Twentieth Century* (trans. A. Harrison and T. Mes), New York: SUNY Press, p. 225.
55. Cohen, *Hearth of Darkness*, p. 9.
56. Amelia Gentleman (2016), 'Hungry, scared and no closer to safety: child refugees failed by Britain', *Guardian* online (Australian edition). Online: https://www.theguardian.com/world/2016/aug/02/child-refugees-calais-failed-by-britain, accessed 2 August 2016.
57. Mark M. Anderson (2007), 'The child victim as witness to the Holocaust: an American story?', *Jewish Social Studies*, 14/1, p. 3.
58. Ibid., pp. 13–14.
59. Surely a reference to Nevil Shute's novel of apocalypse, *On The Beach* (1957).

Chapter 5: *Landscape in the Mist*

1. An earlier version of this chapter was published as '*Landscape in the Mist*: thinking beyond the perimeter fence', in Angelos Koutsourakis and Mark Steven (eds) (2015), *The Cinema of Theo Angelopoulos*, Edinburgh: Edinburgh University Press. I am deeply grateful for the editors' original input and assistance in thinking about the film.

2. For a succinct discussion of Greek history in the twentieth and twenty-first centuries, as explored in Angelopoulos' films, see Angelos Koutsourakis and Mark Steven (2015), 'Angelopoulos and the lingua franca of modernism', in Koutsourakis and Steven, *Angelopoulos*, pp. 2 and 10–15.
3. 'With growing numbers of child deaths at sea, UN agencies call for enhancing safety for refugees and migrants,' Press Release, UNHCR, 19 February 2016. Available online: http://www.unhcr.org/news/press/2016/2/56c6e7676/growing-numbers-child-deaths-sea-un-agencies-call-enhancing-safety-refugees.html, accessed 10 September 2016.
4. Dan Georgakas (2015), 'Megalexandros: authoritarianism and national identity,' in Koutsourakis and Steven, *Angelopoulos*, p. 129.
5. For Angelopoulos' views on the connection between the two films see: Godas, 'The kids take the taste of life … the same happens in the scene of the rape; Voula perceives the hardness of the world.' Christos Godas (2012), 'The Cinema File: the interview', 6/22, *Scholars Association News, International Online Magazine* (May). Online http://www.onassis.org/online-magazine/issue-22/article-6.php, accessed 22 September 2016.
6. Kathleen Murphy (1990), 'Children of paradise', *Film Comment*, 26/6, p. 38.
7. See Godas, *Interview*.
8. Wolfram Schütte (1992), 'Ein zeitreisender Landvermesser', in P.W. Jansen and W. Schütte (eds), *Theo Angelopoulos: Reihe Film 45*, p. 37. The substance of the piece is translated in an online source, Wolfram Schütte, 'Theo Angelopoulos: land-surveyor and time-traveler', http://zakka.dk/euroscreenwriters/interviews/theo_angelopoulos.htm, accessed 16 September 2016.
9. See Chapter 3.
10. Heather Crawley, (n.d.), Gender-related persecution and women's claims to asylum, online information tool, http://www.refugeelegalaidinformation.org/gender-related-persecution-and-womens-claims-asylum, accessed 2 August 2016.
11. i Ταξίδι στα Κύθηρα (*Voyage to Cythera*, 1984), in Το Μετέωρο Βήμα του Πελαργού (*The Suspended Step of the Stork*, 1991), and in Μια Αιωνιότητα και μια Μέρα (*Eternity and a Day*, 1998).
12. Electra is the daughter of Agamemnon and Clytemnestra and the sister of Orestes. In the version of her story as told by Sophocles, she is a passionate, angry woman, obsessed with the memory of her brother and intent on his duty to avenge their father when he returns from exile.
13. Godas, *Interview*.
14. Some writers refer to Angelopoulos as a secular film-maker, but I take my lead from conversations with Vrasidas Karalis who sees a strong Orthodox sentiment in his work, and which I believe is apparent in *Landscape*. He calls the film a 'metaphysical road movie' and asks 'is this the tree in the garden of Eden,

or the luminous tree at the end of Andrey Tarkovsky's *Sacrifice*?', Vrasidas Karalis (2012), *A History of Greek Cinema*, London: Continuum, p. 225.
15. Vassilis Rafailidis (2003), Ταξίδι στο μύθο Δια της ιστορίας και στην ιστορία δια του μύθου (Into the Myth), Athens: Aigokeros, p. 82 (English translation of quotation provided by Angelos Koutsoukaris).
16. Schütte, 'Landvermesser', p. 36.
17. The Book of Genesis 2:17. The first book of the Old Testament, accepted as a 'Law' book by Orthodox Christians. 'The origin of the Orthodox Christian Faith is the self-disclosure of God', is a founding principle that indicates the importance of the Father and revelation in Greek Orthodoxy, Greek Orthodox Diocese of America, 'Our Faith'. Online: http://www.goarch.org/ourfaith/ourfaith7062, accessed 21 September 2016.
18. The Book of Revelations 22:14 (the last book of the New Testament). It is the book that marks the cusp between Judaic tradition and Helenic influence on the early Church.
19. Nikos Kolovos (1990), Θόδωρος Αγγελόπουλος (*Theo Angelopoulos*), Athens: Aigokeros, p. 174. In-text translation provided by Angelos Koutsoukaris.
20. Robert Sinnerbrink (2015), 'Angelopoulos' gaze: modernism, history, cinematic ethics,' in Angelos Koutsoukaris and Mark Steven (eds), *Angelopoulos*, p. 89.
21. Simeon Karafolas (1998), 'Migrant Remittances in Greece and Portugal: Distribution by Country of Provenance and the Role of the Banking Presence', *International Migration*, 36/3, pp. 358–60.
22. John Durham Peters (1999), 'Exile, nomadism and diaspora: the stakes of mobility in the western canon', in Hamid Naficy (ed.), *Home, Exile, Homeland: Film, Media and the Politics of Place*, New York and London: Routledge, p. 20 ff.
23. Hamid Naficy (2001), *An Accented Cinema: Exilic and Diasporic Film*, Princeton: Princeton University Press, p. 219.
24. Murphy, 'Children of Paradise', p. 38.
25. The Gospel according to Luke, 15:24. The New Testament.
26. Joanne Faulkner (2010), *The Importance of Being Innocent: Why We Worry about Children*, Cambridge: Cambridge University Press, p. 127.
27. Adam Phillips (2002), *Equals*, New York: Basic Books, p. 17.
28. Murphet, Julian (2015), 'Cinematography of the group: Angelopoulos and the collective subject of cinema', in A. Koutsourakis and M. Steven (eds), *Angelopoulos*, pp. 162, 168.
29. Jacques Rancière (2009), *The Emancipated Spectator*, trans. Gregory Elliott, London: Verso, p. 107.
30. Hanneke Grootenboer (2011), 'The pensive image: on thought in Jan van Huysum's still life paintings,' *Oxford Art Journal*, 34/1, p. 17.
31. Composer: Eleni Karaindrou.

32. Godas, *Interview*.
33. Naomi Schor (2001), 'Pensive texts and thinking statues: Balzac with Rodin', *Critical Inquiry*, 27/2 (Winter) p. 241.
34. Ibid., p. 240.
35. Andrew Horton (1997), *The Films of Theo Angelopoulos: A Cinema of Contemplation*, Princeton: Princeton University Press.
36. Meir Wigoder (2012), 'The acrobatic gaze and the pensive image in Palestinian morgue photography', *Critical Inquiry*, 38/2, p. 270; see also Roland Barthes (1977/1981), *Camera Lucida–Reflections on Photography*, New York: Hill and Wang.
37. Leo Charney (1998), *Empty Moments: Cinema, Modernity and Drift*, Durham NC: Duke University Press, p. 64.

Chapter 6: *The Leaving of Liverpool*: Empire and religion, poetry and the archive

1. Bertolt Brecht (1947), 'Children's Crusade, 1939', in *Selected Poems of Bertolt Brecht*, (trans. H.R. Hays), New York: Harvest.
2. Prior to the Australian passage, children were sent to Canada. This poem is quoted in a letter from child migrant 'T.C.', Canada, 1890, back to the Liverpool Home from whence he had been sent out, and quoted in an annual report of the Father Berry Homes. Nugent Archives.
3. *The Leaving of Liverpool* was shot in New South Wales, Australia and Liverpool, UK in 1991, and screened as a television mini-series on the Australian Broadcasting Company (ABC) in July 1992. The producer was Steve Knapman, the director, Michael Jenkins, and the writers, Sue Smith and John Alsop. The ABC co-produced the series with the BBC (UK). The ABC funded all production costs whilst BBC Enterprises managed overseas sales. Gerard Knapp (1991), 'On location: *The Leaving of Liverpool*, – *Leaving* uncovers child abuse' *Encore*, 8/18, (15–28 November), cover and p. 6. The show was not screened on British television until 1993, a decision that the producer felt was linked to concerns about the Republican leanings of the male character Bert, in the final sequences of the final episode. 'It is very political and the depiction of a boy turning from a patriot to a republican who tries physically to attack the Queen is controversial,' Tina Ogle (1993), 'Ship of Sorrows', *Time Out* (14–21 July), p. 147.
4. The history of child migration to the colonies spans three centuries, and includes earlier forced migration to Australia through the deportation of convicts (that commenced shortly after the English invasion of Aboriginal land in 1788). Some first arrivals and subsequent convicts were under 16 years old, and

of that number some were as young as nine. Kate Darien-Smith, 'Childhood', *Online Dictionary of Sydney*. Online: http://dictionaryofsydney.org/entry/children#, accessed 10 August 2016. In addition to archival material, accounts of child removals through institutional schemes to send labour and young 'white' colonists to the colonies are included in the autobiographical transcripts of interviews collected in New South Wales: Stewart Lee, transcript online at: http://www.migrationheritage.nsw.gov.au/cms/wp-content/uploads/2009/11/Fairbridge11-StewartLee.pdf; David Hill (2007), *The Forgotten Children: Fairbridge Farm School and its betrayal of Australia's Child Migrants*, Sydney: Random House; in an accessible novel, Robert Dinsdale (2013), *Little Exiles*, Sydney: Harper Collins; and in scholarly works: Gordon Lynch (2014), 'Saving the child for the sake of the nation: moral framing and the civic, moral and religious redemption of children,' *American Journal of Cultural Sociology*, 2/2, pp. 165–96; Shurlee Swain and Margot Hillel (2010), *Child, Nation, Race, and Empire: Child Rescue Discourse, England, Canada and Australia, 1850–1915*, Manchester: Manchester University Press.

5. The mini-series provides an example of the 'degree to which international co-production can advance an organic and critically revisionist, yet popular, sense of multicultural contemporary Australia', Stuart Cunningham and Elizabeth Jacka (1996), *Australian Television and International Mediascapes*, Cambridge: Cambridge University Press, pp. 78, 79, 123, and quote p. 249. The series was part of a 'ratings move by the ABC to create good content' to fight issues of debt and falling advertising revenue, Tom O'Regan (1993), *Australian Television Culture*, Sydney: Allen and Unwin, p. 51.

6. '… it out-rated every other network and was the top-rating mini-series of that year,' Steve Knapman quoted in Ogle: *Encore*, p. 147.

7. Thanks to the ACMI archive and Mediatheque in Melbourne for access to the original letterbox version of both two-hour films that make up the mini-series, and to the AFI archive held at RMIT University also in Melbourne, for access to scripts, press releases and press cuttings. Images were collected through the writer Sue Smith and Lisa French (also RMIT).

8. In 2010, then UK Prime Minister Gordon Brown apologised to British child migrants, noting that the abuse of their childhoods occurred 'in the memories of most of us here today,' and that, 'as children, your voices were not always heard', Child Migrants Trust (CMT), Gordon Brown 'Apology to child migrants', 10 March 2010. Online: http://www.childmigrantstrust.com/news/number10govuk--apology-issued-to-child-migrants, accessed 15 September 2016. The apology was the result of interventions and activism, notably led by the British social worker Margaret Humphreys, whose book *Empty Cradles* (London: Doubleday, 1994) exposed the systematic emigration of children from institutional care. Humphreys also set up the Child Migrants Trust. The

film *Oranges and Sunshine* (Loach, 2010) was based on her experience and those adult survivors with whom she worked in Australia and the UK. For a broad reading of activism and film in Europe see Leshu Torchin (2012), *Creating the Witness: Documenting Genocide on Film, Video and the Internet*, Minneapolis: University of Minnesota Press.
9. For an elaborated discussion on the long-term impact of displacement (post-severe trauma) on families also Marianne Hirsch (2012), *The Generation of Postmemory: Writing and Visual Culture after the Holocaust*, New York: Columbia; and an auto-ficto-biography on a Cambodian survivor: Alice Pung (2011), *Her Father's Daughter*, Melbourne: Black Ink.
10. Jason Hart (2014), 'Children and forced migration', in Elena Fiddian-Qasmiyeh, Gil Loescher, Katy Long and Nando Sigona (eds), *The Oxford Handbook of Refugee and Forced Migration Studies*, Oxford: Oxford University Press, p. 386.
11. Gary Dickson (2007), *The Children's Crusade: Mediaeval History, Modern Mythistory*, Basingstoke: Palgrave Books, pp. 9–14.
12. Ibid., p. 171.
13. Ibid., p. 91.
14. Ibid., p. 142.
15. I include media information here from 2016 as it is not a phenomenon that can be ignored, the counter-rhetorics of a caliphate and child martyrs is too striking to ignore, although with the proviso that longer-term research is required to determine the way in which these children locate within the Pied Piper analogies of the twelfth century. The girl at the centre of the Bethnal Green (2015) investigation, Kadiza Sultana, was reported killed in August 2016. Online http://www.itv.com/news/2016-08-11/bethnal-green-schoolgirl-kadiza-sultana-who-joined-islamic-state-killed-in-airstrike-in-syria/, 11 August 2016, accessed 29 September 2016.
16. Dickson, *The Children's Crusade*, p. 153. A London-based organisation that focuses on countering radicalisation of the young for military purposes cites the Ottoman levy system devised by the Emperor Murad (1326–89) as an inspiration for contemporary kidnapping of Yezidi and Turkmen children for training as soldiers. They also point to distinct differences in the cultural origins and outcomes of the practice for the boys in the fourteenth century onwards against children taken by Daesh today, who 'are more likely to end up as cannon fodder.' Noman Benotman and Nikita Malik (2016), *The Children of Islamic State*, London: Quilliam Foundation, p. 24 (research supported by UNESCO and the UN Office of the Special Representatives of the Secretary-General for Children and Armed Conflict. Available online: https://www.quilliamfoundation.org/wp/wp-content/uploads/publications/free/the-children-of-islamic-state.pdf, accessed 29 September 2016.

17. A measured assessment and description of the policy of offshore assessment and detention of asylum seekers arriving by boat is provided on the Australian Government's own website. Janet Phillips (2012), 'The Pacific Solution revisited: a statistical guide to the asylum seeker caseloads on Nauru and Manus Island.' Report published 4 September 2012. Online: http://parlinfo.aph.gov.au/parlInfo/download/library/prspub/1893669/upload_binary/1893669.pdf;fileType=application percent2Fpdf.

   The policy has provoked increasing legal, medical and popular criticism as detention has continued and impacts on inmates have been proven dangerous to mental health and general wellbeing. Paul Farrell, Nick Evershed and Helen Davidson (2016), 'The Nauru Files: cache of 2000 leaked reports reveal scale of abuse of children in Australian offshore detention', *Guardian* online, 10 August 2016. Online: https://www.theguardian.com/australia-news/2016/aug/10/the-nauru-files-2000-leaked-reports-reveal-scale-of-abuse-of-children-in-australian-offshore-detention, accessed 16 August 2016. A policy response from The Refugee Council promotes an integrated regional response that does not include detention: *Thinking Beyond Offshore Processing: key recommendations from the Refugee Council of Australia*, 12 September 2016, Online: http://www.refugeecouncil.org.au/getfacts/seekingsafety/asylum/offshore-processing/thinking-beyond-offshore-processing-key-recommendations-refugee-council-australia/, accessed 29 September 2016. This builds on an Australian Human Rights Commission report, Gillian Triggs (2014), *The Forgotten Children: National Inquiry into Immigration Detention*. Sydney: HRC. Online: www.humanrights.gov.au/sites/default/files/document/publication/forgotten_children_2014.pdf, accessed 20 September 2016.

18. Ira Katznelson (2003), *Desolation and Enlightenment: Political Knowledge after Total War, Totalitarianism and the Holocaust*, New York: Columbia University Press, p. 50.

19. Swain and Hillel, *Child, Nation, Race and Empire* pp. 88–99 (Canada); and a history of child migration schemes in New South Wales. A complete research guide, (pls note) authorised by the historian of the Catholic Church in Australia, Barry Coldrey, available online at http://guides.naa.gov.au/good-british-stock/index.aspx, accessed 12 May 2016. For an account of the emigration of Catholic children from the 1880s through to the 1920s, see various papers in the Nugent archive (NCA165). 'Father Nugent escorted the first party of Catholic children to Canada 18 August 1870' [NB. Dr Barnardo's had started a similar project in 1882], Bennett, Rev. John, 'The hierarchy and the poor, 1850–1950', typed manuscript, pp. 25–6. (Ref. NCA122). Bennett, Rev. John, 'Emigration of Catholic boys and girls' (pamphlet of The Catholic Emigration Association, reprinted from *The Christian Democrat*, 1929). Thirty five years later the same Rev (now

Monsignor) Bennett visited Australia 'to see relatives and also to gather impressions in the field of migration being closely concerned for the last forty years' (letter to the Archbishop elect of Liverpool G.A. Beck, dated 25 February 1964). Rev. John Bennett (b. 1891 in Skirton, Lancs.) is a useful case study as he had himself lost a parent when young and experienced poverty, fostering and then travel as a soldier, before studying for the priesthood and serving the poor in the Liverpool parish of Bootle. He had experienced displacement as a child and clearly felt it was an appropriate response to the poverty of other Catholics.

20. Imogen Tyler, Nick Gill, Deirdre Conlon and Ceri Oeppen (2014), 'The business of child detention: charitable co-option, migrant advocacy and activist outrage', *Race and Class*, 56/3, pp. 4–6.
21. Ibid., p. 6.
22. Peter Fryer (2010), *Staying Power: The History of Black People in Britain*, London: Pluto Press, p. 60. See also p. 53 ff.
23. Kenneth Morgan (1992), 'Bristol and the Atlantic trade in the eighteenth century', *The English Historical Review*, 107/424, pp. 626–7 and 632.
24. Kenneth Morgan (2016), 'Building British Atlantic Port Cities: Bristol and Liverpool in the Eighteenth Century', in D. Maudlin and B.L. Herman (eds), *Building the British Atlantic World: Spaces, Places and Material Culture, 1600–1850*, Chapel Hill, NC, North Carolina Press, pp. 219–22.
25. According to M.J.D. Roberts, Victorian society was '… a society in which the ideal of individual moral responsibility was gladly accepted among citizens, in which the legitimacy of voluntary associational effort was conceded almost unconditionally, in which the privileges of status were widely accepted as having been earned by conscientious discharge of public duty, and in which there flourished a sense of moral community restored. By the 1880s, it was clear, moral reform voluntarism had successfully entrenched itself as a distinctive – perhaps a defining – characteristic of English public self-image.' M.J.D. Roberts (2004), *Cambridge Social and Cultural Histories: Making English Morals: Voluntary Association and Moral Reform in England, 1787–1886*. Cambridge, Cambridge University Press, pp. 245–6.
26. See lecture notes, Sarah Wise, 'Annie MacPherson and the Gutter children'. Online: http://spitalfieldslife.com/2015/11/25/annie-macpherson-the-gutter-children/, accessed 10 July 2016.
27. Swain and Hillel, *Child, Nation, Race and Empire*, p. 115.
28. Lynch, 'Saving the child', p. 166.
29. *On Their Own: Britain's Child Migrants* (Curator: Kim Tao, Post Federation Migration Australian Maritime Museum in association with The Maritime Museum, Liverpool UK (2011–14) and The Museum of Childhood, Bethnal Green (2015–16)).

Australian installations on tour are recorded on the Immigration Museum Website, Melbourne. Online: https://museumvictoria.com.au/immigration-museum/discoverycentre/stolen-childhoods/, accessed 8 March 2015. The Liverpool installation placed child migration very close to the spot where children would have boarded ships to make the journey to Australia. The Bethnal Green installation (co-curated by Gordon Lynch) broadened the references to the motivations of men and women pushing for migration, and brought in the voices of more survivors as well as stronger emphasis on the voices of the philanthropists and Empire builders.

30. Lynch, 'Saving the child', pp. 165–6.
31. See previous note 22. Bennett noted that Barnardo's work was a response to the awful conditions he encountered as a trainee doctor in London, conditions which changed his original intention to serve as a missionary abroad to one serving the poor at home (and then sending some of them overseas). Bennett, who seems mainly interested in the religious aspect of migration rather than any consideration of Empire building, specifically criticised Dr Barnardo whom he felt ignored the wishes of the Catholic church by at first ignoring children's birth religion in his work, 'in 1887 he admitted that one fifth of the children he rescued were baptised Catholics … he was an extreme Protestant with a missionary zeal who had come to London to Dublin to prepare himself in the London hospital for work in China as a medical missionary … He was an autocrat brooking no interference who regarded it as his bounden duty to bring up all in the religion which he followed.' Rev. John Bennett, 'The hierarchy and the poor', pp. 21–2.
32. Gordon Lynch (2016), *Remembering Child Migration: Faith, Nation-Building and the Wounds of Charity*, London: Bloomsbury, pp. 53–61. Also Lynch, Gordon, 'Child migration schemes to Australia: an historical overview,' undated PDF, lodged on the University of Kent repository. Online: https://kar.kent.ac.uk/47772/1/British%20child%20migration%20schemes%20to%20Australia%20-%20a%20historical%20overview.docx.pdf, accessed 15 July 2016. In a public lecture on the exhibition, Lynch revisited this theme with a passionate denunciation also of the British establishment which connived with the Australian Government to suppress a damning report on the 'homes' in order to save embarrassment to the Royal Family who had supported the Australian initiative (Museum of Childhood, Bethnal Green, 11 June 2016).
33. Giorgio Agamben (1999), *Remnants of Auschwitz: The Witness and the Archive*, New York: Zone Books, p. 24.
34. Reports of emigration held at Nugent archive (NCA 002), Records of the Catholic Reformatory Association 1864–1885; (NCA 005). Records and annual reports of the Father Berry's Homes 1892–1904. '68 boys have emigrated since 1879 and only 3 of those who have remained abroad, as far as I

have been able to ascertain, have been reconvicted – two for riding in a Freight Car from Toronto to Montreal without paying any fare, and the third boy was convicted of stealing.' 22nd Report, presented at annual meeting 26 February 1885, p. 17.

35. Notes on *The Clarence* (opened 15 August 1864) in the Catholic Reformatory Association annual report 1864. Two succeeding ships were destroyed by fire by the boys. 'Destructive fire on board the Reformatory Clarence', *Liverpool Mercury*, 18 January 1884.

36. Arthur Chilton Thomas (1904), 'Wise imperialism: on the advantage of child emigration within the bounds of Empire', public address given to the Catholic Emigration Society, Southport, 25 May. The organisation came under the auspices of The Liverpool Catholic Children's Protection Society. 'For the protection of Catholic children in their religion and from destitution by means of emigration'. Est 1881.

37. The deportees included Irish rebels and their 'widows and orphans', 'shipped wholesale in the Cromwellian period to the West Indies – the boys for slaves – the women and girls for mistresses to the English sugar planters.' Jamie Davie Butler (1896), 'British convicts shipped to American colonies', *The American Historical Review*, 2/1, p. 19. Darien-Smith, 'Childhood': 'It was not until 1847 that British criminal law distinguished between children and adult offenders. Children under 14 years, however, could still be sent to prison until the 1908 Children's Act'.

38. (NCA005) Rev. E. Bans and Arthur Chilton Thomas write, in a supplement on 'Catholic Child Emigration to Canada', that the scarcity of placements in Catholic institutions is a great problem and that children are better off leaving England because they face moral downfall in England. They are also impressed that there are more Catholic clergy per head of population in Canada than in England, Father Berry's Homes, Tenth Annual Report, 1902, pp. 1–5.

39. Victoria Mence, Simone Gengell and Ryan Tebb (2015), *A History of the Department of Immigration: Managing Migration to Australia*, Canberra: Australian Government.

40. I recorded, informally of course, that Lynch's passion when talking about the Ross Report (1955) and the failure to act on its findings (British civil servants and Menzies being crucial players in the cover-up) communicated a welcome solidarity to child migrant survivors present at his lecture (June 2016).

41. Lynch, *Remembering Child Migration*, p. 120.

42. Gwenda Tavan (2012), 'Leadership: Arthur Calwell and the post-war immigration program', *Australian Journal of Politics & History*, 58/2, pp. 204–206.

43. Australian Government, (2009), 'Apology to the forgotten Australians and former child migrants', Canberra, 16 November. Online: https://www.dss.gov.au/our-responsibilities/families-and-children/programs-services/

apology-to-the-forgotten-australians-and-former-child-migrants, accessed 1 October 2016.
44. Mence et al., *A History*, p. 39. See also: Barry Coldrey, Chapter Three, *Good British Stock: Child and Youth Migration to Australia*, National Archives of Australia. Online: http://guides.naa.gov.au/good-british-stock/chapter3/bigbrother.aspx, accessed 5 April 2016.
45. The St Vincent's House for Working Boys sought to provide secure shelter and some education to assist boys in reasonable employment to progress, to graduate boys 'from the street' through to 'respectability'. St Barnard's Home was a 'Training Home'. St Philip's House (established 1892) held 60 beds for street-trading boys, six pence a day for bed and board (eight pence with hot lunch). First annual reports: 1892–3. Nugent Archive NCA 005, p. 10. Father Berry also set up St James' House for Penniless Boys (a night shelter), but the cost of all these ventures exceeded the charity of the Catholic gentry. In 1895 Berry reports, 'The year has not been one of financial success. I am over 400 in debt, not to speak of a mortgage of 600 on the Home in Everton St.' Third Annual Report, p. 4. In the fourth annual report (1897), Berry confesses himself personally in debt to nearly 900 pounds, and later retires in ill health due to stress.
46. Colin McMahon (2014), 'Recrimination and reconciliation: Great Famine memory in Liverpool and Montreal at the turn of the twentieth century', *Atlantic Studies*, 11/3, p. 354 ff.

In 1899, the Catholic newspaper *The Tablet* reports 'A great Catholic gathering in Liverpool', presided over by St Vincent de Paul and convened to seek more funds for the Boys' Homes in general and for older boys to retain their communion and sociability. 12 August 1899, pp. 19–21. For a helpful summary of nineteenth-century provision and objectives of Workhouses, Ragged, Reform, Farm and Industrial Schools in Britain, particularly in London and the North West, responding to Poor Law revision (1834) and the Education Act (1870) and to mounting fear of poverty and criminality in large industrial cities, see Nicola Sheldon (2013), '"Something in the Place of Home": Children in Institutional Care 1850–1918', in Nigel Goose and Katrina Honeyman (eds), *Childhood and Child Labour in Industrial England: Diversity and Agency 1750–1914*, Farnham: Ashgate, pp. 255–76.
47. Danson Archive (V5/2), Invitation and seating plan held at The Maritime Museum, Liverpool.
48. Chilton Thomas, 'Wise Imperialism'.
49. P.E.J. Hemelryk (1904), 'The way in which we should approach the poor,' quoted in report on 'The St Vincent de Paul Society, Annual Meeting in Liverpool', *The Tablet*, 23 July, p. 25.
50. Chilton Smith, 'Wise Imperialism'.
51. Lynch, *Remembering Child Migration*, pp. 65–6.

52. (NCA 057). 'Report of the journey of Mrs M. Lacy on her journey to Canada May/July 1890.' Journey undertaken on behalf of the Catholic Children's Protection Society.
53. Annual Report (1901–02). Nugent Archive.
54. Steven J. Taylor (2014), 'Insanity, philanthropy and emigration: dealing with insane children in late-nineteenth-century north-west England,' *History of Psychiatry*, 25/2, p. 231.
55. Hamid Naficy (2001), *An Accented Cinema: Exilic and Diasporic Film*, Princeton: Princeton University Press.
56. Locations for the filming were Sydney (Redfern), the ABC studios in Frenchs Forest, Newcastle (Carrington) NSW, Lighting Ridge (NSW), and Liverpool, UK. Sea voyage exterior shots were taken on a special 'voyage' of the *S.S. Fairstar* (a vintage ship from the 1950s) that sailed between Sydney and Melbourne for the purpose. The Redfern carriage works, then derelict, were used for dock scenes in Liverpool. 'Perfect setting,' *The Canberra Times*, 16 December 1991, p. 1; Greg Ray (1991), 'Film-makers soak up the Carrington atmosphere,' *Newcastle Herald*, 23 October; Knapp, *Encore*, pp. 7, 9.
57. Thomas Ellison (1886), *The Cotton Trade of Great Britain, including a history of the Liverpool Cotton market and of the Liverpool Cotton Brokers Association*, London: Effingham Wilson, Royal Exchange; Robert Lee (2012), 'Divided loyalties? In-migration, ethnicity and identity: the integration of German merchants in nineteenth century Liverpool,' *Business History*, 54/2, p. 121. Morgan, 'Building British Atlantic Port Cities,' p. 213 ff.
58. Irish peasants were forcibly sent to Liverpool (and the Americas) so that landlords could avoid the costs of their upkeep during the famine. McMahon, 'Recrimination and reconciliation,' p. 347; Irish migrants, many having come over in the famine years, were seen as a troubled and troubling class: Pauline Marne (2001), 'Whose public space was it anyway? Class, gender and ethnicity in the creation of the Sefton and Stanley parks, Liverpool, 1858–1872,' *Social and Cultural Geography*, 2/4, p. 432.
59. Bennett, 'The hierarchy and the poor,' p. 2. See also Catherine Cox, Hilary Marland and Sarah York (2012), 'Emaciated, exhausted and excited: the bodies and minds of the Irish in late nineteenth-century Lancashire asylums,' *Journal of Social History*, 46/2, pp. 501–502.
60. John Mangan, (1992), 'Gripping tragedy of migrant orphans,' *The Age*, Thursday 2 July, p. 5. (The series was aired 8–9 July 1992).
61. Janet Bell, 'Curator's Notes'. Online: http://aso.gov.au/titles/tv/leaving-liverpool/notes/, accessed 14 May 2016.
62. Both roles were taken by inexperienced child actors. Their Liverpool origins, and Lily's Irish/Liverpool parentage and 'scouser' status are crucial to the impact of the drama. Scouser is a term for native residents of Liverpool and is derived

from the meat and biscuit potato stew called 'scouse', which may have been brought to the city by Scandinavian sailors. 'Scally' is a pejorative term used within Liverpool for men and boys who, in the Victorian era, would have been described as street traders and corner men. Most of the boys in the St Vincent's Home would have been in this demographic. The term may derive from the mass immigration of Irish men and women, as Scally is also an Irish surname.

63. This returns us to Chapter 1, in which I discuss the extreme pressure on migrant children to be resilient and to retain their 'innocence', no matter what their experience, in order to still be viewed as children and deserving of protection and help. See Chapter 1, Part Two, and notes 23 and 24 in that chapter.

64. The film suggests that Bert is in the same state as Lily, which would indicate the Fairbridge Farm in Molong, Orange. Yet the Catholic leadership and chapel in Bert's story is more indicative of the Western Australian boys' settlements under the Christian Brothers. To an extent, the exact location is not the point of the script, as the system as a whole was problematic and often criminally negligent. The character of the director of Bert's 'farm' is based on Brother Keaney. One does not usually rely on Wikipedia, but in this case I believe it forms part of the archive: See the Wikipedia entry accessed 14 April 2016. (It has since been re-edited, last accessed 13 July 2016.) At the point of my first access it was clearly written by someone/or several people angered by Brother Paul Keaney's cruelty to boys in his care (the page was marked in a 'Dispute' stage) Its status at the time is extracted below for record of the level of anger in the writing. Online: https://en.wikipedia.org/wiki/Paul_Keaney, 14 April 2016.

'Brother Paul Francis Keaney, MBE, ISO (5 October 1888 – 26 February 1954) was an Irish-born Australian Catholic paedophile who sexually and physically abused male child migrants at a Christian Brothers work camp in Western Australia. Two old boys from the school ended up cutting the head off the statue consequently the statue no longer exists. Keaney was born on 5 October 1888, … In later life he supervised the building and running of child slave labour camps & paedophile rings at Tardun and Bindoon using children forcibly deported from the UK. He died at Subiaco on 26 February 1954, aged 65. A statue was erected to his memory at Bindoon (that should be removed like that of Saddam Hussain in Baghdad). In an obituary he was referred to as "The Orphan's Friend" whereas in reality this sadist routinely inflicted savage attacks and sexual abuse on his wards … The boys' trousers would be pulled down, in front of the other boys, before they received their beatings.'

65. The Maritime Union of Australia was a strongly communist-inspired organisation and fought for workers' rights throughout the twentieth century. The film, *The Hungry Mile* (1953) was one of a number of activist and consciousness-raising documentaries made by the Union's film unit in the 1950s.

66. Liverpool Maritime Museum archives record several dinner invitations and seating plans (these are stored as D/D/V/5/2). Records also indicate his active involvement in the establishment of technical training courses and internationalised education for young men wishing to enter business. P.E.J. Hemelryk (1901), 'The making of a businessman,' *The Tablet*, 20 April, p. 9.
67. P.E.J. Hemelryk (1901), 'The Commercial Bureau', *The Tablet*, 27 April, p. 10. Also accounts of the establishment of an evening and full time technical school requiring foreign language skills, these are held in D/D/V/5/2.
68. Liverpool School of Commerce – the full curriculum is outlined in a document held at Liverpool Maritime Museum.
69. 'Commercial education in Liverpool: Mr Hemelryk's Scheme', *The Tablet*, 23 September, 1899, p. 36.
70. The Irish Catholic areas were mainly on the north of the city, in Everton and in Scotland Road. These were mostly disappeared in the slum clearances of the 1960s, and during the May Blitz of 1941. An account of the residues and the decline of sectarianism in Liverpool in the twentieth century is available in Keith Daniel Roberts (2015), *The Rise and Fall of Liverpool Sectarianism: An Investigation into the Decline of Sectarian Antagonism on Merseyside*, PhD thesis, University of Liverpool repository.
71. FACT (2015), 'What is a libidinal circuit? Elke Grenzer at FACT 2015', http://www.fact.co.uk/news-articles/2015/07/what-is-a-libidinal-circuit.aspx, accessed July 21 2015.
72. The first full-colour documentary made in Australia, *The Queen in Australia*, 1954. Available at the Screen and Sound Archive, Canberra.
73. Yoko Ono approved the script and released the song rights. Knapp, *On Location*, p. 6.
74. A sea shanty – usually 'bound for South Australia', with the verse: 'I'm Liverpool born and Liverpool bred, long in the arm and thick in the head'.
75. John Lennon (1970), 'Working Class Hero', *John Lennon/Plastic Ono Band*, London: Apple Records.
76. Barry C. Coldrey, submission, Senate Inquiry into Child Migration, Canberra (1999–2002), pp. 22–3. http://www.aph.gov.au/Parliamentary_Business/Committees/Senate/Community_Affairs/Completed_inquiries/1999-02/child_migrat/submissions/sublist, accessed 3 October 2016.
77. Jean-Francois Lyotard (1991), 'The sublime and the avant-garde, trans. L. Liebmann, G. Bennington and M. Hobson, *The Inhuman* (Cambridge: Polity Press), p. 99.

Chapter 7: *Diamonds of the Night*

1. Primo Levi (2013), *The Drowned and the Saved*, London: Abacus, p. 101.

2. Pauline Oliveros (1989/2005), *Deep Listening: A Composer's Sound Practice*, Lincoln NE: iUniverse, Inc., p. 44.
3. Aaron Kerner names these 'surrealistic digressions' but I think that they offer emphasis, perspective, and focus rather than 'digression'. Aaron Kerner (2011), *Film and the Holocaust: New Perspectives on Dramas, Documentaries and Experimental Films*, London: Continuum, p. 63.
4. Arnošt Lustig (1976), *Darkness Casts No Shadow*, Evanston, IL: Northwestern University Press, p. 173.
5. For an extensive and brilliant account of the haunted image, see Saxton, Libby (2008), *Haunted Images: Film, Ethics, Testimony and the Holocaust*, London: Wallflower, in particular pp. 56–67.
6. William Osborne (n.d.), 'Under the abyss of otherness: Pauline Oliveros' deep listening and the *Sonic Meditations*', published online http://www.osborne-conant.org/index.html, pp. 4/17. Also available in Dorothy Johnson and Wendy Oliver (eds) (2000), *Women Making Art: Women in the Literary, Visual and Performing Arts Since 1960*, New York: Lang, pp. 65–86.
7. Alena Heitlinger (2005), 'Politicizing Jewish memory in postwar Czechoslovakia,' *East European Jewish Affairs*, 35/2, p. 138.
8. Ibid., p. 136.
9. Book of Proverbs, 3:15. The Old Testament (*King James Bible*).
10. Hans Christian Anderson (1872), 'The red shoes', in *Hans Christian Anderson: Fairy Tales and Stories* (trans. H.P. Paull), http://www.digregor.com/FairyTales/redshoes.html, accessed 1 November 2016
11. Elie Wiesel (1958/2006), *Night*, London: Penguin Classics, p. 82.
12. Ibid., p. 91.
13. Ibid., p. 107.
14. Lustig, *Darkness*, pp. 29–30. Lustig and Němec also collaborated on *Transport from Paradise* (1962).
15. Silverman, *Palimpsestic Memory*, pp. 54–60.
16. Marianne Hirsch (2008), 'The generation of postmemory', *Poetics Today*, 29/1, p. 112. See also: Marianne Hirsch (2012), *The Generation of Postmemory: Writing and Visual Culture after the Holocaust*, New York: Columbia.
17. Alison Landsberg (2004), *Prosthetic Memory: The Transformation of American Remembrance in the Age of Mass Culture*, New York: Columbia University Press, p. 2.
18. Michael Rothberg (2009), *Multidirectional Memory: Remembering the Holocaust in the Age of Decolonization*. Stanford: Stanford University Press.
19. While the film uses flashbacks and moments of surrealism to indicate Manny's thought processes as the boys try to make their escape, the book has more dialogue between the two boys and a more complex hinter-plot that involves their complex relationship with Frank, a much older fellow prisoner, and Manny's

recollections of his father's arrest and death. However, the ambiguous ending is common to film and novella.
20. Lustig, *Darkness*, p. 163.
21. Lauren Berlant (2011), *Cruel Optimism*, Durham, NC: Duke University Press, p. 90.
22. Landsberg, *Prosthetic Memory*, p. 98.
23. Ibid., p. 98.
24. Silverman, *Palimpsestic Memory*, p. 60.
25. Wilhelm H. Riehl (1852), cited in Harrison, Robert Pogue (1992), *Forests: The Shadow of Civilisation*, Chicago: University of Chicago Press, p. 176.
26. Harrison, *Forests*, p. 176.
27. Jane T. Costlow (2013), *Heart-Pine Russia: Walking and Writing the Nineteenth Century Forest*, Ithaca, NY: Cornell University Press, p. 87.
28. Karen Lury discusses *Ivan's Childhood* and *Diamonds of the Night*, and points out the resonance between forests as a backdrop and the fairy tale as a common narrative structure for talking about the child in wartime. Karen Lury (2010), *The Child in Film*, London: I.B.Tauris, pp. 125–32.
29. Primo Levi (2015), 'The Truce', *The Complete Works of Primo Levi, Volume One* (trans. Ann Goldstein), London: Penguin, p. 339.
30. *The Truce* (Francesco Rosi, Italy/France, 1997); 1/36. Alternative translation: Levi: 'The Truce', p. 227.
31. Levi, 'The Truce', p. 340; see also on postwar Soviet orphan/childhoods: Juliane Fürst (2008), 'Between salvation and liquidation: homeless and vagrant children and the reconstruction of Soviet society', *The Slavonic and East European Review*, 86/2 (April), pp. 232–58.
32. Althea Williams and Sarah Ehrlich (2013), 'Escaping the train to Auschwitz', *BBC News online*, 20 April. Online: http://www.bbc.com/news/magazine-22188075, accessed 4 October 2016.
33. The prayer is the oldest daily prayer in Judaism and it is specifically commanded in the Torah (and in the words of the prayer itself) that parents should teach it to their children.
34. A film by the Australian Cate Shortland, based on Rachel Seiffert's novella 'Lore', which forms Part Two of Seiffert's *The Dark Room* (2001). It draws on Shortland's German heritage as well as on her Australian cinematic sensibility to land, maturity, homesickness (akin to the uncanny, *Unheimlich*), and the walkabout.
35. The loneliness of exclusion led some pre-war German Jewish film-makers to incorporate an idea of *Heimat* into their work, with the hope that urban belonging could be constructed as equivalent to the villages, mountains and forests. Ofer Askenazi (2015), 'The non-Heimat Heimat, Jewish film-makers

and German nationality from Weimar to the GDR,' *New German Critique*, 126, 42/3 (November), pp. 177–20 ff.
36. Fred Camper (1985), 'Sound and silence', in Elisabeth Weis and John Belton (eds), *Film Sound: Theory and Practice*, New York: Colombia University Press, p. 372.
37. Ibid., p. 380.
38. George Kouvaros (2015), 'As if it were for the last time, Wim Wenders – film and photography', *New German Critique*, 125/42/2, (August) p. 93.
39. Silverman, *Palimpsestic Memory*, p. 48.
40. Ibid., p. 40.
41. Ibid., p. 125.

Afterword: where have all the children gone?

1. Giorgio Agamben (1995), 'We refugees', *Symposium*, 49/2, (Summer), p. 119.
2. Walter Benjamin, 'Surrealism', quoted in Merrick Burrow (2004–05), 'Dialectical fairyland, cosmic advertising and the mimetic faculty in the Arcades Project', *New Formations*, 54, p. 108.
3. Gregory Dart (2010), 'Daydreaming' in M. Beaumont and G. Dart (eds), *Restless Cities*, London: Verso, p. 79.
4. Ibid., p. 91.
5. Dai Jinhua (2002), 'Invisible writing: the politics of Chinese mass culture in the 1990s', *Cinema and Desire: Feminist Marxism and Cultural Politics in the Work of Dai Jinhua*, London: Verso, p. 220.
6. Walter Benjamin (1999), *The Arcades Project*, Cambridge, MA: The Belknap Press, H4a, 2, p. 436.
7. Bonnie Honig (2001), *Democracy and the Foreigner*, Princeton University Press, p. 17.
8. Heaven Crawley (n.d.), Gender-related persecution and women's claims to asylum. Online information tool, http://www.refugeelegalaidinformation.org/gender-related-persecution-and-women's-claims-asylum, accessed 2 August 2016.

Bibliography

ABC News (2016), 'Football fan banned after banana thrown at Indigenous AFL star Eddie Betts', *ABC News,* 21 August. Online http://www.abc.net.au/news/2016-08-21/fan-banned-banana-thrown-at-eddie-betts-port/7769766, accessed 29 August 2016.

Ackers, Louise and Helen Stalford (2004), *A Community for Children? Children, Citizenship and Internal Migration in the EU,* Aldershot: Ashgate Publishing.

Agamben, Giorgio (1995), 'We refugees', *Symposium,* 49/2, (Summer), pp. 114–19.

―――― (1998), *Homo Sacer: Sovereign Power and Bare Life.* Stanford, CA: Stanford University Press.

―――― (1999), *Remnants of Auschwitz: The Witness and the Archive.* New York: Zone Books.

―――― (2009), *The Signature of All Things: A Note on Method* (trans. Luc D'Isanto and Kevin Attell), Cambridge, MA: MIT Press.

Ahmed, Sara (2004), 'Collective feelings', *Theory, Culture & Society,* 21/2, pp. 25–42.

Anagnost, Ann (1997), 'Children and national transcendence in China,' in *Constructing China: The Interaction of Culture and Economics,* Kenneth G. Lieberthal, Shuen-fu Lin, and Ernest P. Young (eds), Ann Arbor: University of Michigan Press, pp. 195–222.

―――― (2004), 'The corporeal politics of quality (suzhi)', *Public Culture,* 16/2, pp. 189–208.

Anderson, Hans Christian (1872), 'The red shoes', in *Hans Christian Anderson: Fairy Tales and Stories* (trans. H.P. Paull). Online http://www.digregor.com/FairyTales/redshoes.html, accessed 1 November 2016.

Anderson, Mark C. (2014), 'Zombies and cowboys: how to win the apocalypse', *European Scientific Journal,* 2 (September), pp. 207–15.

Anderson, Mark M. (2007), 'The child victim as witness to the Holocaust: an American story?', *Jewish Social Studies,* 14/1, (Fall) pp. 1–22.

Ansell, Nicola (2009), 'Childhood and the politics of scale: descaling children's geographies', *Progress in Human Geography,* 33/2, pp. 190–209.

Appadurai, Arjun (2006), *Fear of Small Numbers: An Essay on the Geography of Anger,* Durham, NC: Duke University Press.

Askenazi, Ofer (2015), 'The non-Heimat Heimat, Jewish film-makers and German nationality from Weimar to the GDR,' *New German Critique,* 126, 42/3 (November), pp. 115–43.

Bibliography

Augé, Marc (1995), *Non-Places: Introduction to an Anthropology of Super-Modernity* (trans. John Howe), London: Verso.

Auguste, Isabelle (2009), 'On the significance of saying "Sorry" – politics of memory and Aboriginal reconciliation in Australia', *Coolabah*, 3, pp. 43–50.

Australian Government (2009), 'Apology to the forgotten Australians and former child migrants', Canberra, 16 November 2009. Online https://www.dss.gov.au/our-responsibilities/families-and-children/programs-services/apology-to-the-forgotten-australians-and-former-child-migrants, accessed 1 October 2016.

Bachelard, Gaston (1971), *The Poetics of Reverie: Childhood, Language, and the Cosmos* (trans. David Russell), Boston: Beacon Press.

Bai, Limin (2008), 'Children as the youthful hope of an old empire: race, nationalism, and elementary education in China 1895–1915,' *The Journal of the History of Childhood and Youth*, 1/2, pp. 210–31.

Barret, James R. (1992), 'Americanization from the bottom-up, immigration and the remaking of the working class in the United States: 1880–1930,' *Discovering America*, 79/3, pp. 996–1020.

Barsalou, Kathleen P. (2008), *The Age of William A. Dunning: The Realm of Myth Meets the Yellow Brick Road*, (unpublished PhD thesis), Florida Atlantic University, UMI Number: 3339601.

Barthes, Roland (1977/1981), *Camera Lucida—Reflections on Photography*, New York: Hill and Wang.

Baum, L. Frank (1900/1960), *The Wonderful Wizard of Oz*, New York: Dover Books.

Berghahn, Daniela (2013), *Far-flung Families in Film: The Diasporic Family in Contemporary European Cinema*, Edinburgh: Edinburgh University Press.

Biao, Xiang (2007), 'How far are the left-behind left behind? A preliminary study in rural China', *Population, Space and Place*, 13, pp. 179–91.

Beck, Ulrich (2009), 'Critical theory of world risk society: a cosmopolitan vision', *Constellations*, 16/1, pp. 3–22.

Behnke Kinney, Anne (1995), *Chinese Views of Childhood*, Honolulu: Hawaii University Press.

—— (1995), 'Dyed silk, Han notions of the moral development of children,' in Behnke Kinney, Anne, *Chinese Views of Childhood*, Honolulu: Hawaii University Press, pp. 17–56.

Benhabib, Seyla, with Jeremy Waldron, Bonnie Koenig and William Kymlicka (2006), *Another Cosmopolitanism*, Oxford: Oxford University Press.

Benjamin, Walter (1999), *The Arcades Project*, (trans. Howard Eiland and Kevin McLaughlin), Cambridge, MA: The Belknap Press of Harvard University Press.

Bennett, Rev. John (n.d.), 'The hierarchy and the poor, 1850–1950', typed manuscript. pp. 25–6. Nugent Archive, Ref. NCA122.

—— (1929), 'Emigration of Catholic boys and girls', pamphlet of The Catholic Emigration Association, reprinted from *The Christian Democrat*.

Bibliography

Benotman, Noman and Nikita Malik (2016), *The Children of Islamic State*, London: Quilliam Foundation.
Bequelin, Nicholas (2004), 'Staged development in Xinjiang,' *China Quarterly*, clxxviii, pp. 358–78.
Berlant, Lauren (2011), *Cruel Optimism*, Durham, NC: Duke University Press.
Bhabha, Jacqueline (2009), 'The "mere fortuity of birth"? children, mothers, borders and the meaning of citizenship', in Seyla Benhabib and Judith Resnik (eds), *Migrations and Mobilities: Citizenship, Borders and Gender*, New York: New York University Press, pp. 187–227.
Blunt, Alison (2007), 'Cultural geographies of migration: mobility, transnationality, and diaspora', *Progress in Human Geography*, 31/5, pp. 684–94.
Bohland, Markus P.J. and Sean Moreland (2014), '"If you rip the fronts off houses": killing innocence in Alfred Hitchcock's *Shadow of a Doubt* (1943)', in Debbie Olsen (ed.), *Children in the Films of Alfred Hitchcock*, New York: Palgrave, pp. 87–112.
Bourne, Stephen (2001/2005), *Black in the British Frame: The Black Experience in British Film and Television*, London: Bloomsbury.
Brecht, Bertolt (1947), 'Children's Crusade, 1939' in *Selected Poems of Bertolt Brecht* (trans. H.R. Hays), New York: Harvest, pp. 148–59.
Brosius, Christiane and Nicolas Yazgi (2007), 'Is there no place like home?': contesting cinematographic constructions of Indian diasporic experiences', *Contributions to Indian Sociology*, 41, pp. 355–86.
Buckingham, David (2007), 'Selling childhood? Children and consumer culture', *Journal of Children and Media*, 1/1, pp. 15–24.
Buck-Morss, Susan (1989), *The Dialectics of Seeing: Walter Benjamin and the Arcades Project*, Cambridge, MA: MIT.
—— (2011), 'Communism and ethics', in *Communism, A New Beginning*, Conference paper, Cooper Union, New York. Online video http://www.versobooks.com/blogs/706-communism-a-new-beginning-alain-badiou-and-slavoj-zizek-with-verso-books-at-cooper-union-new-york-october-14th-16th-2011, accessed 16 October 2011.
Burrow, Merrick (2004), 'Dialectical fairyland, cosmic advertising and the mimetic faculty in the Arcades Project', *New Formations*, 54, pp. 108–25.
Buti, Antonio (2007), *Sir Ronald Wilson: A Matter of Conscience*. Crawley, WA: University of Western Australia Publishing.
Butler, Jamie Davie (1896), 'British convicts shipped to American colonies', *The American Historical Review*, 2/1, pp. 12–33.
Calvino, Italo (2011), *Into the War*, London: Picador.
Camper, Fred (1985) 'Sound and silence', in Elisabeth Weis and John Belton (eds), *Film Sound: Theory and Practice*, New York: Columbia, pp. 369–81.
Carthy, Eliza, 'The Big Machine' by Eliza Carthy & The Wayward Band, The Music Room, Liverpool Philharmonic, 18 November 2016.

Bibliography

Castañeda, Claudia (2002), *Figurations: Child, Bodies, Worlds*, Durham, NC: Duke University Press.
Charney, Leo (1998), *Empty Moments: Cinema, Modernity and Drift*, Durham, NC: Duke University Press.
Chen, Kuan-hsing (2010), *Asia as Method: Toward Deimperialization*, Durham, NC: Duke University Press.
Child Migrants Trust (CMT) (2010), Gordon Brown 'Apology to child migrants', 10 March. Online http://www.childmigrantstrust.com/news/number10govuk--apology-issued-to-child-migrants, accessed 15 September 2016.
Chilton Thomas, Arthur (1904), 'Wise imperialism: on the advantage of child emigration within the bounds of empire', public address given to the Catholic Emigration Society, Southport, 25 May. Nugent Archive.
Chin, Ann-ping (1988), *Children of China: Voices from Recent Years*, New York: Knopf.
Chu, Y.C., Stephanie Hemelryk Donald and Andrea Witcomb (2003), 'Children, media, and the public sphere in Chinese Australia', in Rawnsley G.; Rawnsley M. (ed.), *Political Communications in Greater China: The Construction and Reflection of Identity*, original edn., London: Routledge Curzon, pp. 261–74.
Cliff, Tom (2016), *Oil and Water, Being Han in Xinjiang*, Chicago: University of Chicago Press.
Cohen, Boaz and Rita Horvath (2010), 'Young witnesses in the DP camps: children's Holocaust testimony in context', *Journal of Modern Jewish Studies*, 11/1, pp. 103–25.
Cohen, Sara Simcha (2013), *Hearth of Darkness: the Familiar, the Familial, and the Zombie*, PhD Diss. Submitted to University of California. Accessible via Proquest.
Coldrey, Barry (n.d.), *Good British Stock: Child and Youth Migration to Australia*, National Archives of Australia. Online http://guides.naa.gov.au/good-british-stock/chapter3/big-brother.aspx, accessed 5 April 2016.
Comaroff, John (2006), 'Reflections on youth, from the past to the post-colony', in Greg Downey and Melissa S.Fisher (eds), *Frontiers of Capital: Ethnographic Reflections on the New Economy*, Durham, NC: Duke University Press, pp. 267–81.
Community Affairs References Committee (29 February 2012), *Commonwealth Contribution to Former Forced Adoption Policies and Practices*. Canberra: Australian Senate, accessed 20 August 2016.
Conan, Éric and Henri Rousso (1998), *Vichy: An Ever-Present Past*, Hanover: Dartmouth College, University of New England Press.
Coote, Diana (2010), 'The inertia of matter and the generativity of flesh', in Diana Coote and S. Frost (eds), *New Materialisms: Ontology, Agency and Politics*, Durham, NC: Duke University Press, pp. 92–115.

Bibliography

Costlow, Jane T. (2013), *Heart-Pine Russia: Walking and Writing the Nineteenth Century Forest*, Ithaca, NY: Cornell University Press.

Cox, Catherine, Hilary Marland and Sarah York (2012), 'Emaciated, exhausted and excited: the bodies and minds of the Irish in late nineteenth-century Lancashire asylums', *Journal of Social History*, 46/2, pp. 500–24.

Crawley, Heaven (2000), 'Gender, persecution and the concept of politics in the asylum determination process', *Forced Migration Review*, 9, pp. 17–20. Online www.fmreview.org/FMRpdfs/FMR09/fmr9.6.pdf, accessed 16 July 2016.

—— (2001), *Refugees and Gender: Law and Process*, Bristol: Jordan Publishing.

—— (n.d.), 'Gender-related persecution and women's claims to asylum'. Online information tool, http://www.refugeelegalaidinformation.org/gender-related-persecution-and-women's-claims-asylum, accessed 2 August 2016.

Cresswell, Timothy (2010), 'Towards a politics of mobility', *Environment and Planning D: Society and Space*, 28, pp. 17–31.

Crock, Mary (2006), *Seeking Asylum Alone: A Study of Australian Law, Policy and Practice Regarding Unaccompanied and Separated Children*, Sydney: Themis Press.

Cunningham, Stuart and Elizabeth Jacka (1996), *Australian Television and International Mediascapes*, Cambridge: Cambridge University Press.

Dai, Jinhua (2002), 'Invisible writing: the politics of Chinese mass culture in the 1990s', in Tani E. Barlow and Jing Wang (trans.), *Cinema and Desire: Feminist Marxism and Cultural Politics in the Work of Dai Jinhua*, London: Verso, pp. 213–34.

Dart, Gregory (2010), 'Daydreaming', in Matthew Beaumont and Gregory Dart (eds), *Restless Cities*, London: Verso, pp. 79–97.

De Bruyn, Ben (2010), 'Borrowed time, borrowed world and borrowed eyes: care, ruin and vision in McCarthy's *The Road* and Harrison's *Ecocriticism*', *English Studies*, 91/7 (November), pp. 776–89.

Del Favero, Dennis (2015), 'Tampa 2001', Libidinal Circuits Exhibition and Conference, 2015, FACT Liverpool. Online /www.fact.co.uk/projects/libidinal-circuits-scenes-of-urban-innovation-iii/dennis-del-favero-tampa-2001-2015.aspx, accessed 1 April 2017.

Denov, Myriam (2010), *Child Soldiers: Syria's Revolutionary United Front*, Cambridge: Cambridge University Press.

Dickson, Gary (2007), *The Children's Crusade: Mediaeval History, Modern Mythistory*, Basingstoke: Palgrave Books.

Dinsdale, Robert (2013), *Little Exiles*, Sydney: Harper Collins.

Donà, Georgia and Angela Veale (2011), 'Divergent discourses, children and forced migration', *Journal of Ethnic and Migration Studies*, 37/8, pp. 1273–89.

Donald, Stephanie Hemelryk (2000), *Public Secrets, Public Spaces: Cinema and Civility in China*, Lanham: Rowman and Littlefield.

Bibliography

———— (2001), '"History, entertainment, education and *jiaoyu*": a Western Australian perspective on Australian children's media, and some Chinese alternatives', *International Journal of Cultural Studies*, 4, pp. 279–99.

———— (2005), *Little Friends: Children's Film and Media Culture in China*, Lanham: Rowman and Littlefield.

———— (2010), 'Global Beijing: *The World* is a violent place', in Christoph Lindner (ed.), *Globalization, Violence and the Visual Culture of Cities*. London: Routledge, pp. 122–34.

———— (2014), 'Inertia and ethical urban relations: the living, the dying and the dead', in Stephanie Hemelryk Donald and Christoph. P. Lindner (eds), *Inert Cities: Globalization, Mobility and Suspension in Visual Culture*, London: I.B.Tauris, pp. 153–70.

———— (2015), 'Cosmopolitan endurance: migrant children and film spectatorship', in K. Beeler and S. Beeler (eds), *Children's Film in the Digital Age: Essays on Audience, Adaption and Consumer Culture*, London: McFarland and Company, pp. 133–47.

———— (2015), '*Landscape in the Mist*: thinking beyond the perimeter fence', in Angelos Koutsourakis and Mark Steven (eds), *The Cinema of Theo Angelopoulos*, Edinburgh: Edinburgh University Press, pp. 206–18.

Donald, Stephanie Hemelryk, Eleonore Kofman and Catherine Kevin (eds) (2012), *Branding Cities: Cosmopolitanism, Parochialism, and Social Change*, 2nd edn., New York: Routledge Academic.

———— (2012), 'Processes of Cosmopolitanism and Parochialism,' in Stephanie Hemelryk Donald, Elenore Kofman and Cathering Kevin (eds), *Branding Cities: Cosmopolitanism, Parochialism and Social Change*, 2nd edn., New York: Routledge Academic, pp. 1–13.

Donald, Stephanie Hemelryk and Christoph P. Lindner (eds) (2014), *Inert Cities: Globalization, Mobility and Suspension in Visual Culture*, London: I.B.Tauris.

Donald, Stephanie Hemelryk, Emma Wilson and Sarah Wright (eds) (2017), *Childhood and Nation in Contemporary World Cinema: Borders and Encounters*, London: Bloomsbury.

Doty, Alexander (2000), *Flaming Classics: Queering the Film Canon*, London: Routledge.

Ellison, Thomas (1886), *The Cotton Trade of Great Britain, including a history of the Liverpool Cotton market and of the Liverpool Cotton Brokers Association*, London: Effingham Wilson, Royal Exchange.

Elsaesser, Thomas (2005), 'Double occupancy and small adjustments: Space, place and policy in the New European Cinema since the 1990s', in Thomas Elsaesser, *European Cinema: Face to Face with Hollywood*, Amsterdam: Amsterdam University Press.

Bibliography

Evans, Richard (2016), 'Throwing bananas at black sportsmen has been recognised as racism across Europe for decades', *The Advertiser* online, 2 August. Online: http://www.adelaidenow.com.au/news/opinion/richard-evans-throwing-bananas-at-black-sportsmen-has-been-recognised-as-racism-across-europe-for-decades/news-story/afcb5d4a634119b327507e7616755e0b, accessed 1 September 2016.

FACT (2015), 'What is a libidinal circuit? Elke Grenzer at FACT 2015', http://www.fact.co.uk/news-articles/2015/07/what-is-a-libidinal-circuit.aspx, accessed 21 July 2015.

Farrell, Paul, Nick Evershed and Helen Davidson (2016), 'The Nauru Files: cache of 2000 leaked reports reveal scale of abuse of children in Australian offshore detention', *Guardian* online, 10 August.

Faulkner, Joanne (2010), *The Importance of Being Innocent: Why We Worry about Children*, Cambridge: Cambridge University Press.

Flanagan, Richard (2016), *Notes on an Exodus*, Sydney: Vintage Books.

Flusser, Vilém (2013), *The Freedom of the Migrant: Objections to Nationalism* (trans. Kenneth Kronenberg), Champaign, IL: University of Illinois Press.

Friedberg, Anne (2002), 'Urban mobility and cinematic visuality: the screens of Los Angeles – endless cinema or private telematics', *Journal of Visual Culture*, 1, pp. 183–204.

Frodon, Jean-Michel (2010), 'Referent images', in Jean-Michel Frodon (ed.), *Cinema and the Shoah: An Art Confronts the Tragedy of the Twentieth Century* (trans. Anna Harrison and Tom Mes), New York: SUNY Press, pp. 219–54.

Fryer, Peter (2010), *Staying Power: The History of Black People in Britain*, London: Pluto Press.

Funchion, John (2010), 'When Dorothy became history: L. Frank Baum's enduring fantasy of cosmopolitan nostalgia', *Modern Language Quarterly*, 71/4, pp. 429–51.

Furia, Annalisa (2012), *Victims or Criminals? The Vulnerability of Separated Children in the Context of Migration in the United Kingdom and Italy*, Working Paper 69, Farnham: Sussex Centre for Migration Research.

Fürst, Juliane (2008), 'Between salvation and liquidation: homeless and vagrant children and the reconstruction of Soviet society', *The Slavonic and East European Review*, 86/2, (April), pp. 232–58.

Gensburger, Sarah (2014), 'Witnessing the looting of Jewish belongings during the Holocaust: what can history do with images?', *Dapim: Studies on the Holocaust*, 28/2, pp. 74–96.

Gentleman, Amelia (2016), 'Hungry, scared and no closer to safety: child refugees failed by Britain', *Guardian* online (Australian edition). Online https://www.theguardian.com/world/2016/aug/02/child-refugees-calais-failed-by-britain, accessed 2 August 2016.

Bibliography

Georgakas, Dan (2015), 'Megalexandros: authoritarianism and national identity', in Angelos Koutsourakis and Mark Steven (eds), *The Cinema of Theo Angelopoulos*, Edinburgh: Edinburgh University Press, pp. 129–40.

Gilman, Todd S. (2003), '"Aunty Em, Hate You! Hate Kansas! Taking the Dog, Dorothy," conscious and unconscious desire in The Wizard of Oz', in Suzanne Rahn (ed.), *L. Frank Baum's World of Oz, A Classic Series at 100*, Lanham, MD: Children's Literature Association and Scarecrow Press, pp. 127–45.

Gilroy, Paul (2011), 'Great games: film, history and working-through Britain's colonial legacy', in Lee Grieveson and Colin McCabe (eds), *Film and the End of Empire*, London: BFI, pp. 13–32.

Godas, Christos (2012), 'The Cinema File: the interview', 6/22, *Scholars Association News, International Online Magazine*, (May). Online http://www.onassis.org/online-magazine/issue-22/article-6.php, accessed 22 September 2016.

Gold, Thomas, Doug Guthrie and David Wank (eds) (2004), *Social Connections in China: Institutions, Culture and the Changing Nature of Guanxi*, Cambridge: Cambridge University Press.

Goodman, David S.G. (2004), 'The campaign to "open up the west": national, provincial and local perspectives', *China Quarterly*, clxxviii, pp. 317–34.

—— (2008), 'Why China has no new middle class: cadres, managers and entrepreneurs,' in David S.G. Goodman (ed.), *The New Rich in China: Future Rulers, Present Lives*, London: Routledge, pp. 23–37.

—— (2014), *Class in Contemporary China*, Cambridge: Polity.

Graf, Christine (2013), 'Childhood lost: Australia's stolen generation'. *Faces*, 29, pp. 12–13.

Grootenboer, Hanneke (2001), 'The pensive image: on thought in Jan van Huysum's still life paintings', *Oxford Art Journal*, 34/1, pp. 13–30.

Hack, Karl (1991), 'Decolonisation and the Pergau Dam affair', *History Today*, 44/11, pp. 9–12.

Hall, Stuart (2004), 'Calypso Kings', in Michael Bull and Les Back (eds), *The Auditory Culture Reader*, Oxford: Berg, pp. 419–26. (Originally published in the *Guardian*, 27 June 2002).

Hamer, John H. (1998), 'Money and the moral order in late nineteenth and early twentieth century American capitalism,' *Anthropological Quarterly*, 71/3, pp. 138–49.

Hao, Yufan, and Liu Weihua (2012), 'Xinjiang: increasing pain in the heart of China's borderland', *Journal of Contemporary China*, 21/74, pp. 205–25.

Harrison, Robert Pogue (1992), *Forests: The Shadow of Civilization*, University of Chicago Press.

Hart, Jason (2014), 'Children and forced migration', in Elena Fiddian-Qasmiyeh, Gil Loescher, Katy Long and Nando Sigona (eds), *The Oxford Handbook of Refugee and Forced Migration Studies*, Oxford: Oxford University Press, pp. 383–94.

Bibliography

Hassler-Forest, Dan (2014), 'Zombie spaces', in Edward P. Comentale and Aaron Jaffe (eds), *The Year's Work at the Zombie Research Centre*, Bloomington: Indiana University Press.
Heitlinger, Alena (2005), 'Politicizing Jewish memory in postwar Czechoslovakia,' *East European Jewish Affairs*, 35/2, pp. 135–53.
Hemelryk, P.E.J. (1901), 'The making of a businessman,' *The Tablet*, 20 April.
—— (1901), 'The Commercial Bureau' *The Tablet*, 27 April.
Hill, David (2007), *The Forgotten Children: Fairbridge Farm School and its Betrayal of Australia's Child Migrants*, Sydney: Random House.
Hirsch, Marianne (1997), *Family Frames: Photography, Narrative, and Postmemory*, Cambridge, MA: Harvard University Press.
—— (2008), 'The generation of postmemory', *Poetics Today*, 29/1, pp. 103–28.
—— (2012), *The Generation of Postmemory: Writing and Visual Culture after the Holocaust*, New York: Columbia.
Honig, Bonnie (2001), *Democracy and the Foreigner*, Princeton: Princeton University Press.
Hörschelmann, Kathrin and Lorraine van Blerk (2012), *Children, Youth and the City*, London: Routledge.
Horton, Andrew (1997), *The Films of Theo Angelopoulos: A Cinema of Contemplation*, Princeton: Princeton University Press.
Humphreys, Margaret (1994), *Empty Cradles*, London: Doubleday Books.
Jacka, Tamara (2009), 'Cultivating citizens: *suzhi* (quality) discourse in the PRC', *positions*, 17/3, pp. 523–35.
Jenkins, Henry (1998), *The Children's Culture Reader*, New York: NYU Press.
Jing, Xiaolei (2008), 'Tragedy prompts action, *Beijing Review* online, 48 (25 November). Online http://www.bjreview.com.cn/nation/txt/2008-11/25/content_166482.htm, accessed 2 September 2016.
Johnson, Deborah and Wendy Oliver (eds) (2000), *Women Making Art: Women in the Literary, Visual and Performing Arts Since 1960*, New York: Lang.
Jones, Andrew F. (2002), 'The child as history in republican China: a discourse on development', *positions: east asia cultures critique*, 10/3, pp. 695–727.
Kant, Immanuel (1986), 'The third definitive article of perpetual peace between states' (1902 translation), section of Immanuel Kant, 'Perpetual Peace', in Ernst Behler (ed.), *Immanuel Kant: Philosophical Writings*, New York: Continuum, third definitive article: pp. 284–6; whole section: pp. 270–311.
Karafolas, Simeon (1998), 'Migrant remittances in Greece and Portugal: distribution by country of provenance and the role of the banking presence', *International Migration*, 36/3, pp. 357–82.
Karalis, Vrasidas (2012), *A History of Greek Cinema*, London: Continuum.
Katznelson, Ira (2003), *Desolation and Enlightenment: Political Knowledge after Total War, Totalitarianism and the Holocaust*, New York: Columbia University Press.

Bibliography

Kearney, Kevin (2012), 'Cormac McCarthy's *The Road* and the frontier of the human', *Lit: Literature Interpretation Theory*, 23/2, pp. 160–78.

Kerner, Aaron (2011), *Film and the Holocaust: New Perspectives on Dramas, Documentaries, and Experimental Films*, London: Continuum.

Kilduff, Hannah (2017), 'The child as hyphen: Yamina Benguigui's *Inch'allah Dimanche*', in Stephanie Hemelryk Donald, Emma Wilson and Sarah Wright, (eds), *Childhood and Nation in Contemporary World Cinema: Borders and Encounters*, New York: Bloomsbury, pp. 200–14.

Kipnis, Andrew B. (2004), 'Practices of *guanxi* production and practices of *ganqing* avoidance', in Gold, Thomas, Doug Guthrie and David Wank (eds), *Social Connections in China: Institutions, Culture and the Changing Nature of Guanxi*, Cambridge: Cambridge University Press, pp. 21–34.

—— (2006), '*Suzhi*: A keyword approach', *China Quarterly*, 186, pp. 295–313.

Knapp, Gerard (1991), 'On location: *The Leaving of Liverpool* – Leaving uncovers child abuse' *Encore*, 8/18, 15–28 November.

Koefoed, Andreas (dir.) (2015), *At Home in the World*, Sonntag Films. Online http://www.athomeintheworldfilm.com/#a-home-in-the-world, accessed 19 November 2016.

Kofman, Eleonore (2005), 'Migration, citizenship and the reassertion of the nation-state in Europe', *Citizenship Studies*, special issue on Spaces, Places and Scales of Citizenship, 9/6, pp. 453–67.

Koutsourakis, Angelos and Mark Steven (2015), 'Angelopoulos and the lingua franca of modernism', in Angelos Koutsourakis and Mark Steven (eds), *The Cinema of Theo Angelopoulos*, Edinburgh: Edinburgh University Press, pp. 1–19.

Kouvaros, George (2015), 'As if it were for the last time, Wim Wenders – film and photography', *New German Critique*, 125/42/2, (August), pp. 81–95.

Kleinman, Arthur and Joan Kleinman (1994), 'How bodies remember: social memory and bodily experience of criticism, resistance, and delegitimation following China's Cultural Revolution', *New Literary History*, 25/3/1, pp. 707–23.

Kolovos, Nikos (1990), Θόδωρος Αγγελόπουλος [Theo Angelopoulos], Athens: Aigokeros, p. 174. In-text translation provided by Angelos Koutsoukaris.

Lake, Marilyn (1999), 'Childbearers as rights-bearers: feminist discourse on the rights of Aboriginal and non-Aboriginal mothers in Australia, 1920–1950', *Women's History Review*, 8/2, pp. 347–63.

Landsberg, Alison (2004), *Prosthetic Memory: The Transformation of American Remembrance in the Age of Mass Culture*, New York: Columbia University Press.

Lavarch, Michael (1997), *Bringing Them Home: Report of the National Enquiry into the Separation of Aboroginal and Torres Strait Islander Children from their Families*, Canberra: Commonwealth of Australia.

Lebeau, Vicky (1995), *Lost Angels: Psychoanalysis and Cinema*, London: Routledge.

Bibliography

Lee, Nicholas (2001), *Childhood and Society: Growing Up in an Age of Uncertainty*, Buckingham: Open University Press.

Lee, Robert (2012), 'Divided loyalties? In-migration, ethnicity and identity: the integration of German merchants in nineteenth century Liverpool', *Business History*, 54/2, pp. 117–53.

Lefebvre, Henri (1968/1996), *Writings on Cities*, 5th edn. (eds/trans. Eleonore Kofman and Elisabeth Lebas), Oxford: Blackwell.

Lennon, John (1970), 'Working Class Hero', *John Lennon/Plastic Ono Band*, London: Apple Records.

Levi, Primo (2013), *The Drowned and the Saved*, trans. Raymond Rosenthal, London: Abacus.

—— (2015), 'The Truce', *The Complete Works of Primo Levi, Volume One* (trans. Ann Goldstein), London: Penguin.

Li, Na, Wei-hsin Lin, Xiaobing Wang (2012), 'From rural poverty to urban deprivation? The plight of Chinese rural-urban migrants through the lens of *Last Train Home*', *East Asia*, 29, pp. 173–86.

Littlefield, Henry M. (1964), '*The Wizard of Oz*: parable on populism', *American Quarterly*, 16/1 (Spring), pp. 47–58.

Liu, Xinyu (2005), 'Ruins of the future: class and history in Wang Bing's Tiexi district', *New Left Review*, 31 pp. 125–36.

Lu, Xun (Hsun) (1921/1960/1972), 'My old home', *Selected Stories of Lu Hsun*, Beijing (Peking): Foreign Languages Press.

Luckhurst, Roger (2015), *Zombies: A Cultural History*, London: Reaktion Books.

Lury, Karen (2010), *The Child in Film: Tears, Fears and Fairy Tales*. London, New York: I.B.Tauris.

—— (2016), 'Children, objects and motion … balloons, bikes, kites and tethered flight', presentation at Royal Holloway London, 19 April 2016. Audiofile available online at http://childnationcinema.org/events/international-conference/, accessed 10 June 2016.

—— (2012), 'A high wind in Jamaica: blank looks and missing voices', *Screen*, 53/4, pp. 447–52.

Lustig, Arnost (1976), *Darkness Casts No Shadow* (trans. Jeanne Němcová), Evanston, IL: Northwestern University Press.

Lynch, Gordon (2014), 'Saving the child for the sake of the nation: moral framing and the civic, moral and religious redemption of children', *American Journal of Cultural Sociology*, 2/2, pp. 165–96.

—— (n.d.), 'Child migration schemes to Australia: an historical overview', PDF, lodged on the University of Kent repository. Online https://kar.kent.ac.uk/47772/1/British%20child%20migration%20schemes%20to%20Australia%20-%20a%20historical%20overview.docx.pdf, accessed 15 July 2016.

—— (2016), *Remembering Child Migration: Faith, Nation-Building and the Wounds of Charity*, London: Bloomsbury.

Lyotard, Jean-Francois (1991), 'The Sublime and the Avant-Garde,' (trans. Lisa Liebmann, Geoffrey Bennington and Marian Hobson), *The Inhuman*, Cambridge: Polity Press.

Ma, Jean (2010), *Melancholy Drift: Marking Time in Chinese Cinema*, Hong Kong: Hong Kong University Press, pp. 86–7.

Makine, Andrei (1995), *Le Testament Français*, Paris: Mercure de France.

Malik, Sarita (2002), *Representing Black Britain: Black and Asian Images on Television*, London: Sage.

Mangan, John (1992), 'Gripping tragedy of migrant orphans', *The Age*, 2 July, p. 5.

Marciniak, Katarzyna (2008), 'Foreign women and toilets', *Feminist Media Studies*, 8/4, pp. 337–56.

Marks, Laura U. (2000), *The Skin of the Film: Intercultural Cinema, Embodiment and the Senses*, Durham, NC: Duke University Press.

Marne, Pauline (2001), 'Whose public space was it anyway? Class, gender and ethnicity in the creation of the Sefton and Stanley parks, Liverpool, 1858–1872,' *Social and Cultural Geography*, 2/4, pp. 421–43.

McAdam, Jane and Fiona Chong (2014), *Refugees: Why Seeking Asylum is Legal and Australia's Policies Are Not*, Sydney: UNSW Press.

McAllister, Kirsten Emiko (2011), 'Asylum in the margins of contemporary Britain: the spatial practices of desire in *Gypo*,' *Space and Culture*, 14/2, pp. 165–82.

McCarthy, Cormac (2006), *The Road*, London: Picador.

McMahon, Colin (2014), 'Recrimination and reconciliation: Great Famine memory in Liverpool and Montreal at the turn of the twentieth century', *Atlantic Studies*, 11/3, pp. 344–64.

Mence, Victoria, Simone Gengell and Ryan Tebb (2015), *A History of the Department of Immigration: Managing Migration to Australia*, Australian Government: Canberra.

Mieder, Wolfgang (2016), *Tradition and Innovation in Folk Literature*, Oxford: Routledge (Revivals).

Millward, James A. (2007), *Eurasian Crossroads: A History of Xinjiang*, New York: Columbia University Press.

Morey, Anne (1995) '"A whole book for a nickel"? L. Frank Baum as filmmaker', *Children's Literature Association Quarterly*, 20/4 (Winter), pp. 155–60.

Morgan, Kenneth (1992), 'Bristol and the Atlantic trade in the eighteenth century', *The English Historical Review*, 107/424, pp. 626–50.

—— (2016), 'Building British Atlantic Port Cities: Bristol and Liverpool in the Eighteenth Century', in Daniel Maudlin and Bernard L Herman (eds), *Building the British Atlantic World: Spaces, Places and Material Culture, 1600–1850*, Chapel Hill, NC: North Carolina Press, pp. 212–28.

Bibliography

Morris, Lydia (2010), *Asylum, Welfare and the Cosmopolitan Ideal: A Sociology of Rights*, Oxford: Routledge.

Muller, Adam (2007), 'Notes toward a theory of nostalgia: childhood and the evocation of the past in two European "heritage" films', *New Literary History*, 37, pp. 739–60.

Murphet, Julian (2015), 'Cinematography of the group: Angelopoulos and the collective subject of cinema', in Angelos Koutsourakis and Mark Steven (eds), *The Cinema of Theo Angelopoulos*, Edinburgh: Edinburgh University Press, pp. 159–74.

Murphy, Kathleen (1990), 'Children of paradise', *Film Comment*, 26/6, pp. 38–9.

Naficy, Hamid (2001), *An Accented Cinema: Exilic and Diasporic Film*, Princeton: Princeton University Press.

Naftali, Orna (2016), *Children in China*, London: Polity Press.

Nava, Mica (2007), *Visceral Cosmopolitanism: Gender, Culture and the Normalization of Difference*, Oxford: Berg.

Nestingen, Andrew (2013), *The Cinema of Ari Kaurismäki; Contrarian Stories*, New York: Bloomsbury.

Nicol, Trish and Dominic Case (2001), 'Let's Talk Business Phillip Noyce Right At Home With Atlab's New Talent and Technology', *Metro Magazine*, 131/132, pp. 286–9.

Nowell Smith, Geoffrey (2012), 'From realism to neo-realism', in Lúcia Nagib, Chris Perriam and Rajinder Dudrah (eds), *Theorizing World Cinema*, New York: I.B.Tauris, pp. 147–59.

Noyes, Alexander D. (1894), 'The banks and the panic of 1893', *Political Science Quarterly*, 9/1, (March), pp. 12–30.

Nussbaum, Martha (1997), 'Capabilities and human rights', *Fordham Law Review*, 6/2, 197, pp. 273–300.

O'Connor, Ian (1993), 'Aboriginal child welfare law, policies and practices in Queensland: 1865–1989', *Australian Social Work*, 46/3, pp. 11–22.

Ogle, Tina (1993), 'Ship of Sorrows', *Time Out*, 14–21 July.

Oliveros, Pauline (1989/2005), *Deep Listening: A Composer's Sound Practice*, iUniverse Inc: New York.

O'Regan, Tom (1993), *Australian Television Culture*, Sydney: Allen and Unwin.

Osborne, William (2000), 'Under the abyss of otherness: Pauline Oliveros' deep listening and the *Sonic Meditations*', in Deborah Johnson and Wendy Oliver, (eds), *Women Making Art: Women in the Literary, Visual and Performing Arts Since 1960*, New York: Lang, pp. 65–86.

Pearson, Maeve (2004), 'Arcadian children: Benjamin, Fourier and the child of the Arcades', New Formations, 54, pp. 126–38.

——— (2007), 'Re-exposing the Jamesian Child: the paradox of children's privacy', *The Henry James Review*, 28/2 (Spring), pp. 101–19.

Bibliography

Perera, Suvendrini (2001), 'A line in the sea: the Tampa, boat stories and the border', *Cultural Studies Review*, 8/1, May, pp. 11–27.

Petek, Polona (2010), 'Highways, byways and dead ends: towards a non-Eurocentric cosmopolitanism through Yugonostalgia and Slovenian cinema', *New Review of Film and Television Studies*, 8/2, pp. 218–32.

Peters, John Durham (1999), 'Exile, nomadism and diaspora: the stakes of mobility in the western canon', in Hamid Naficy (ed.), *Home, Exile, Homeland: Film, Media and the Politics of Place*, New York and London: Routledge, pp. 17–41.

Phillips, Adam (2007), *Side Effects*, London: Penguin Books.

——— (2005), 'The forgetting museum', *Index on Censorship*, Vol 2. *Eurozine*. Online: http://www.eurozine.com/articles/2005-06-24-phillips-en.html, accessed 30 October 2016.

——— (2002), *Equals*, New York: Basic Books.

Phillips, Janet (2012), 'The Pacific Solution revisited: a statistical guide to the asylum seeker caseloads on Nauru and Manus Island.' Report published 4 September 2012. Online: http://parlinfo.aph.gov.au/parlInfo/download/library/prspub/1893669/upload_binary/1893669.pdf;fileType=application percent2Fpdf, accessed 1 April 2017.

Philo, Chris (2003), '"To go back up the side hill", memories, imaginations and reveries of childhood', *Children's Geographies*, 1/1, pp. 7–23.

Pickowicz, Paul G. (2011), 'Independent Chinese film: seeing the not-usually-visible in rural China,' in Lynch, Catherine, Robert B. Marks, and Paul G. Pickowicz, *Radicalism, Revolution, and Reform in Modern China*, Plymouth: Lexington, pp. 161–84.

Pierpoint, Mary (2000), 'Was Frank Baum a racist or just the creator of Oz?' Indian Country: today media network.com 25 October 2000. Online https://indiancountrymedianetwork.com/news/was-frank-baum-a-racist-or-just-the-creator-of-oz/, accessed 1st April 2017.

Pilkington, Doris/Nugi Garimara (1996), *Follow the Rabbit-Proof Fence*, Brisbane: University of Queensland Press.

Plaks, Andrew H. (1976), *Archetype and Allegory in the Dream of the Red Chamber*, Princeton: Princeton University Press.

Poznanski, Renée (2014), 'Anti-semitism and the rescue of Jews in France', in Jacques Semelin, Claire Andrieu and Sarah Gensburger (eds), *Resisting Genocide: The Multiple Forms of Rescue*, Oxford Scholarship Online, pp. 1–22.

Prout, Alan (2005), *The Future of Childhood*, Abingdon/Falmer: Routledge.

Pung, Alice (2011), *Her Father's Daughter*, Melbourne: Black Ink.

Puwar Nirmal (2007), 'Social cinema scenes', *Space and Culture*, 10, pp. 253–70.

Qiu, Zitong and Maria Elena Indelicato (2017), 'Beiqing, kuqing and national sentimentality in Liu Junyi's *Left Behind Children*', in Donald, Stephanie Hemelryk,

Bibliography

Emma Wilson and Sarah Wright (eds), *Childhood and Nation in Contemporary World Cinema: Borders and Encounters*, New York Bloomsbury, pp. 215–24.

Quinlivan, Davina (2012), *The Place of Breath in Cinema*, Edinburgh: Edinburgh University Press.

Qvortrup, Jens (2007), 'Editorial: a reminder', *Childhood*, 14/4, pp. 395–400.

Rafailidis, Vassilis (2003), Ταξίδι στο μύθο Δια της ιστορίας και στην ιστορία δια του μύθου [Into the Myth], Athens: Aigokeros.

Rancière, Jacques (2009), *The Emancipated Spectator* (trans. Gregory Elliott), London: Verso.

Rascaroli, Laura (2013), 'Becoming-minor in a sustainable Europe: the contemporary European art film and Aki Kaurismäki's *Le Havre*', Screen, 54/3, (Autumn), pp. 324–40.

Rashkin, Esther (2009), 'Psychoanalysis, cinema, history: personal and national loss in René Clément's *Forbidden Games*', *Projections*, 3/1 (Summer), pp. 53–76.

Ray, Greg (1991), 'Film-makers soak up the Carrington atmosphere', *Newcastle Herald*, 23 October.

Refugee Council of Australia (2016), *Thinking Beyond Offshore Processing: key recommendations from the Refugee Council of Australia*, 12 September. Online: http://www.refugeecouncil.org.au/getfacts/seekingsafety/asylum/offshore-processing/thinking-beyond-offshore-processing-key-recommendations-refugee-council-australia/, accessed 29 September 2016.

Ricoeur, Paul (2004), *Memory, History, Forgetting* (trans Kathleen Blamey and David Pellauer), Chicago: University of Chicago Press.

Roberts, Keith Daniel (2015), *The Rise and Fall of Liverpool Sectarianism: An Investigation into the Decline of Sectarian Antagonism on Merseyside*, PhD thesis, University of Liverpool repository.

Roberts, M.J.D. (2004). *Cambridge Social and Cultural Histories: Making English Morals: Voluntary Association and Moral Reform in England, 1787–1886*. Cambridge, Cambridge University Press.

Robinson, Luke (2013), *Independent Chinese Documentary: From the Studio to the Street*, London: Palgrave.

Robinson, Shirleene (2013), 'Regulating the Race: Aboriginal children in private European homes in colonial Australia', *Journal of Australian Studies*, 37/3, pp. 303–305.

Rose, Jacqueline S. (1984), *The Case of Peter Pan: Or, the Impossibility of Children's Fiction*. London: Macmillan.

Rothberg, Michael (2009), *Multidirectional Memory: Remembering the Holocaust in the Age of Decolonization*. Stanford: Stanford University Press.

Rudd, Kevin (2008), *Apology to Australia's Indigenous Peoples*, 13 February. Online http://www.aph.gov.au/house/rudd_speech.pdf, accessed 16 November 2010.

Bibliography

Rushdie, Salman (1992), *The Wizard of Oz: An Appreciation*, London: BFI Publishing (BFI Film Classics).

Ryono, Angel, and Matthew Galway (2015), 'Xinjiang under China: reflections on the multiple dimensions of the 2009 Urumqi uprising', *Asian Ethnicity*, 16/2, pp. 235–55.

Schor, Naomi (2001), 'Pensive texts and thinking statues: Balzac with Rodin', *Critical Inquiry*, 27/2 (Winter), pp. 239–65.

Schütte, Wolfram (1992), 'Ein zeitreisender Landvermesser', in Peter W. Jansen and W. Schütte (eds), *Theo Angelopoulos: Reihe Film 45*, Munchen, Wien: Carl Hanser, pp. 9–42.

—— 'Theo Angelopoulos: land-surveyor and time-traveler' http://zakka.dk/euroscreenwriters/interviews/theo_angelopoulos.htm, accessed 16 September 2016

Seiffert, Rachel (2001), *The Dark Room*, London: Random House.

—— (2013), *Lore*, London: Vintage International (Movie Tie-In).

Selcer, Richard F. (1990), 'From Tara to Oz and home again: home sweet movies', *Journal of Popular Film and Television*, 18/2, pp. 52–63.

Sen, Amartya (2006), *Identity and Violence: The Illusion of Destiny*, New York: Allen and Lane.

Serraillier, Ian (1956/2012), *The Silver Sword*, London: Vintage.

Seymour, David/UNESCO (1949), *Children of Europe*, Paris: UNESCO, publication 403. Online http://unesdoc.unesco.org/images/0013/001332/133216eb.pdf, accessed 7 September 2016.

Sheehan, Paul (2012), 'Road, fire, trees: Cormac McCarthy's post-America,' in Julian Murphet and Mark Steven (eds), *Styles of Extinction: Cormac McCarthy's The Road*, London: Continuum, pp. 89–108.

Sheldon, Nicola (2013), '"Something in the place of home": children in institutional care 1850–1918', in Nigel Goose and Katrina Honeyman (eds), *Childhood and Child Labour in Industrial England: Diversity and Agency 1750–1914*, Farnham: Ashgate, pp. 255–76.

Shute, Nevil (1957/2010), *On The Beach*, New York: Vintage International.

Silverman, Max (2015), *Palimpsestic Memory: The Holocaust and Colonialism in French and Francophone Fiction and Film*, Oxford: Berghahn.

Sinnerbrink, Robert (2015), Angelopoulos' gaze: modernism, history, cinematic ethics,' in Angelos Koutsoukaris and Mark Steven (eds), *Angelopoulos*, pp. 80–96.

Skelton, Tracey (2007), 'Children, young people, UNICEF and participation', *Children's Geographies*, 5/1, pp. 165–81.

Slater, Katherine Simons (2013), *Little Geographies: Children's Literature and Local Place*, University of California, San Diego. Unpublished PhD thesis. UMI Number: 3601902.

Bibliography

Smith, Simon C. (2007), 'Integration and disintegration: the attempted incorporation of Malta into the United Kingdom in the 1950s', *The Journal of Imperial and Commonwealth History*, 35/1, pp. 49–71.

Stoker, Bram (1993/1897), *Dracula*. London: Wordsworth Editions.

Su, Yang (2011), *Collective Killings in Rural China during the Cultural Revolution*, Cambridge: Cambridge University Press.

Swain, Shurlee and Margot Hillel (2010), *Child, Nation, Race, and Empire: Child Rescue Discourse, England, Canada and Australia, 1850-1915*, Manchester: Manchester University Press.

Tao, Lina (2014), 'Media representation of internal migrant children in China between 1990 and 2012', Masters Dissertation, UNSW.

Tavan, Gwenda (2012), 'Leadership: Arthur Calwell and the post-war immigration program', *Australian Journal of Politics & History*, 58/2, pp. 203–20.

Taylor, Steven J. (2014), 'Insanity, philanthropy and emigration: dealing with insane children in late-nineteenth-century north-west England,' *History of Psychiatry*, 25/2, pp. 224–36.

Tisdall, E. Kay M. and Samantha Punch (2012), 'Not so "new", looking critically at childhood studies,' *Children's Geographies*, 10/3, pp. 249–64.

Tomba, Luigi (2009), 'Of quality, harmony, and community: civilisation and the middle class in urban China', *positions*, 17/3, pp. 591–616.

Torchin, Leshu (2012), *Creating the Witness: Documenting Genocide on Film, Video and the Internet*, Minneapolis: University of Minnesota Press.

Treacher, Amal (2006), 'Children's imaginings and narratives: inhabiting complexity', *Feminist Review*, 82, pp. 96–113.

Triggs, Gillian (2014), *The Forgotten Children: National Inquiry into Immigration Detention*. Sydney: HRC. Online: www.humanrights.gov.au/sites/default/files/document/publication/forgotten_children_2014.pdf, accessed 20 September 2016.

Tyler, Imogen, Nick Gill, Deirdre Conlon and Ceri Oeppen (2014), 'The business of child detention: charitable co-option, migrant advocacy and activist outrage', *Race and Class*, 56/3, pp. 3–21.

Unger, Jonathan (2002), *The Transformation of Rural China*, New York: M.E.Sharpe.

UNICEF (1996), 'The Trauma of War'. Online http://www.unicef.org/sowc96/7trauma.htm, accessed 7 September 2016. (UNICEF re-organisaion of webpages underway 2017.)

UNICEF, (1996) 'Children in War'. Online http://www.unicef.org/sowc96/1cinwar.htm, accessed 7 September 2016. (UNICEF re-organisaion of webpages underway 2017.)

UNICEF (2015), 'Refugee and Migrant Children in Europe'. Online http://www.unicef.org/publicpartnerships/files/Refugee_and_migrant_children_in_Europe-_Sept_2015.pdf, accessed 13 July 2016. (UNICEF re-organisaion of webpages underway 2017.)

Bibliography

Wacquant, Loïc (2008), *Urban Outcasts: A Comparative Sociology of Urban Marginality*, London: Polity.

Watkin, William (2014), 'The signature of all things: Agamben's philosophical archaeology', *MLN*, 129/1, (January), pp. 139-61.

Werbner, Pnina (2006), 'Understanding vernacular cosmopolitanism', *Anthropology News* 47/5, pp. 7-11.

Wiesel, Elie (1958/2006), *Night* (trans. Marion Wiesel), London: Penguin Classics.

Wigoder, Meir (2012), 'The acrobatic gaze and the pensive image in Palestinian morgue photography', *Critical Inquiry*, 38/2, pp. 267-88.

Wilkes Tucker, Anne, Will Michaels and Natalie Zelt (2012), *War Photography: Images of Armed Conflict and its Aftermath*, Museum of Contemporary Art, New Haven: Yale University Press.

Wilson, Emma (2003), *Cinema's Missing Children*, London: Wallflower Press.

Williams, Althea and Sarah Ehrlich (2013), 'Escaping the train to Auschwitz', *BBC News Online*, 20 April. Online http://www.bbc.com/news/magazine-22188075, accessed 4 October 2016.

Woronov, Terry E. (2004), 'In the eye of the chicken: hierarchy and marginality among Beijing's migrant schoolchildren', *Ethnography*, 5/3, pp. 289-313.

—— (2007), 'Performing the nation, China's children as Little Red Pioneers,' *Anthropological Quarterly*, 80/3, pp. 647-72.

—— (2009), 'Governing China's children: governmentality and "Education for Quality"', *Positions: East Asia Cultures Critique*,17/3, pp. 567-89.

Yan, Hairong (2003), 'Spectralization of the rural: reinterpreting the labor mobility of rural young women in post-Mao China', *American Ethnologist*, 30/4, pp. 1-19.

Yang, Mayfair Mei-hui (1994), *Gifts, Favors and Banquets: The Art of Social Relationships in China*, Ithaca, NY: Cornell University Press.

Ye, Jingzhong and Lu, Pan (2011), 'Differentiated childhoods: impacts of rural labor migration on left-behind children in China', *Journal of Peasant Studies*, 38/2, pp. 355-77.

Zhang, Xudong (2012), 'The will to allegory and the origin of Chinese modernism: rereading Lu Xun's Ah Q - the real story', in M. Wolleager and M. Eatough, *The Oxford Handbook of Global Modernisms*, Oxford: Oxford University Press (Oxford Handbooks). Online. http://www.oxfordhandbooks.com/view/10.1093/oxfordhb/9780195338904.001.0001/oxfordhb-9780195338904-e-7?print=pdf, accessed 16 September 2016.

Zhang, Yingjin (2012), 'Directors, aesthetics, genres: Chinese postsocialist cinema, 1979-2010', in Yingjin Wang (ed), *A Companion to Chinese Cinema*, Oxford: Wiley Blackwell, pp. 57-74.

Žižek, Slavoj (2007), *Enjoy Your Symptom!: Jacques Lacan in Hollywood and Out*, London: Routledge.

Filmography

28 Days Later (Danny Boyle, UK, 2012)
At Home in the World (Andreas Koefoed, Denmark, 2015) [*Et hjem i verden*]
Au Revoir Les Enfants (Louis Malle, France, 1987)
Australia (Baz Luhrmann, USA/Australia, 2008)
Beekeeper, The (Theo Angelopoulos, Greece/France/Italy, 1986) [Ο Μελισσοκόμος]
Bicycle Thieves (Vittorio de Sica, Italy, 1948)
Book Thief, The (Brian Percival, USA, Germany, 2013)
Bran Nue Dae (Rachel Perkins, Australia, 2009)
Caché (Michael Haneke, France/Austria/Germany/Italy, 2005)
Chitty Chitty Bang Bang (Ken Hughes, UK, 1968)
Chocolat (Claire Denis, France/West Germany Cameroon, 1988)
Citizen Kane (Orson Welles, USA, 1941)
Diamonds of the Night (Jan Němec, Czechoslovakia, 1964) [*Démanty noci*]
Emerald City (Michael Jenkins, Australia, 1988)
Eternity and a Day (Theo Angelopoulos, Greece, 1998)
Forbidden Games (Rene Clement, France, 1952) [*Les Jeux Interdits*]
Four Hundred Blows /Les Quatre Cent Coups (François Truffaut, France, 1959)
Frozen (Chris Buck and Jennifer Lee, USA, 2013)
Germany Year Zero (Roberto Rossellini, Italy, 1948)
Harry Potter and the Chamber of Secrets (Chris Columbus, USA, 2002)
Home Alone 2 (Chis Columbus, USA, 1992)
Hunger Games – Catching Fire, The (Francis Lawrence, USA, 2013).
Hunters, The (Theo Angelopoulos, Greece, 1977)
I am Legend (Francis Lawrence, USA, 2007)
Ice Storm, The (Ang Lee, USA, 1997)
In This World (Michael Winterbottom, UK, 2002)
Ivan's Childhood (Andrei Tarkovsky, USSR, 1962)
Jacquot de Nantes (Agnès Varda, France, 1991)
Jemima and Johnny (Lionel Ngakane, South Africa/UK, 1966)
Ju Dou (Zhang Yimou, China, 1988)
Kisses (Lance Daly, Ireland, 2008)
Landscape in the Mist (Theo Angelopoulos, Greece, 1988) [Τοπίοστην Ομίχλη]
Last Train, The (Joseph Vilmaier and Dana Vávrová, Germany/Czech Republic, 2006) [*Der Letzte Zug*]

Filmography

Last Train Home (Fan Lixin, Canada, 2009)
Le Havre (Aki Kaurismäki, France, 2011)
Leaving of Liverpool, The (Michael Jenkins, Australia/UK, 1992)
Lin Puzi's Shop (Shui Ha, China, 1959)
Little Moth (Peng Tao, China, 2007)
Lore (Cate Shortland, Australia/Germany, 2012)
Ma Liang and his Magic Paintbrush (*Magic Brush*) (Jin Xi, China, 1955) [*Shen bi*]
Mad Max (George Miller, Australia, 1979)
Muriel (Alain Resnais, France, 1963) [*Le temps de retour*]
Night and Fog (Alain Resnais, France, 1956) [*Nuit et brouillard*]
Night of the Living Dead, The (George A. Romero, USA, 1968)
On the Beach (Stanley Kramer, USA, 1959)
Once My Mother (Sophia Turkiewicz, Australia, 2013)
Oranges and Sunshine (Jim Loach, UK/Australia, 2010)
Rabbit-Proof Fence (Philip Noyes, Australia, 2002)
Railroad of Hope (Ning Ying, China, 2002) [Xiwang zhi you 希望之旅]
Reconstruction (Theo Angelopoulos, Greece, 1970) [Αναπαράσταση]
Red Balloon, The (Henri Lamourisse, France, 1956) *Le ballon rouge*
Red Dog (Kriv Stenders, Australia, 2011)
River's Edge (Tim Hunter, USA, 1986)
Road, The (John Hillcoat, USA, 2009)
Sanmao's Travels (Zhao Ming and Yan Gong, China, 1949) [*Sanmao liu lang ji*]
Shining, The (Stanley Kubrick, USA, 1980)
Shoeshine (Vittorio de Sica, Italy, 1946) [*Sciuscià*]
Springtime in an English Village (Colonial Film Unit, UK, 1944)
Stand By Me (Rob Reiner, USA, 1987)
Travelling Players, The (Theo Angelopoulos, Greece, 1975) [Ο Θίασος]
Truce, The (Francesco Rosi, Italy/France, 1997)
Turtles Can Fly (Bahman Ghobadi, Kurdish Iraq, 2004) [*Kûsî Jî Dikarin Bifirin*]
Twilight (Catherine Hardwicke, USA, 2008)
Un Chien Andalou (Luis Buñuel, France, 1928)
Voyage to Cythera (Theo Angelopoulos, Greece/Italy/UK/West Germany, 1984) [Ταξίδι στα Κύθηρα]
Walkabout (Nic Roeg, UK/Australia, 1971)
War Horse (Steven Spielberg, USA, 2011)
Welcome (Philippe Lioret, France, 2009)
White Material (Claire Denis, France, 2009)
Wild Child (Nick Moore, UK/USA/France, 2008)
Wings of Desire (Wim Wenders, Germany, 1987) [*Der Himmel über Berlin*]
Wizard of Oz, The (Victor Fleming, George Cukor (uncredited), USA, 1939)
Yellow Balloon, The (J. Lee Thompson, UK, 1953)

Index

28 Days Later, 114

abandonment, 30, 92, 73, 80, 85, 92, 104–5, 188, 189
Aboriginal Australians, 47, 50, 57, 153
  on film, 39–40, 48
  see also Indigenous Australians
activism/activist, 143–4, 148, 165, 208 n.27
  for children, 3, 12, 26
  films, 6, 62, 161–2, 213 n.26
adaptability, 2, 72
adolescence *see* teenage/rs
adult(s), 13, 21–2, 36, 46, 48, 73, 84, 105, 107, 123
  audience, 18, 19, 23, 98
  authority/power, 26, 69, 72, 62, 72
  becoming an, 23, 40, 72, 79, 88, 198
  companions, 6, 91–2
  criminality and violence, 4, 6, 14–15, 38, 78, 124, 162, 169–70, 201
  failure, 16, 41, 54, 81, 112, 133, 138
  nostalgia and fantasy, 7, 8–11, 27–8, 90
  as performative, 23–5, 57, 68
  as peripheral and limited, 64, 69, 77, 128, 132, 134, 139, 167
  untrustworthy, 97, 162
  world, 3, 10, 22–3, 72, 126, 131, 136–7, 147
  writing a child, 5, 45–6, 81

Afghanistan, 4, 53
Africa, 4, 6, 12, 83
  France in, 28
Agamben, Giorgio, 4, 7, 20, 151
Ahmed, Sara, 9–10, 16, 46
Algeria, 77, 183, 185
America(n), 18–19, 25, 26–7, 44, 96
  abroad, 27, 30, 35, 89
  family, 117, 119, 121
  nightmares, 112, 115, 116
Anderson, Mark M., 117
angel, 15, 139, 187, 189
  guardian, 123–5, 126, 128, 129
  of history, 27, 122, 130
  whispers of, 126, 128
  see also Wings of Desire
Angelopoulos, Theo, 8, 121–4, 126–7, 129–31, 134, 136–9
Ansell, Nicola, 22, 50
anxiety, 88, 96, 106, 183, 186
  adult, 26, 81, 90
  separation, 12, 160
apocalyptic world, 110, 115, 117
  fear of, 106
  post-, 112
Arcades project, 13, 199
  see also Benjamin, Walter
archive, the, 6, 9, 142–4, 156, 158, 170–1, 185–6
  no, 112

Index

arrival
  Dorothy's, 16, 17–18, 30, 41–2, 142
  journey to, and from, 12–13, 21, 25–6, 51, 73–4, 83, 188
  space of, 6, 16, 57, 72, 85–7, 94, 116, 122, 129, 144, 150, 171
  see also home; migration; waiting
Asia-as-method, 22
asylum seekers, 7, 12, 92, 123, 204 no.6
At Home in the World, 12
Au Revoir Les Enfants, 78–9
Auschwitz, 151, 177, 187–8, 217 n.27
Australia, 38–40
Australia
  child migration to, 3, 4, 34, 73, 142–3, 146, 147–8, 150–3, 160–9
  as Oz, 38–40
  postwar, 20, 25, 153
  see also Aboriginal Australians; film, workshops; Indigenous Australians; *Oranges and Sunshine*; *Rabbit-Proof Fence*; Stolen Generations

Banardo's, 149–51
bare life, 4, 7, 108, 113, 132
  see also Agamben, Georgio
Baum, Frank, 1, 8–19, 24, 27, 44, 81
becoming, 22–3, 24, 33, 40
Beekeeper, The, 126
being, 22–3, 24, 133, 135
  'at home', 59
  non/not, 24, 33
  state of, 52, 129, 191
  ways of, 18
being-in-the-world, 7, 18

belonging, 2, 16, 21, 33, 49, 72, 78, 86, 94, 97, 131, 184
  colonialism and, 27, 28, 44
  national, 131, 167
Benjamin, Walter, 10, 13–14, 138, 193, 199–200
Berghahn, Daniela, 1–2
Berlant, Lauren, 100
betrayal, 8, 48, 53, 78, 83, 103, 132, 146, 162, 170, 177
Bicycle Thieves, 88
Book of Rites, 9, 10
Book Thief, The, 59
border(s)
  controls, 26, 128, 133, 149, 171
  crossings, 4, 7, 8, 48, 72, 81, 86, 105, 122, 160
  less, 72, 126
  personal/non-physical, 87, 103, 130–1, 134, 139
  soft/hard, 8, 88, 90
Boyle, Danny, 114
Bran Nue Dae, 59
breath/ing
  not, 68, 92
  not safe to/holding, 86–7, 90–1, 93, 193, 201–2
  space for, 4, 94, 173–4, 177–8, 191
  strained, 174–5
  see also listening; waiting
Buchenwald, 177, 180
Buck-Morss, Susan, 10
Bullied Teacher, 60–1
bullying, 15, 46, 56, 60, 163
Buñuel, Luis, 174–6, 179, 182

Caché, 77
Calvino, Italo, 14–15

Index

camera, the, 31, 33, 68
  as eye, 12, 86, 97, 108, 146, 174
Camper, Fred, 191
Canada, 25, 142, 148, 150, 152, 156, 157, 160
  see also migration, forced
cannibals, 111, 112–15, 119, 123
capitalism, 10, 112, 114
  accelerated, 96
Carthy, Eliza, 15
Castañeda, Claudia, 46
Catholic(s), 152–4, 165–9, 171
  French, 78
  philanthropy, 153–9, 161
  reformatories, 151–2
  school, 57, 61, 163
  see also Leaving of Liverpool, The
Chen Kuan-hsing, 22
child
  as collector, 10–11, 13–14, 15, 200
  cosmopolitan, 45–7, 54, 72–3, 94
  emigration (from England), 150, 152–3, 156, 164, 165, 168–9, 170–1
  homelessness, 5, 34, 46, 184
  migrant, 3–5, 16, 30, 34–5, 38, 46, 67, 71–5, 92, 146, 148–50, 153–8
  refugee, 3, 45–7, 71, 79, 81, 122, 130, 131, 133, 146, 201
  resilience, 6, 8
  soldiers, 5, 28–9, 147, 230 n.16
  travelling alone, 6, 32–4, 54, 80, 88, 92, 131, 133, 145
  voice, 4, 23, 45, 68, 143
child abuse, 131, 144
  rape, 123, 125, 127, 129, 133, 139, 147
  systemic, 151, 160, 161–2, 167, 169–71

  see also Little Moth
child detention, 26, 50, 72, 148–9, 151, 170–1
  in Australia, 47, 146, 164
child life, 7–9, 11–12, 45, 13, 197, 201
Child Migrants Trust (UK), 3, 169
childhood, 2, 6, 7, 8–10, 13–14, 20, 73, 74, 105, 123, 133, 137, 165, 166, 169
  cinematic politics of, 17, 24
  ephemerality and, 195–6, 198, 200
  flattened ontology of, 28, 33, 72, 76, 90
  immobility and, 108–9
  lost, 142, 162, 198, 201
  memories of, 82–3, 85
  as method, 22–3, 69, 76, 101
  in social discourse, 25–6, 46, 132
  transitions, 21–2, 72
  in war, 29, 77, 80–1
  see also child, migrant; child life
Children of Europe, 3, 80
children's crusade/Children's Crusade, the, 144–6
Children's Crusade, The, 142, 146
Chilton Thomas, Arthur, 152, 153, 156–7
China, Peoples Republic of
  domestic migration in, 8, 20, 25, 30–1, 34, 45, 67, 198
  Liberation, 30, 51, 102
  modernisation in, 4, 8, 12, 95, 97–8, 99–105, 109, 117, 201
  see also film, workshops; guanxi; *Little Moth*; *Railroad of Hope*; *Sanmao's Travels*
Chitty Chitty Bang Bang, 90
Chocolat, 40

Index

cinema, 14, 138, 174, 176, 183–4
    child (migrant) in, 3–4, 8, 13, 17, 20–5, 35, 50, 72, 76, 101, 105
    imagination and storytelling, 19, 47, 51, 85, 89, 92, 126–7, 129, 131, 134
    missing child in, 17, 33
    see also colour; Dorothy, as signature; Dorothy Complex, the; film
Citizen Kane, 9
citizenship, 46, 74
city, 12, 36–8, 59, 66, 76–7, 89
    right to, 42, 74, 79, 86
Cliff, Tom, 35
Cohen, Sara Simcha, 114–15
collection(s), 9–10, 13, 101
    image/film, 3, 6, 7, 56, 63, 198, 200
    Red Balloon, 63, 65
    see also archive, the; child, as collector; memory
colonial
    expansion, 44, 142, 148–9, 151–6, 171
    privilege and belonging, 5, 22, 27–30, 39, 59, 89
    see also Empire; imperial(ism); post-colonial
colour
    coding for emotion, 45, 47–50, 55, 59
    in film, 36, 56, 64, 76–7, 87, 93, 170
    Technicolor, 19, 38, 40
comedy, 54, 58
    slapstick, 51, 63, 69
Commonwealth, 142, 146, 147, 151, 161, 167, 184
    see also Empire

concentration camps, 113, 115–16, 151, 177, 178, 182, 192
Confucian values, 21, 33, 110
Convention of the Rights of the Child, 79
Coote, Diana, 98
cosmopolitan, 31, 40, 78–9
    child migrants as, 45–7, 54, 72–3, 94
    consciousness, 75, 76, 86
    Dorothy as, 27, 30, 41, 44
    gaze, 81, 85, 92
courage, 5, 26, 37, 72, 88, 121, 126, 131, 135, 147, 180

Daly, Lance, 23, 35–6
Dart, Gregory, 199
daydreaming, 14, 195, 198–201
De Bruyn, 111–12
death
    of a child, 106, 121
    life and, 52, 87, 108, 110, 115
    see also concentration camps; Lazarus
Death of Yasar, 56
Debord, Guy, 199
dehumanisation, 170, 181, 186
Denis, Claire, 5, 28, 40, 198
deportation, 13, 78, 82–3, 149, 152, 188
despair, 54, 80, 100, 102, 110, 125, 127, 131, 136, 138, 168, 176
Diamonds of the Night, 175, 176–87, 190, 192–3
Dickson, Gary, 144–6
diegetic, 92, 127, 137, 176
    agency, 122
    experience, 179
    extra-, 108, 123
    sound, 177, 191, 193

Index

documentary, 3, 9, 81
  see also At Home in the World; In This World; Once My Mother; Railroad of Hope
doll(s), 10, 58, 61, 108, 109
  see also toys
Dorothy (Gale), 4, 16, 17–19, 26, 40–2, 44, 71
  figure, 5, 6, 41, 142, 202
  friends of, 37
  Garland's, 19, 24, 58
  sign of, 19, 24, 43, 89
  as signature, 6, 15, 20–2, 24–5, 27–9, 33, 36, 72, 81, 89, 121, 200, 202
  see also ruby slippers; *Wizard of Oz, The*
Dorothy Complex, the, 6, 7, 17, 21–2, 26–7, 30, 33, 178, 198
double occupancy, 36, 87, 88–9
Dracula, 114
drained of life, 191–2, 193
dreams/dreaming, 131, 167
  of children, 13–14, 88, 111, 198–200
  Dorothy, 6, 20, 27, 40, 44, 201
  migrant, 67, 116, 117, 126, 130, 184
  sequence, 61, 178, 187–8, 192
  state, 98, 179, 182
drowning, 39, 146, 147, 170, 173, 199

Elsaesser, Thomas, 36
Emerald City, 39
Emerald City, 18, 29, 37, 89
empathy, 3, 79, 104, 112, 114, 117
Empire (British), 2, 38, 75, 199
  building, 146, 150–2, 155–7, 165–6, 169–71

  see also Australia, migration to; imperial(ism); *Leaving of Liverpool, The*
enchantment, 10, 14, 29, 136, 180
ephemerality, 7–8, 9–15, 176, 195, 198, 200–1
Eternity and a Day, 126

fairytale, 5, 18–19, 180, 186–8
  narrative, 4, 87, 124, 129, 131–2, 135
family
  belonging, 2, 24, 58, 78
  as dangerous, 23, 36, 38
  fragmentation, 41, 69, 101
  losing, 56, 184
  pressures on, 51, 62
  separated from, 33–5, 53, 132, 142, 144, 156–60
  substitute, 16, 80, 116–17
  see also Confucian values
famine, 41
  Chinese, 105, 198
  Irish, 154, 161
fantasy
  child/teen, 13, 15, 132
  colonial, 5, 27–8, 29
  of escape, 17, 18, 81, 200
  realism and, 19, 35, 40
  structure, 21–2, 44, 80, 85
Fascists, 14, 15
F(f)ather, 124, 126–8, 130, 135, 139
fathers, 2, 13, 36, 102, 110, 116, 136, 177, 180
  death of, 52, 57, 181
  figure, 113, 117, 127
  reunion with, 79, 189
  see also Road, The

267

Index

fear, 68, 80–1, 90, 97, 98, 105–6, 168, 202
  driven by, 25, 58
  visualising, 5, 55, 113, 115
feeling(s)
  access to, 9, 47
  human, 103–4, 110, 112, 117
  structure of, 92, 148
  see also human, feeling; renqing
film
  and emotion, 9, 33, 46–9, 54, 85, 101, 160
  -maker, 5, 12–13, 31, 76, 81, 85, 122–3, 131–2, 134, 175, 180
  spectator, 8, 12, 23, 36, 75, 92, 110, 124–5, 191
  workshops, 7, 45, 46–69, 113
  see also childhood, as method
Flannagan, Richard, 55
flattened ontology, 36, 50, 63, 68, 74, 75, 77, 85
  of childhood, 28, 33, 72, 76, 90
  definition, 22
Flusser, Vilém, 97, 98
Forbidden Games, 77, 81
forgetting, 11, 85, 96, 182
  profound, 9
Four Hundred Blows/Les Quatre Cent Coups, 88
fragility, 8, 11, 81, 103, 121
Frank, Anne, 117
Freud, Sigmund, 12, 14, 199
Friedberg, Anne, 12
friendship, 4, 26, 29, 54, 63, 64, 91
  bonds of, 78–9, 107, 133
  on film, 46, 56–7, 61, 76
Frozen, 59
Funchion, John, 27, 30, 35

Garland, Judy *see* Dorothy, Garland's
gaze, 20, 81, 84, 98, 130
  collective cosmopolitan, 85
genocide, 175, 184
  see also Auschwitz; Buchenwald; concentration camps
Germany, 122, 126, 130, 186, 190
Germany Year Zero, 105
Ghost Story, 52–3, 60
ghosts, 36, 46, 52–3, 58, 60, 68, 85, 121, 130, 176, 179, 191, 196–7
Gilroy, Paul, 72, 74, 75–6, 86
global
  change, 4, 20, 22
  conflict, 53
  imagination, 38, 64
  migration, 3, 74, 144, 149, 166, 200
  networks and flows, 50, 54, 108, 148
  understandings, 46, 60
God, 68, 113, 138, 150, 168, 176
  death of, 176, 180
  silence of, 121, 126, 128
gods, 135, 138
Great Depression, 18–19, 27
Greece, 121–3, 126, 128, 129–30, 132, 134, 137–8
  Civil War, 8, 122, 130
grief, 130, 132, 135, 160, 167
  national, 5, 8
Grootenboer, Hanneke, 135
growing up, 21, 24, 25, 47
  in war, 79, 201
Guangzhou, 62–3, 99
guanxi, 100–1, 103, 117
guilt, 30, 133, 151
Gulpilil, David, 39–40, 48

268

Index

Han Chinese, 30–1, 33, 35
happy endings, 39, 77, 88, 109, 116–17, 177
Harry Potter, 59, 60
heimat, 190
Hemelryk, P.E.J., 155, 156, 164–5
heroic, 39, 106–7, 122–3, 185
   Dorothy as, 18, 26, 44
   non-, 29
   tropes, 4, 37, 146
   working class, 168–9, 170
Hitchcock, Alfred, 107, 110
Holocaust, 115, 117, 183
home, 2, 22, 61, 78, 115
   being at, 39, 59, 72, 74
   leaving, 17, 58, 122, 142, 178
   no place like, 6, 18, 20, 26, 30, 90, 112, 170, 202
   place called, 5, 38, 41, 86–7, 143, 177, 184, 187–8
   return to, 24, 27, 42, 43, 71, 139, 168–9, 175, 189
   search for, 4, 5, 80, 84, 126, 128, 130–1, 167
Home Alone 2 54
homelessness, 97, 122
   child/hood, 5, 34, 46, 184
   mobility-as-, 2, 16, 17
Honig, Bonnie, 202
hope, 17, 80
   childish, 10, 13, 111, 112, 201
   despair and, 53, 54, 81, 99
   destruction of, 7, 26, 113
hospitality,
   failure of, 6, 15–16, 30
human, 7, 116, 121
   condition, 11, 19, 22, 24
   feeling, 103–4, 110, 112, 117
   not human, 28, 112–15
   see also zombies
humanity, 8, 96, 101, 106
   in-, 113–16, 176
Humphreys, Margaret, 162, 169, 229 n.8
Hunger Games – Catching Fire, The, 59

I am Legend, 113–14, 117
Ice Storm, The, 23–4
identity, 156
   cultural, 26, 27, 46, 57, 60
   fragmented/loss of, 97, 138, 165
   place and, 74, 96
imaginary, 1, 13, 19, 28, 113, 126, 133, 167, 190
   border/boundaries, 62, 133
   geo-spatial, 64, 72, 130
imagination, 104, 112
   cinematic, 19
   children's, 6, 68, 79, 200
   cosmopolitan, 76
   local/national/international, 38, 75, 99
   migrant, 26, 44, 71, 86, 89, 143
immobility, 97–8, 105, 108, 109
imperial(ism), 27, 142, 150, 161, 164, 170–1
   imagination, 75
   post-, 25, 143, 144, 148, 153, 165
   threat, 35, 74
In This World, 45, 85–7, 90, 92
Indigenous Australians
   high school students, 45, 57–62
   violence towards/dispossession of, 38–9, 184, 196, 199
   see also Rabbit-Proof Fence; Stolen Generations

Index

inertia, 97–8, 106, 108–9, 126
innocence
   dangerous, 137, 139
   losing, 50, 107, 109, 131, 132
   as problematic/fantasy, 5, 26, 27–8, 30, 46, 117, 132–3, 167
Ireland, 35–6
Ivan's Childhood, 187–8

Jacquot de Nantes, 50
Jemima and Johnny, 76–8
Jewish people, 115, 117, 157, 186, 188–90
   Czech, 177, 178
   French, 77–8, 218 n.36
Jin Nü, 195–8
Ju Dou, 21

Kansas, 6, 18–20, 27, 30, 40–1, 44, 59, 110, 200
Kaurismäki, Ari, 87–8, 89, 93
Kearney, Kevin, 111–12
Kilduff, Hannah, 108
Kisses, 23, 35–6, 199
Kubrick, Stanley, 36

Landsberg, Alison, 183–4
Landscape in the Mist, 8, 54, 121–39
Last Train, The, 188–9, 190
Last Train Home, 67
Lazarus, 113
Le Havre, 87–90, 92–4
Le Testament Français, 10
Leaving of Liverpool, The, 143–4, 147, 157, 160, 162–71
   see also Australia; migration to; Catholic(s); Liverpool
Lebeau, Vicky, 105–6, 112

Lee, Ang, 22–3
left-behind-children, 34, 99, 105
Levi, Primo, 113, 177, 178, 187–8
liberty, 4, 78, 153
Lin Puzi's Shop, 102
listening, 4, 193
   children, 108, 198
   deep, 173, 177–8, 191
   to silence, 175
Little Moth, 8, 95–8, 100–10, 112, 116–19, 124, 147
Littlefield, Henry, 18–19
Liverpool, 143, 150, 154–7, 161, 164–71
Loach, Ken, 73, 162
London, 76, 89, 90–1, 149–50
   see also film, workshops
loneliness, 28, 56, 111, 116, 181
   away from home, 5, 13, 33, 131, 160, 161, 188
Lore, 187, 189–90
Lost, 56
Luhrmann, Baz, 38–9
Lury, Karen, 5, 207 n.19, 224 n.34
Lustig, Arnošt, 176–8, 181, 184
Lynch, Gordon, 150–1, 152, 157

Ma Liang and his Magic Paintbrush, 199, 200
McCarthy, Cormac, 11, 110–12, 116
Mad Max, 112, 115
magic, 199, 202
   of cinema, 18, 126–7, 129
   migrant, 39, 179, 187
   places, 15, 37, 40, 89, 121, 124, 135–6
Makine, Andreï, 10
Malle, Louis, 78–9

Index

Marks, Laura, 25
maturation, 39, 50, 123, 124, 131, 189
  accelerated, 6, 79-80, 127
  in Dorothy Complex, 6, 17, 21, 26, 37, 72, 121, 178
  melancholy, 106-8, 112
  memory, 25, 116, 143, 148, 173, 177, 192, 193
    adult, 6, 9, 90, 132
    collective historical, 112, 129-30, 161, 184
    embodied, 79, 129, 188
    layered/palimpsestic, 85, 183, 185
    visualising, 52, 55, 151, 179, 180
    work, 11-12, 14, 82
    see also forgetting; nostalgia
migrant(s), 31-2, 35, 37, 44, 62-3, 68, 86-8, 90, 98-9, 139
  child, 3-5, 16, 30, 34-5, 38, 46, 67, 71-5, 92, 146, 148-50, 153-8
  Dorothy as, 20, 22, 26, 40-2, 44, 72, 81, 202
  experiences of, 25-6, 47, 50, 54, 65, 85, 105, 123, 129, 168-9
  see also cosmopolitan; Dorothy Complex, the
migration, 25-6, 42, 43, 89, 101, 103, 116, 130-1, 201
  to Australia (forced), 3, 4, 34, 73, 142-3, 146, 147-8, 150-3, 160-9
  child, 3-6, 8, 46, 74, 90, 144-5, 156
  domestic, 30-5, 44, 67
  forced, 17, 20, 39, 54, 86, 170-1, 180, 199
  as journey/process, 12, 18, 30, 42, 47, 83, 87
  onscreen, 6, 8, 13, 20, 21, 24, 33, 45-6, 51, 76, 81, 101, 124, 188

  rural-urban, 51, 96, 98
  see also double occupancy; home
mobility, 16, 46, 71-4, 90, 93, 130, 138, 200
  children's, 17, 64, 84, 124, 149
  as journeying, 45, 47, 54
  stories of, 90, 92, 132, 144
  waves of, 25, 165
  see also cosmopolitan; homelessness; immobility; migration
monsters, 4, 54, 113, 114
morality, 95
  life without, 96, 114
  national, 26
mothers, 21, 36, 104
  and daughters, 8, 58, 82, 84-5
  leaving, 122-30, 133, 169, 190
  looking for, 87, 160
  losing/taken from, 9, 39, 47, 141, 153, 187
mourn/ing, 63, 85, 107-8, 111
  failure to, 105-6, 108-9, 112
  loss of a child, 6
  passing of childhood, 7, 10
Muriel, 183, 185
mutuality, 46, 100-1, 112
My Old Home, 99-100

Němec, Jan, 175-8, 183-5, 193
New School, 56, 57
Ngakane, Lionel, 76, 78
Night and Fog, 192
Night of the Living Dead, The, 114
Ning, Ying, 21, 30-1, 33-4
nostalgia, 39-40, 107, 170
  adult, 6, 8-11
  for place, 27, 130, 186
  postcolonial, 195

Index

object(s), 1, 9–11, 15, 46, 60, 138, 170
  beloved, 59, 64, 91
  ephemeral, 14
  transitional, 10, 13, 28, 58, 59
  treated as an, 102, 109
  see also collection(s);
    ephemerality; memory
obligation, 151, 164
Oedipus complex, 21
Oliveros, Pauline, 177–8, 191
On the Beach, 112
Once My Mother, 82–5, 169
optimism, 81, 129
  American (Western), 19, 27, 30, 117
  children and, 13, 14, 54, 108–9, 163
  cruel, 100
  lack of, 86, 95
Oranges and Sunshine, 73, 142, 162, 164
  see also Humphreys, Margaret
orphan(s)
  'managing,' 153, 156
  on screen, 17–18, 77, 116, 167, 180, 187
orphanage, 83, 85
  Liverpool, 147, 160, 164, 169
Oz, 16, 18, 29, 44, 121
  allusions to, 36–7, 38–40, 112, 168
  arrival/departure, 16, 24, 59, 130
  and Kansas, 19–20, 110, 200

Palaiologou, Tania, 122–3, 127, 134, 139
Peng Tao, 95, 97, 100, 102–3, 105, 108, 109–10
philanthropy, 144, 148, 150, 151, 157, 160, 164–5, 171
Phillips, Adam, 11, 132, 133

photographs, 85, 138, 189, 192
  documenting through, 8, 9, 35, 80, 83, 115, 185
Pied Piper, 90, 145–6, 177
place, 68, 75, 98, 167
  non-, 12, 29, 96–7, 104
  safe, 16, 53
  see also arrival; cosmopolitan; double occupancy; home
playing, 14, 25, 56–7, 63–4, 76–7, 79, 137, 188
poetry, 142, 146–7, 168, 200
post-colonial, 20, 28, 30, 44, 46, 75, 76, 170–1, 195, 198
  whiteness, 27, 38–9, 62
poverty, 74, 145
  in China, 68, 96, 99, 100, 102
  in Dorothy's America, 18, 26, 44, 142
  in Liverpool, 161
  see also Great Depression
Prague, 177, 178–9, 182, 193
Puwar, Nirmal, 85

quality, 8, 98–9
  without, 104
(Q)queen, 75, 155, 167
  in Oz, 5, 40
queer/ing, 20–1, 24, 26–7, 33
  the text, 19
Qvortrup Jens, 46

Rabbit-Proof Fence, 47–50, 59, 73, 153
Railroad of Hope, 21, 30, 32, 33–5
Rascaroli, Laura, 89
reciprocity, 23–4, 101, 112
Red Balloon, the, 63–4, 76–7, 99
redemption, 14, 124, 127, 131–2
refugee(s), 90, 102, 195, 202

272

Index

camps/detention centres, 12, 164, 170–1
children, 3, 45–7, 71, 79, 81, 122, 130, 131, 133, 146, 201
  journeys, 77, 83, 86–7, 111, 116, 189
  programmes, 7, 55, 153
  see also breath/ing; child, migrant; *Silver Sword, The*; waiting
religion, 57
  and ceremonies, 46, 59
  Christian symbolism, 61, 126–31, 134
  and empire, 142–5, 148, 151, 161, 165, 170
  see also Catholic(s); Children's Crusade; Empire; Jewish people
renqing, 103, 107, 112, 222 no.21
residency
  rights, 12, 89, 99
  undocumented, 68
Resnais, Alain, 183, 185, 192
Ricoeur, Paul, 9, 12
Rivers Edge, 105–7, 112
Road, The
  book, 11, 110–12
  film, 112–18, 123
Rose, Jacqueline, 45, 63
Rothberg, Michael, 185
ruby slippers, 30, 37, 38, 179–80, 199
  see also shoes
Rushdie, Salman, 18, 20, 24, 72, 202

sacrifice, 4, 53, 113, 114, 116, 124, 128–9, 139
safety
  lack of, 24
  places of, 16, 75, 77, 78, 131
  precarious, 12, 52, 129
  seeking, 4, 94, 122, 170

Sanmao's Travels, 51, 63
school, 63, 67
  classroom, 52, 198–200
  farm, 147, 152, 162, 163
  journey, to 32, 34
  spaces of, 52–3, 57–9, 60–2, 78
Schütte, Wolfram, 128
security/insecurity, 51–2, 54, 69, 72, 105, 132
  and defencelessness, 132, 133
Serraillier, Ian, 79, 80
Sheehan, Paul, 114
Shining, The, 36
shoes, 15, 30, 37, 179–80, 181, 183, 192, 199
siblings, 5, 123, 147, 158, 189, 198
Sichuan, 30, 31
silence, 125–6, 129, 138, 170, 175, 177–8, 183, 185, 188
  of death, 10
  of God, 121, 126, 128
  of snow, 135–6
  sound of, 191, 193
Silver Sword, The, 79–80
Silverman, Max, 113, 183, 185, 192, 211 n.44
Slater, Katherine, 44
slavery, 149–50, 184
  child, 38, 47, 105, 146, 153, 161
Springtime in an English Village, 75–6
Squirt's Journey, 61–2
Stand By Me, 106, 133
stigmatisation, 99, 145, 171
Stolen Generations, 3, 47, 73
storyboard, 51–3, 64, 66, 67, 88
stranger(s), 42, 73, 91, 103
  welcoming, 15, 37, 88

273

Index

survival, 39–40, 72–3, 86, 171, 177, 185
  family/friendship and, 4, 24, 79–81
  price of, 26, 98, 112–14, 123, 136, 167, 201
  see also concentration camps
Sydney
  Biennale, 195–6, 199
  children's films, 55–6, 57, 59, 69
  migration to, 160–3, 165, 168
  see also Australia; *Emerald City*; *Leaving of Liverpool, The*
Syria, 27
  conflict in, 4, 146
  refugees from, 55, 71

teenage/rs, 14–15, 23, 27, 35, 106–7, 146
  Dorothy as, 20, 24
  love, 127
toys, 9–10, 59, 61, 68, 81, 167, 224 n.34, 224 n.35
transcendence, 122, 124, 131, 133, 167
transformations, 10, 30, 114
  through mobility, 46, 75, 87
  see also vampires; zombies
transitional object, 10, 13, 28, 58, 59
trauma, 80, 81, 162, 183, 201
  inherited, 143, 188
  migration and displacement, 5, 7, 79, 84
  narratives of, 11, 20, 74, 133
travelling players, 129, 130, 133, 138
Travelling Players, The, 122, 133, 137
treasure, 8, 14, 197
  hunts, 46, 66
Tree of Life, 121, 124, 125, 126, 127, 129, 130

Truce, The, 187–8, 190
Truffaut, François, 88, 110
trust, 54, 57, 100–1, 103, 112
  lack of, 64, 96–7, 108, 117
truth(s), 47, 126, 133, 143, 147, 190
  as uncomfortable, 84
Turkiewicz Sophia, 82–5
Turtles Can Fly, 147
Twilight, 53

Uighurs, 31, 35
Un Chien Andalou, 174, 176
United Kingdom (UK), 7, 39, 45, 90, 143, 146, 148–9, 151–3, 169
  see also Commonwealth; Empire; Liverpool; London; *Leaving of Liverpool, The*
urban, 8, 76
  amorality/fragmentation, 95, 97, 99, 103, 161, 166
  migrants/refugees, 46, 51, 62–3, 67, 68, 102, 110
  space, 76–7, 96, 105, 108

vampires, 53, 96, 113, 114, 115–16, 183, 185
Voyage to Cythera, 125
vulnerability, 106, 132, 143–4, 147
  in-, 28
White, 44

waiting, 93, 109, 119, 174, 187, 202
  in migration, 32, 83, 86–7, 88, 111, 129, 139
  refusing to, 91, 127
Walkabout, 39–40

Index

war
  child in, 3, 4, 15, 29, 77, 116, 142, 144, 201
  collaborators, 88, 90
  growing up in, 50, 79–81
  post, 27, 76, 78, 132, 164
  see also World War I; World War II
War Horse, 59
Wedding, the, 51, 52
Welcome, 88, 90–2
Wenders, Wim, 123, 126, 192
White Australia policy, 152–3
White Material, 5, 28–30, 35, 36, 41, 42, 198, 202
whiteness, 28, 38, 44, 62, 76, 89, 153
Wild Child, 59
Wilson, Emma, 17, 33
Wings of Desire, 123, 126
Winnicott, D.W., 14, 199
Winterbottom, Michael, 45, 85, 86, 92
witch, 37, 38–9, 88, 89–90, 112, 116, 189–90
  Dorothy as, 5, 27, 30, 40, 202
  in Wizard of Oz, 15, 18, 19, 29–30, 180
Without You, 56, 57
witness/ing, 12, 79, 94, 98, 143, 187
  to the Holocaust, 117, 151, 176–7, 180, 182, 184–5
Wizard of Oz, The, 4, 17–18, 35, 48
  and colonial inference, 27, 30
  identification with, 21, 35, 39, 58, 59, 61
  and migration, 40–2, 44, 72
  see also Baum, Frank; Dorothy; Dorothy Complex, the; Oz
Wonderful Wizard of Oz, The,
  book, 18, 27
  film, 24
World War I, 166
World War II, 4, 10, 46, 115, 175–6, 178
  and children, 3, 22, 77, 79, 187
  and destruction/migration, 122, 186
  see also concentration camps; *Diamonds of the Night*; Holocaust; *Silver Sword, The*; *Springtime in an English Village*

Xiao E'zisee *Little Moth*
Xinjiang, 30–2, 35

Yang Jinling 195–6, 198–201
Yellow Balloon, The, 105
yellow brick road, 17–18, 26, 27, 29, 35, 44
  see also Wizard of Oz, The

Zhuangzhuang, Tian, 45, 63
Žižek, Slavoj, 96
zombies, 46, 51–2, 53–4, 68, 96, 108, 112–16

www.ingramcontent.com/pod-product-compliance
Lightning Source LLC
Chambersburg PA
CBHW072128290426
44111CB00012B/1825